The Lab

Hey...Test This!!!

The Astonish Factory
Remember your childhood...and pass it on

Published by The Astonish Factory Inc. 2004

THIS BOOK IS DEDICATED TO MY PARENTS
WHO LET ME GROW UP ON 3 STOOGES AND
LOONEY TUNES! FOR DONNA, BRENDAN, AND
LOGAN...MY PERSONAL 3 STOOGES! TO THE KUNKELS
MIKE, DANIELLE, ALEC, AND LEIGHA FOR BEING THE
BEST LAB PARTNERS ANYONE COULD ASK FOR. TO ALL
OF MY FRIENDS AND FAMILY WHO LAUGHED WITH
ME ALONG THE WAY IN MY LIFE!

AND ESPECIALLY TO GOD FOR ALLOWING ME
TO SEE THE HUMOR IN THIS WONDERFUL WORLD
OF HIS!

THE LAB: HEY...TEST THIS!!!
COPYRIGHT 2004 SCOTT CHRISTIAN SAVA
ALL RIGHTS RESERVED
ISBN: 0-9721259-3-0
LIBRARY OF CONGRESS CONTROL NUMBER:
2004093436
PUBLISHED BY THE ASTONISH FACTORY INC.
PLEASE VISIT US ON THE WEB AT:
WWW.THEASTONISHFACTORY.COM

THE ASTONISH FACTORY
Remember your childhood...and pass it on

The Lab

Welcome...and Stuff!

Hi! Welcome to the Lab!

Esteban and Livingston first saw print in 2001 when The Lab 1 was published by Astonish Comics.

The comedy continued in 2002 with The Lab 2 Electric Boogaloo!

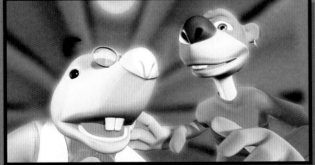

Now...for the first time in the history of the universe... The Lab is now it's very own book with 120 pages of fun and laughter! Thanks for reading...and have a great time!

Scott Christian Sava
April, 2004

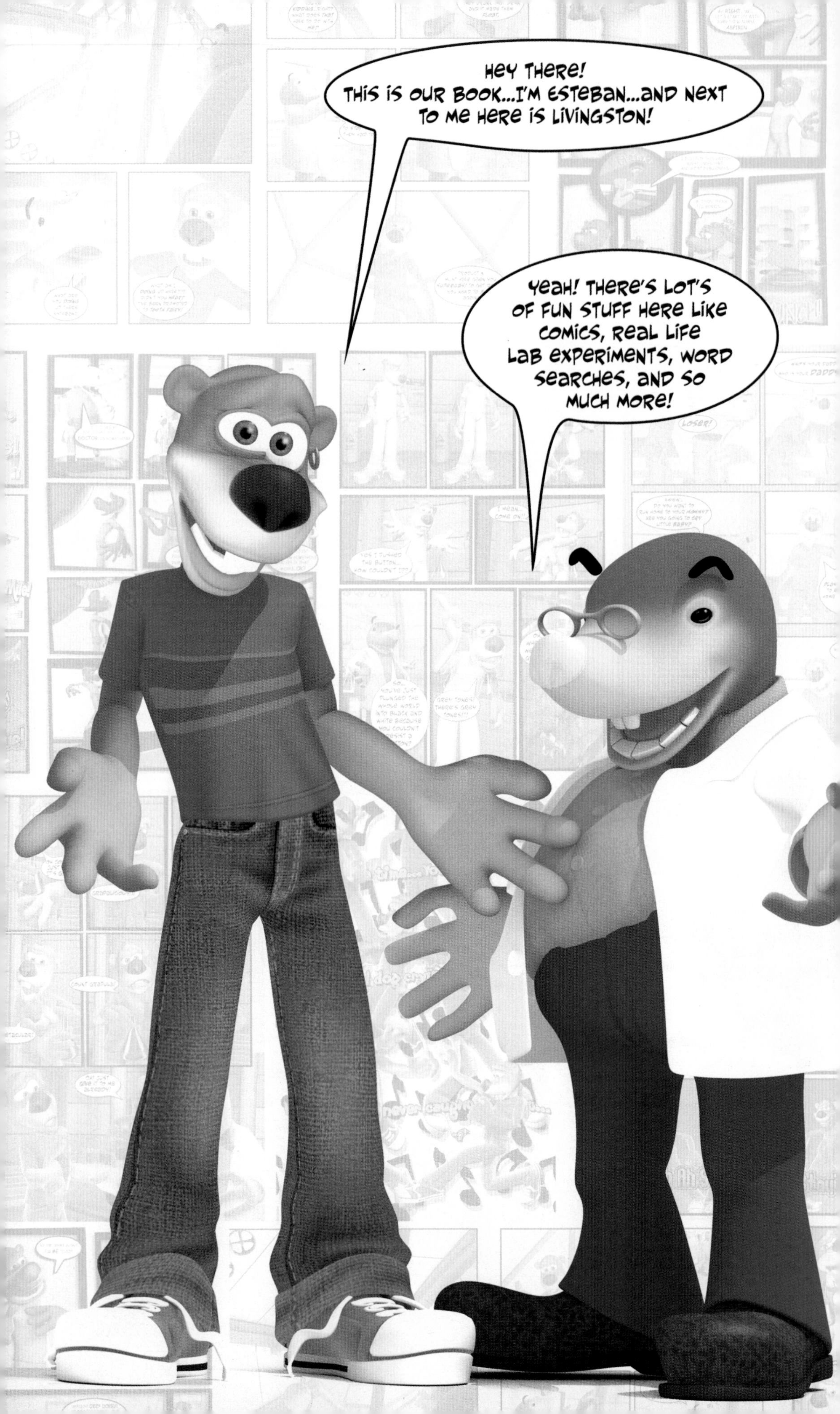
HEY THERE! THIS IS OUR BOOK...I'M ESTEBAN...AND NEXT TO ME HERE IS LIVINGSTON!
YEAH! THERE'S LOT'S OF FUN STUFF HERE LIKE COMICS, REAL LIFE LAB EXPERIMENTS, WORD SEARCHES, AND SO MUCH MORE!

THE HIGH PRICE OF GAS

IN THIS ORIGINAL STORY...WE GET TO MEET OUR FAVORITE MOLE AND WEASEL.

SEE...
LIVINGSTON WELCOME YOU TO BURNS AND ITCHEZ LABS!

MARVEL AT...
INCREDIBLE FLYING WEASELS!

BE DUMBFOUNDED BY...
JUST HOW STUPID THEY REALLY ARE!

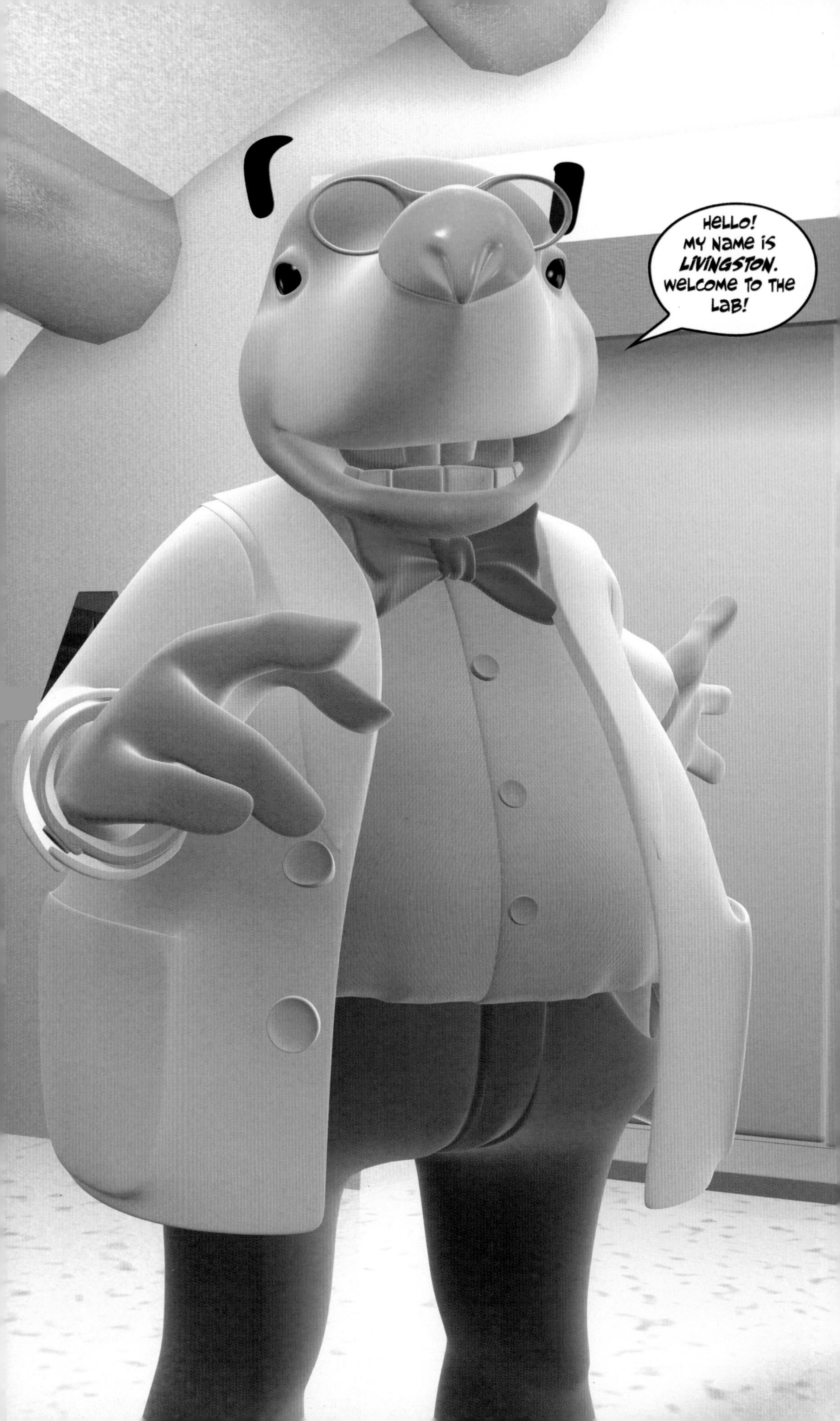
HELLO! MY NAME IS LIVINGSTON. WELCOME TO THE LAB!

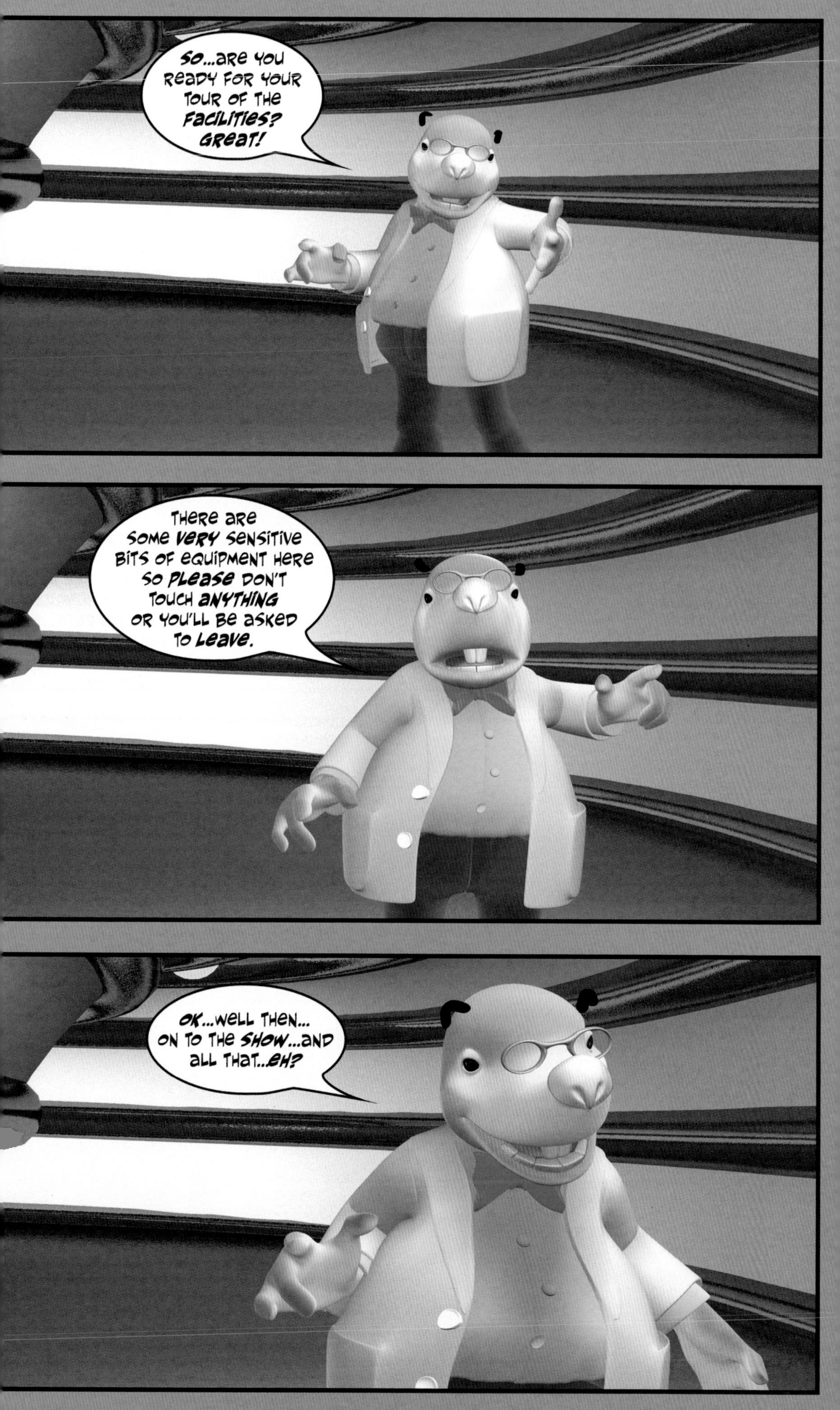
SO...ARE YOU READY FOR YOUR TOUR OF THE FACILITIES? GREAT!
THERE ARE SOME VERY SENSITIVE BITS OF EQUIPMENT HERE SO PLEASE DON'T TOUCH ANYTHING OR YOU'LL BE ASKED TO LEAVE.
OK...WELL THEN... ON TO THE SHOW...AND ALL THAT..EH?

HERE AT BURNS AND ITCHEZ PRODUCT TESTING I'M THE LEAD TESTER...MY SPECIALTY IS DEODORANTS...BUT WE'LL GET TO THAT LATER.
THIS IS WHERE THE MAGIC HAPPENS...SO TO SPEAK...HA HA.

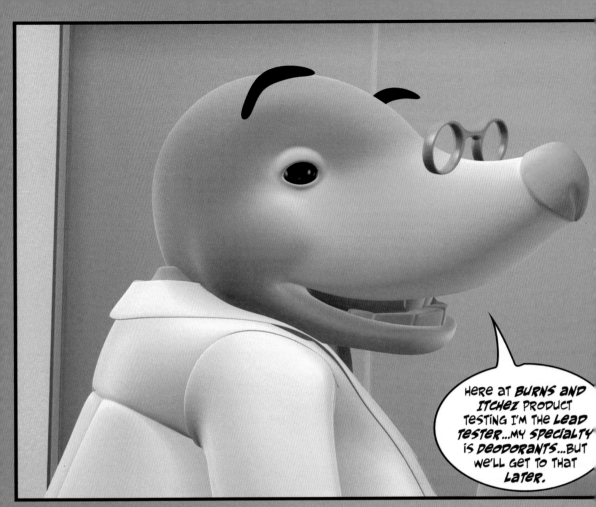

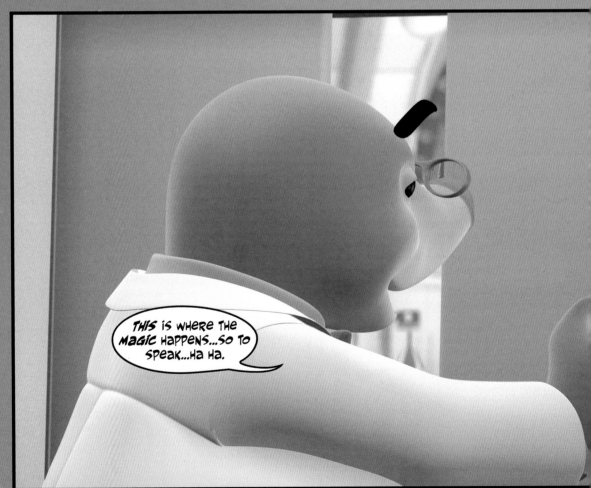

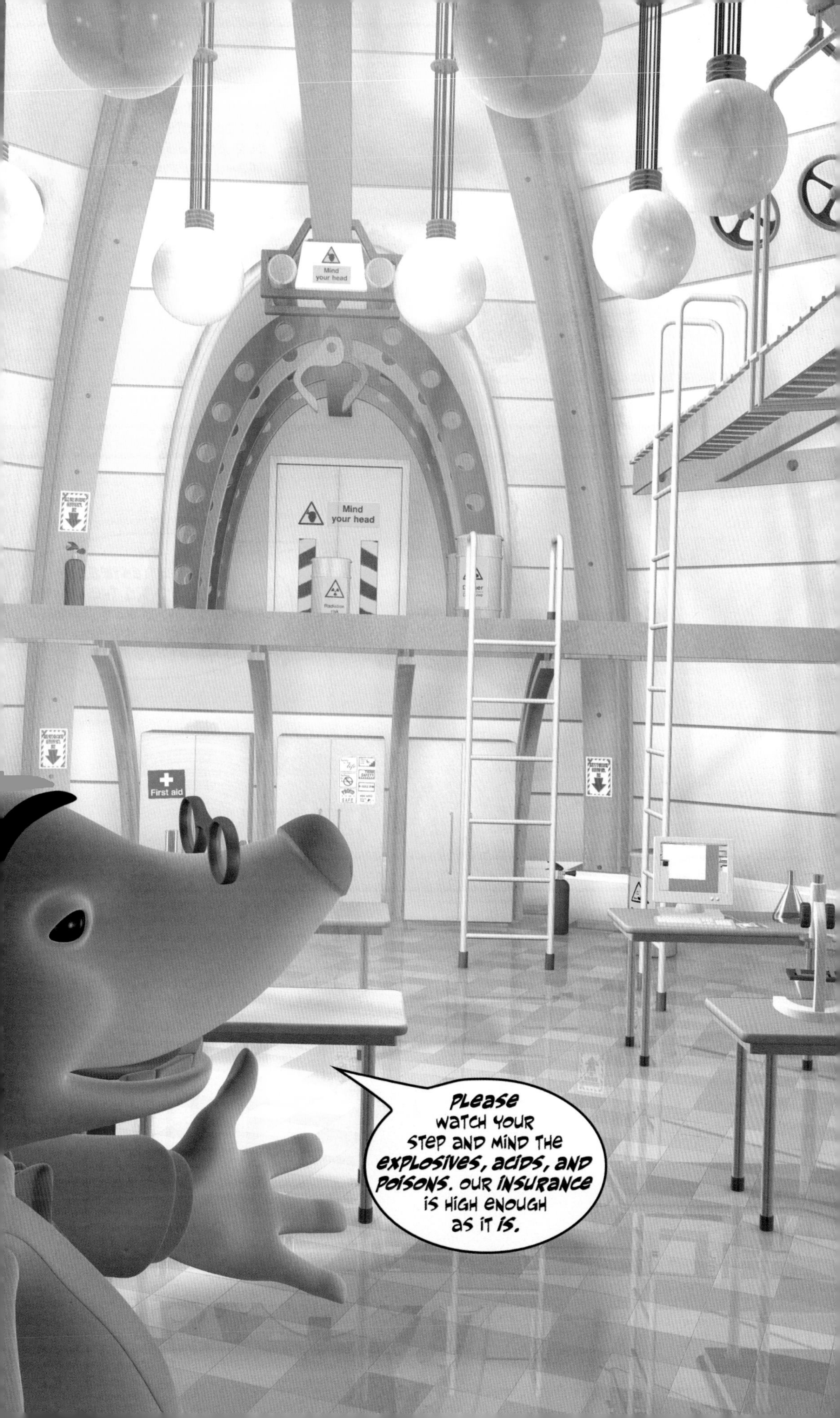
Mind your head
Mind your head
First aid
PLEASE WATCH YOUR STEP AND MIND THE EXPLOSIVES, ACIDS, AND POISONS. OUR INSURANCE IS HIGH ENOUGH AS IT IS.

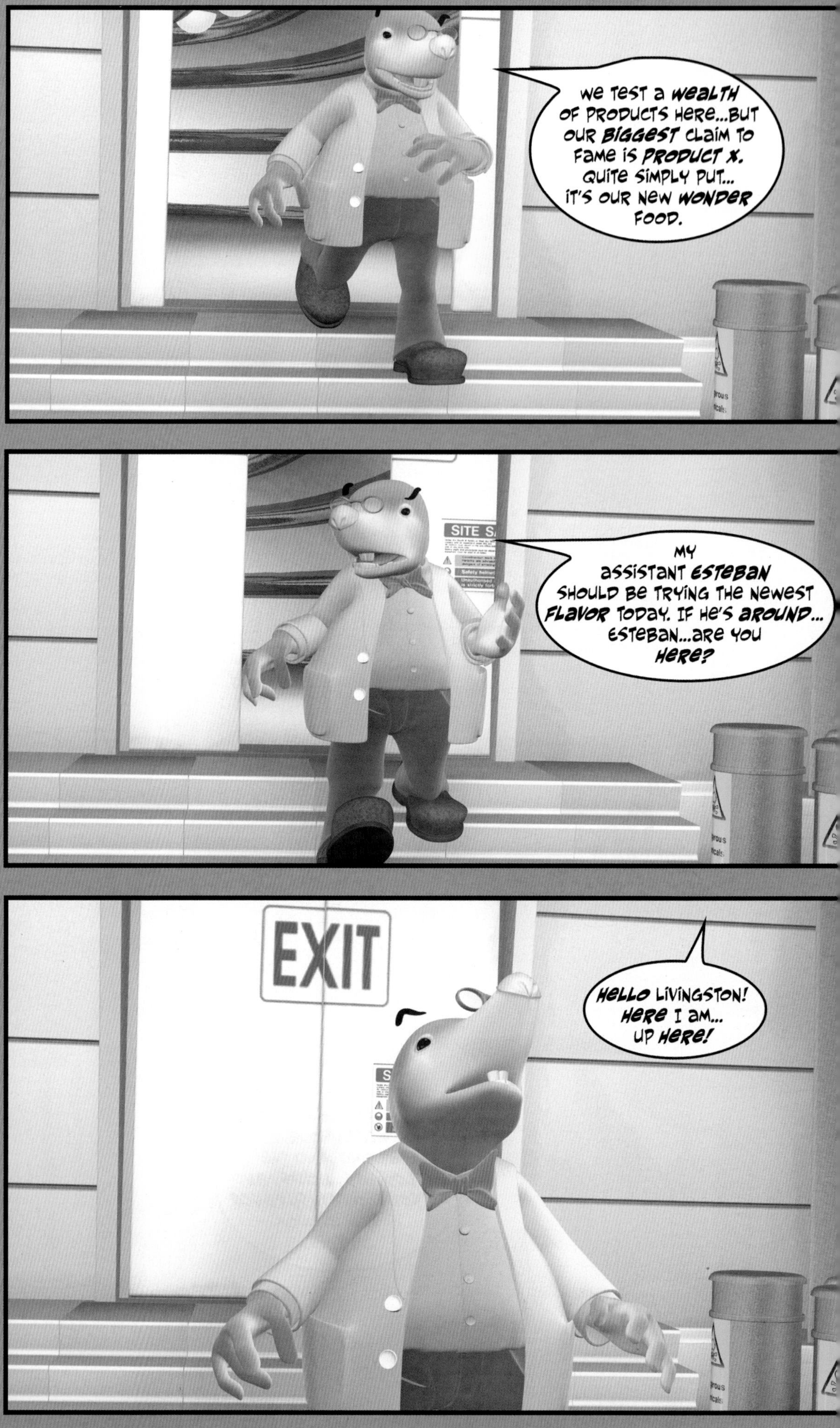
WE TEST A WEALTH OF PRODUCTS HERE...BUT OUR BIGGEST CLAIM TO FAME IS PRODUCT X. QUITE SIMPLY PUT... IT'S OUR NEW WONDER FOOD.
MY ASSISTANT ESTEBAN SHOULD BE TRYING THE NEWEST FLAVOR TODAY. IF HE'S AROUND... ESTEBAN...ARE YOU HERE?
EXIT
HELLO LIVINGSTON! HERE I AM... UP HERE!

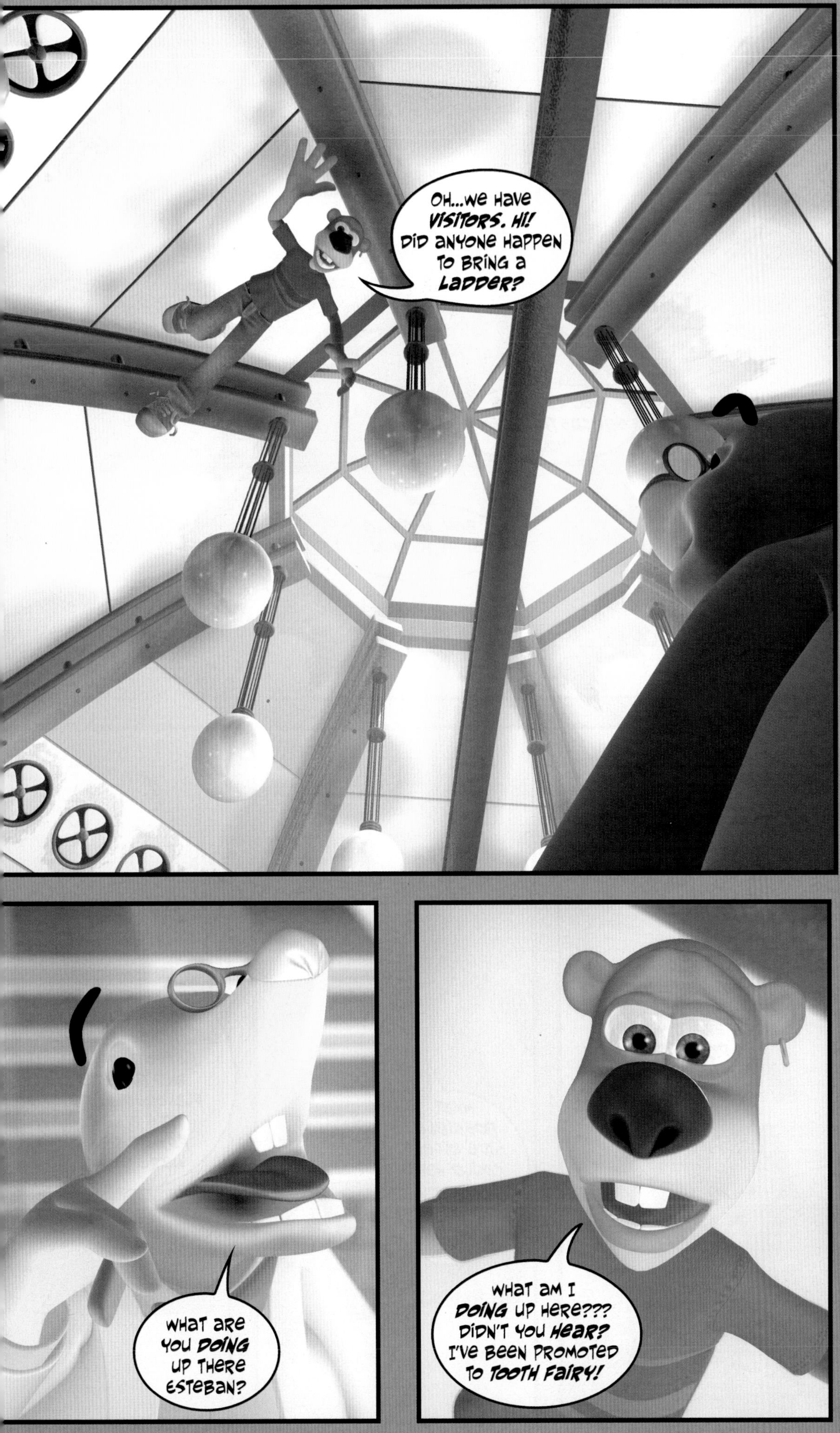
OH...WE HAVE VISITORS. HI! DID ANYONE HAPPEN TO BRING A LADDER?
WHAT ARE YOU DOING UP THERE ESTEBAN?
WHAT AM I DOING UP HERE??? DIDN'T YOU HEAR? I'VE BEEN PROMOTED TO TOOTH FAIRY!

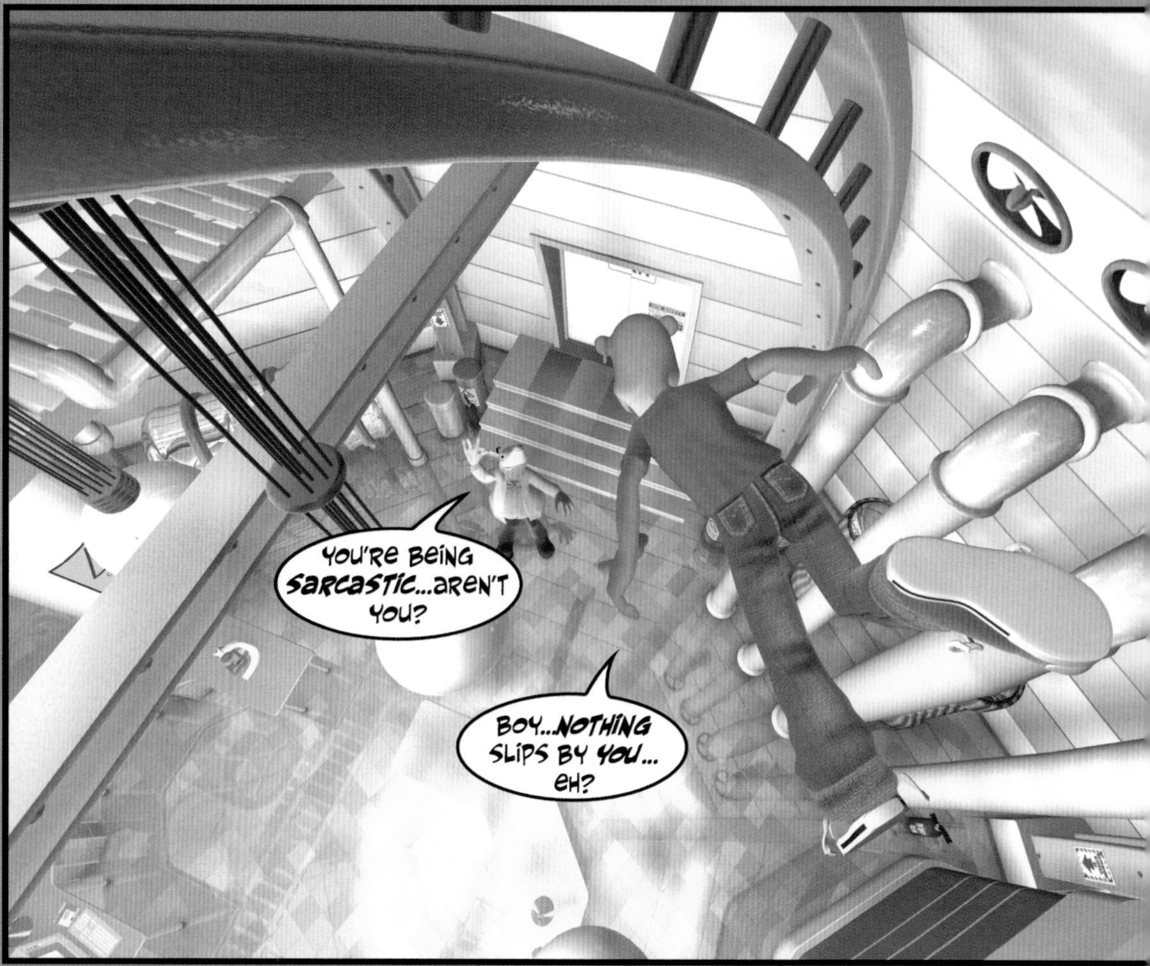

YOU'RE BEING SARCASTIC...AREN'T YOU?
BOY...NOTHING SLIPS BY YOU... EH?

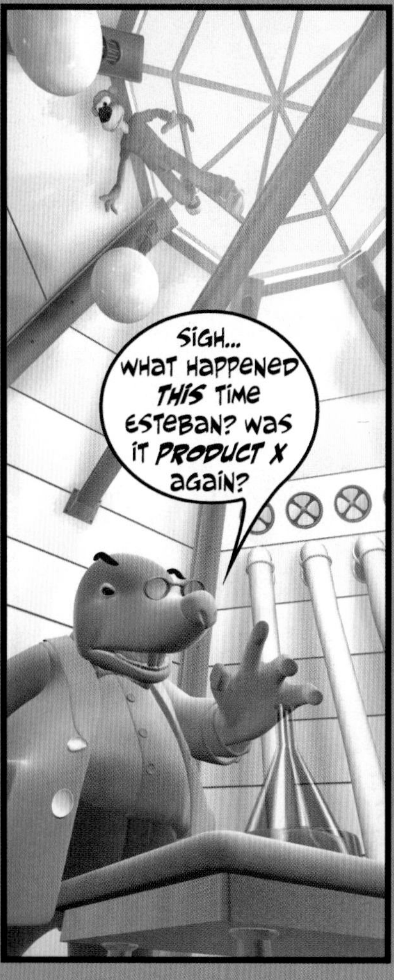

SIGH... WHAT HAPPENED THIS TIME ESTEBAN? WAS IT PRODUCT X AGAIN?

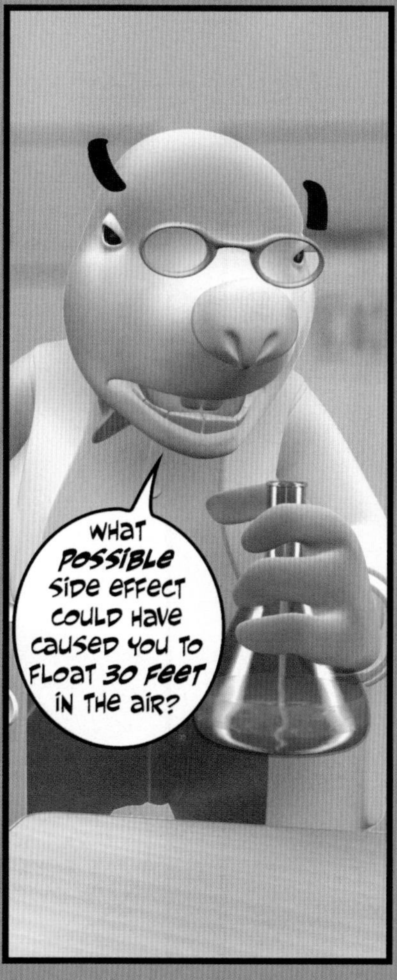

WHAT POSSIBLE SIDE EFFECT COULD HAVE CAUSED YOU TO FLOAT 30 FEET IN THE AIR?

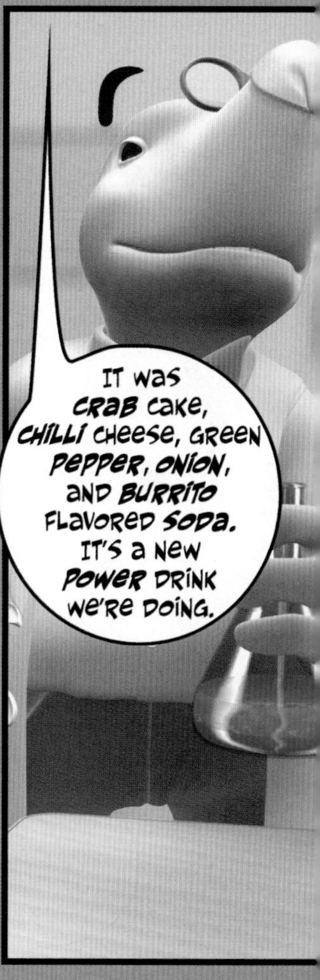

IT WAS CRAB CAKE, CHILLI CHEESE, GREEN PEPPER, ONION, AND BURRITO FLAVORED SODA. IT'S A NEW POWER DRINK WE'RE DOING.

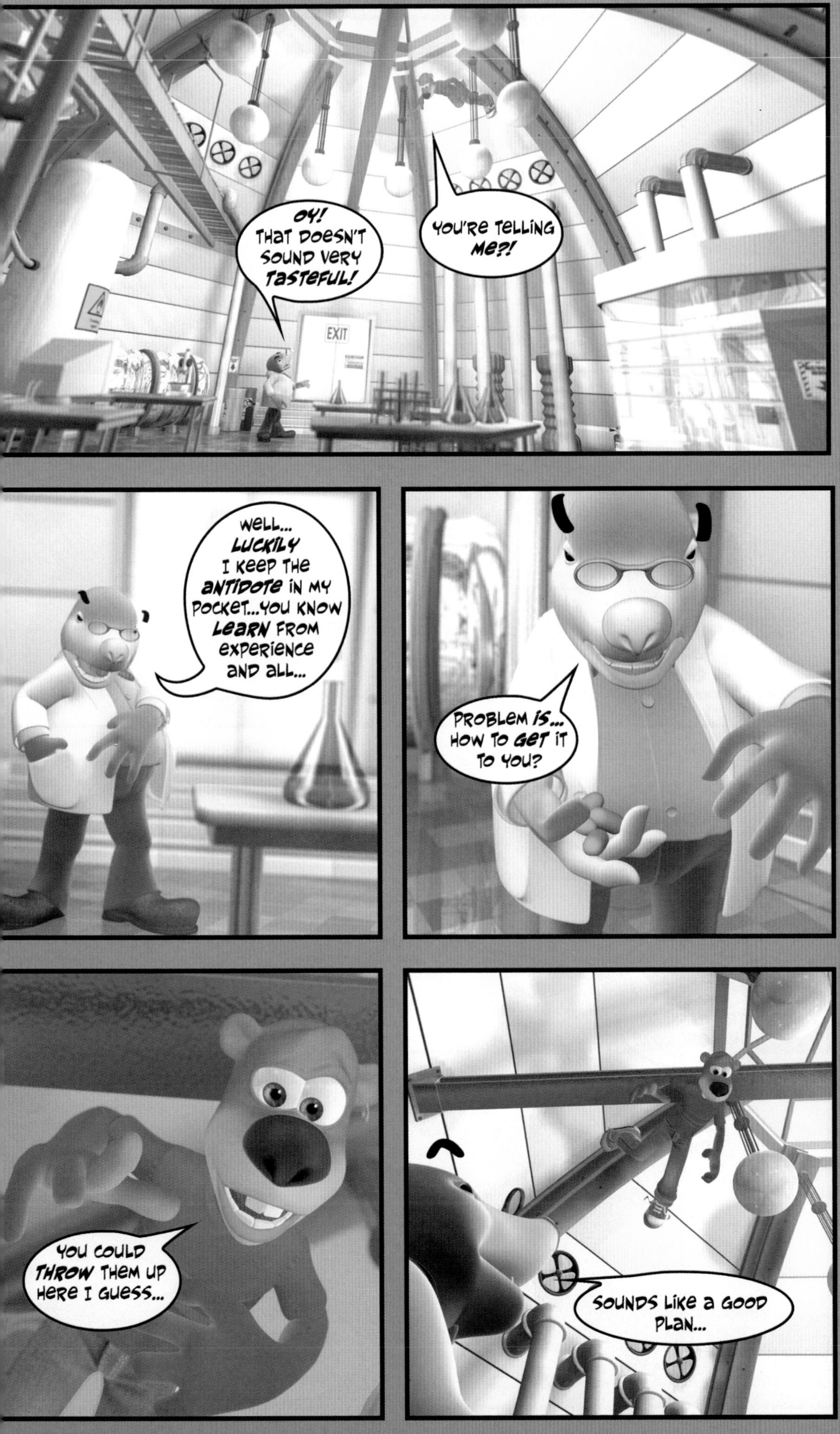
OY! THAT DOESN'T SOUND VERY TASTEFUL!
YOU'RE TELLING ME?!
EXIT
WELL... LUCKILY I KEEP THE ANTIDOTE IN MY POCKET...YOU KNOW LEARN FROM EXPERIENCE AND ALL...
PROBLEM IS... HOW TO GET IT TO YOU?
YOU COULD THROW THEM UP HERE I GUESS...
SOUNDS LIKE A GOOD PLAN...

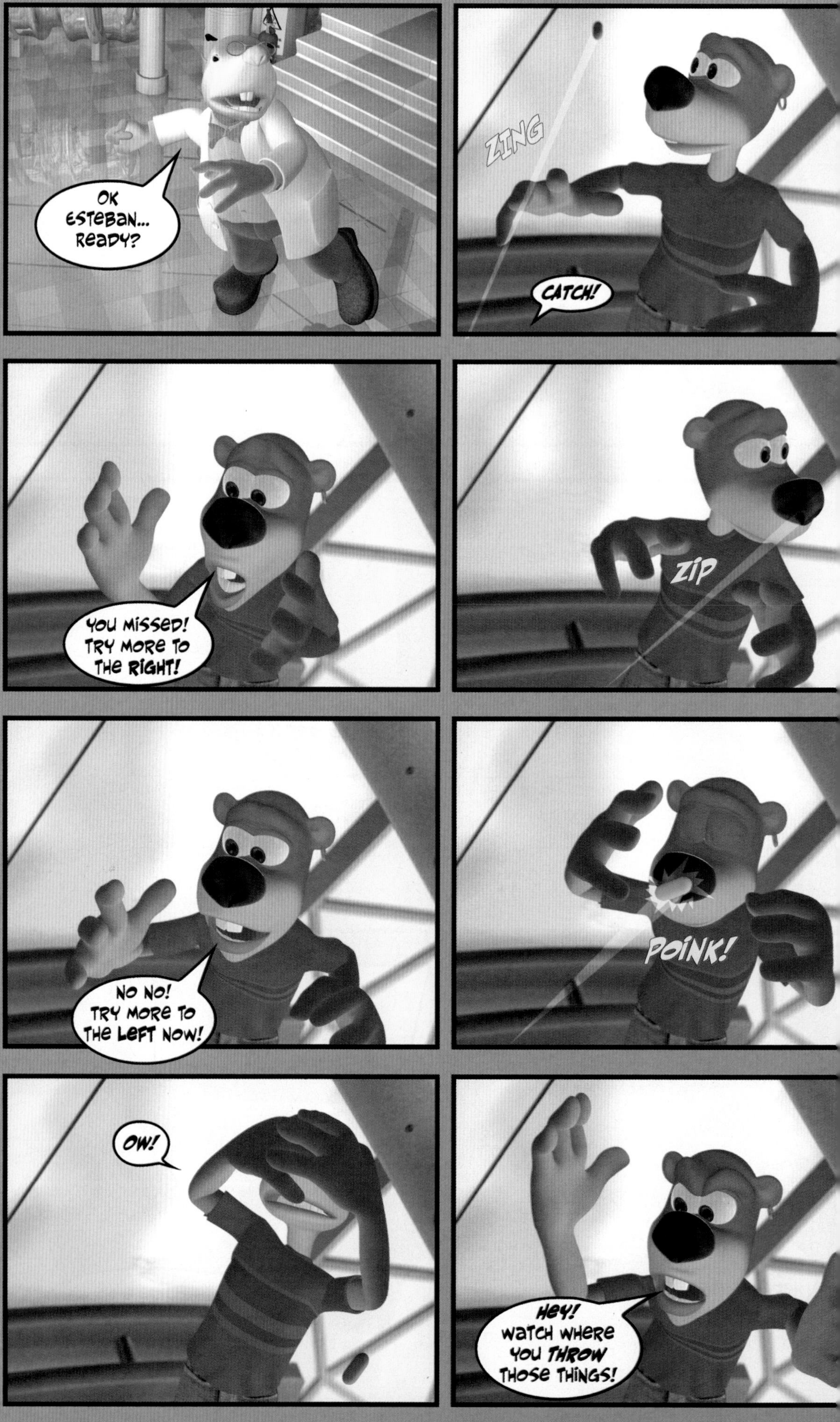
OK ESTEBAN... READY?
ZING
CATCH!
YOU MISSED! TRY MORE TO THE RIGHT!
ZIP
NO NO! TRY MORE TO THE LEFT NOW!
POINK!
OW!
HEY! WATCH WHERE YOU THROW THOSE THINGS!

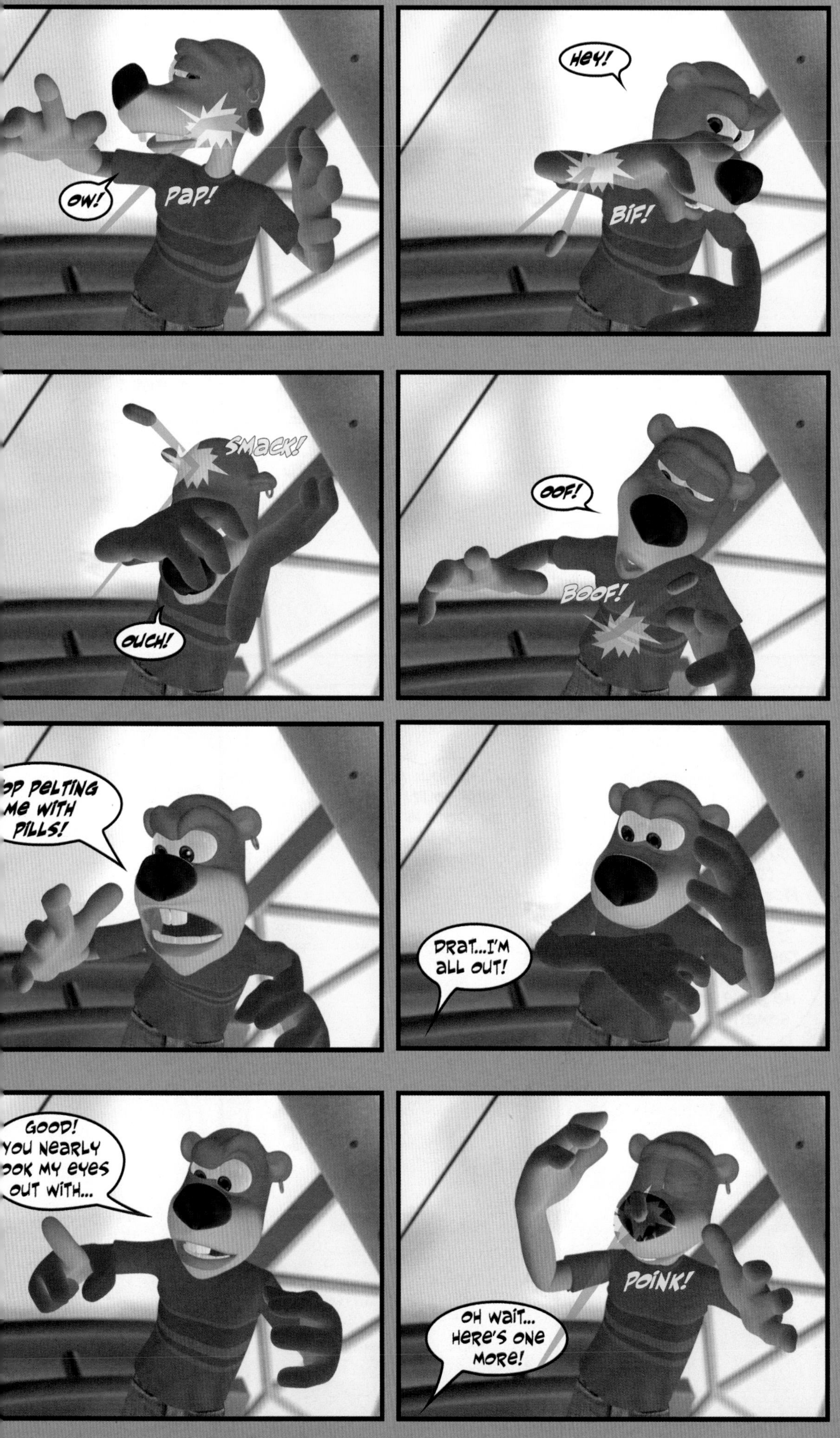
OW!
PAP!
HEY!
BIF!
SMACK!
OUCH!
OOF!
BOOF!
OP PELTING ME WITH PILLS!
DRAT...I'M ALL OUT!
GOOD! YOU NEARLY OOK MY EYES OUT WITH...
POINK!
OH WAIT... HERE'S ONE MORE!

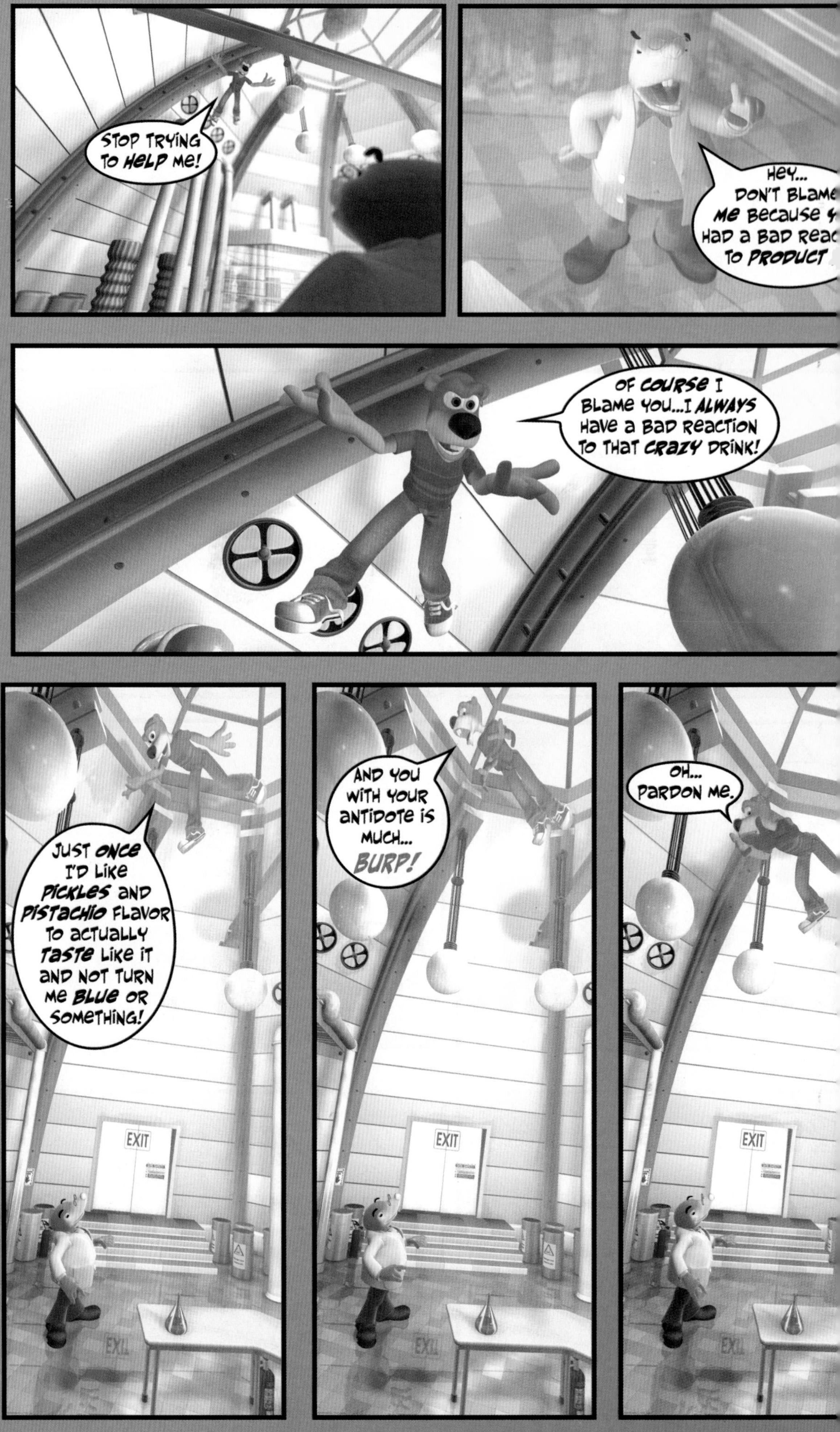
STOP TRYING TO HELP ME!
HEY... DON'T BLAME ME BECAUSE Y HAD A BAD REAC TO PRODUCT
OF COURSE I BLAME YOU...I ALWAYS HAVE A BAD REACTION TO THAT CRAZY DRINK!
JUST ONCE I'D LIKE PICKLES AND PISTACHIO FLAVOR TO ACTUALLY TASTE LIKE IT AND NOT TURN ME BLUE OR SOMETHING!
AND YOU WITH YOUR ANTIDOTE IS MUCH... BURP!
OH... PARDON ME.
EXIT
EXIT
EXIT

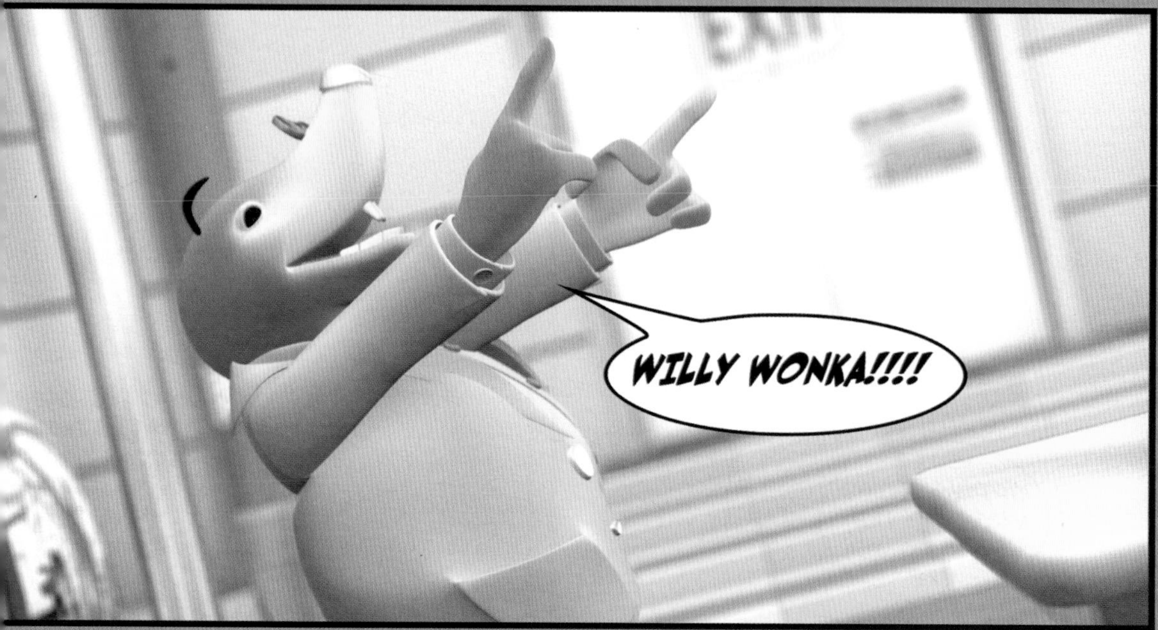
WILLY WONKA!!!!

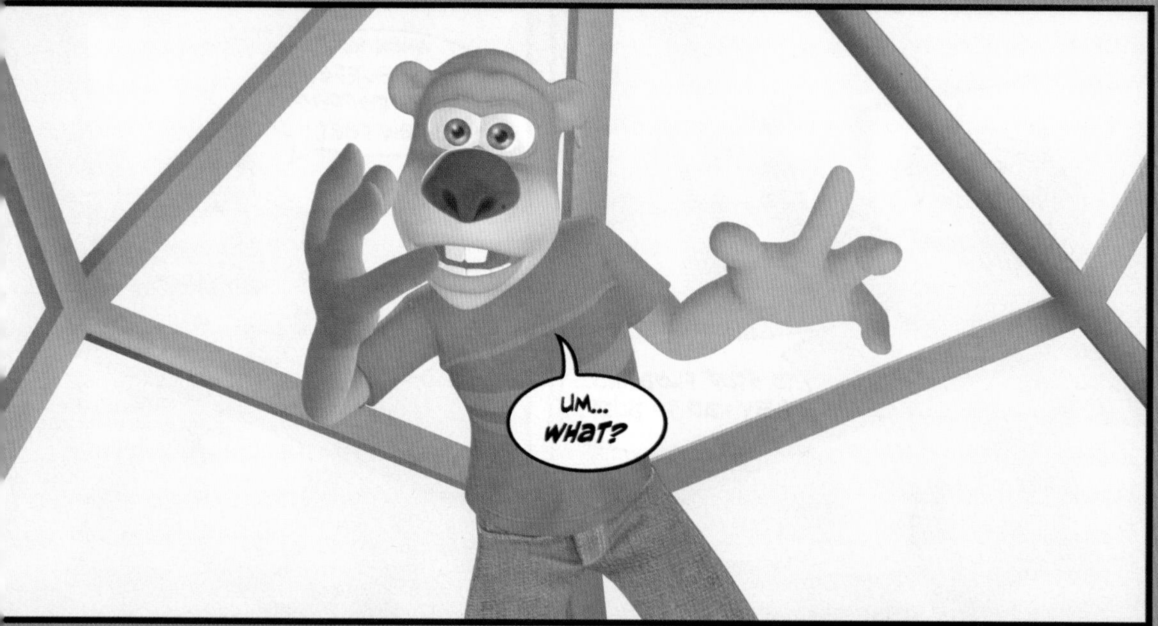
UM...
WHAT?

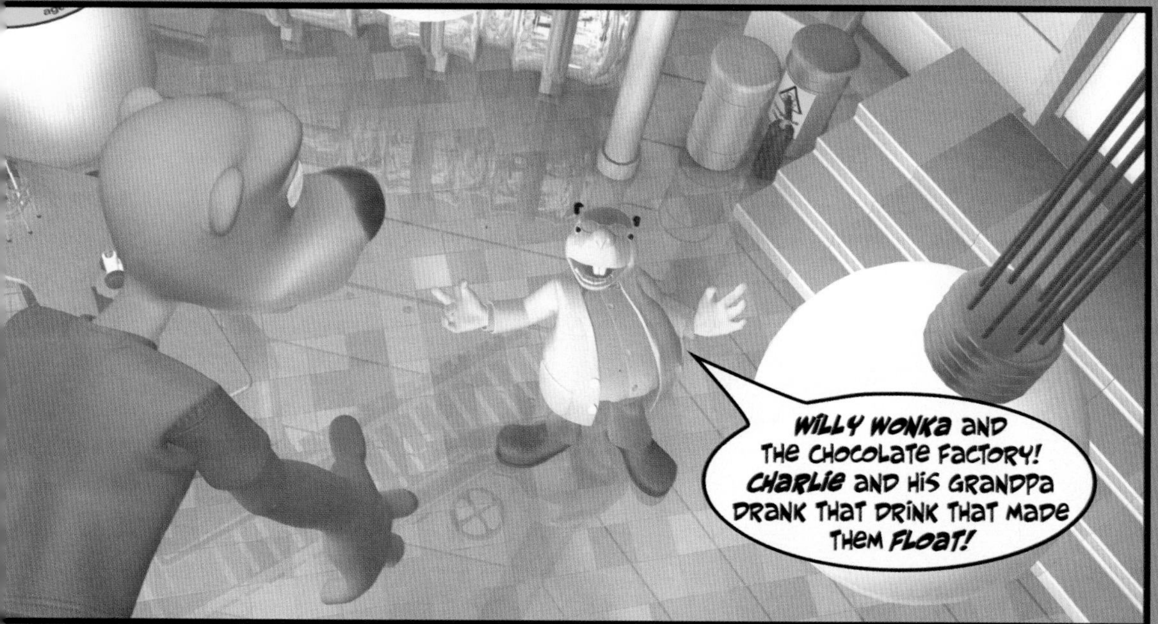
WILLY WONKA AND THE CHOCOLATE FACTORY! CHARLIE AND HIS GRANDPA DRANK THAT DRINK THAT MADE THEM FLOAT!

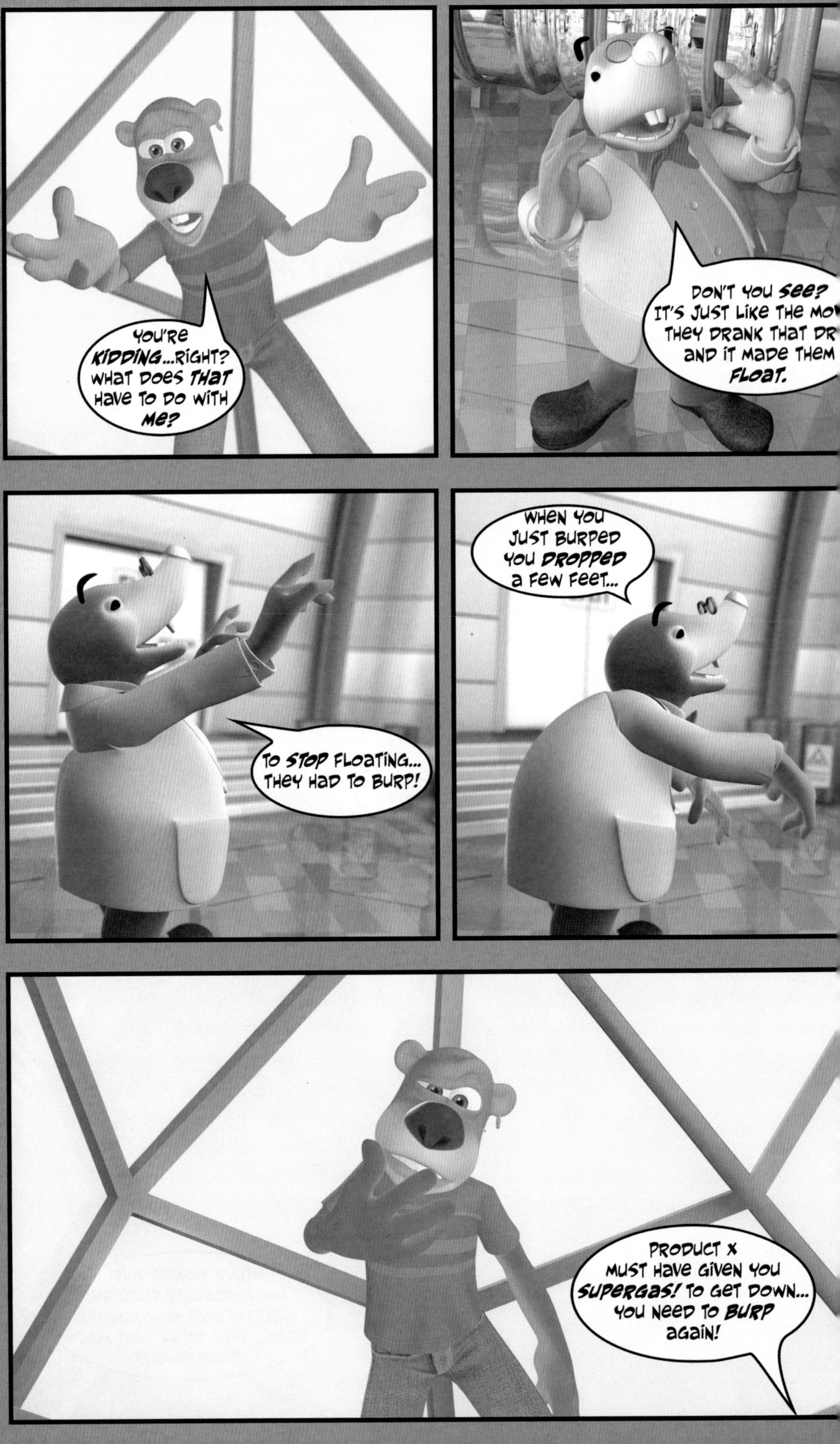

YOU'RE KIDDING...RIGHT? WHAT DOES THAT HAVE TO DO WITH ME?
DON'T YOU SEE? IT'S JUST LIKE THE MO THEY DRANK THAT DR AND IT MADE THEM FLOAT.
TO STOP FLOATING... THEY HAD TO BURP!
WHEN YOU JUST BURPED YOU DROPPED A FEW FEET...
PRODUCT X MUST HAVE GIVEN YOU SUPERGAS! TO GET DOWN... YOU NEED TO BURP AGAIN!

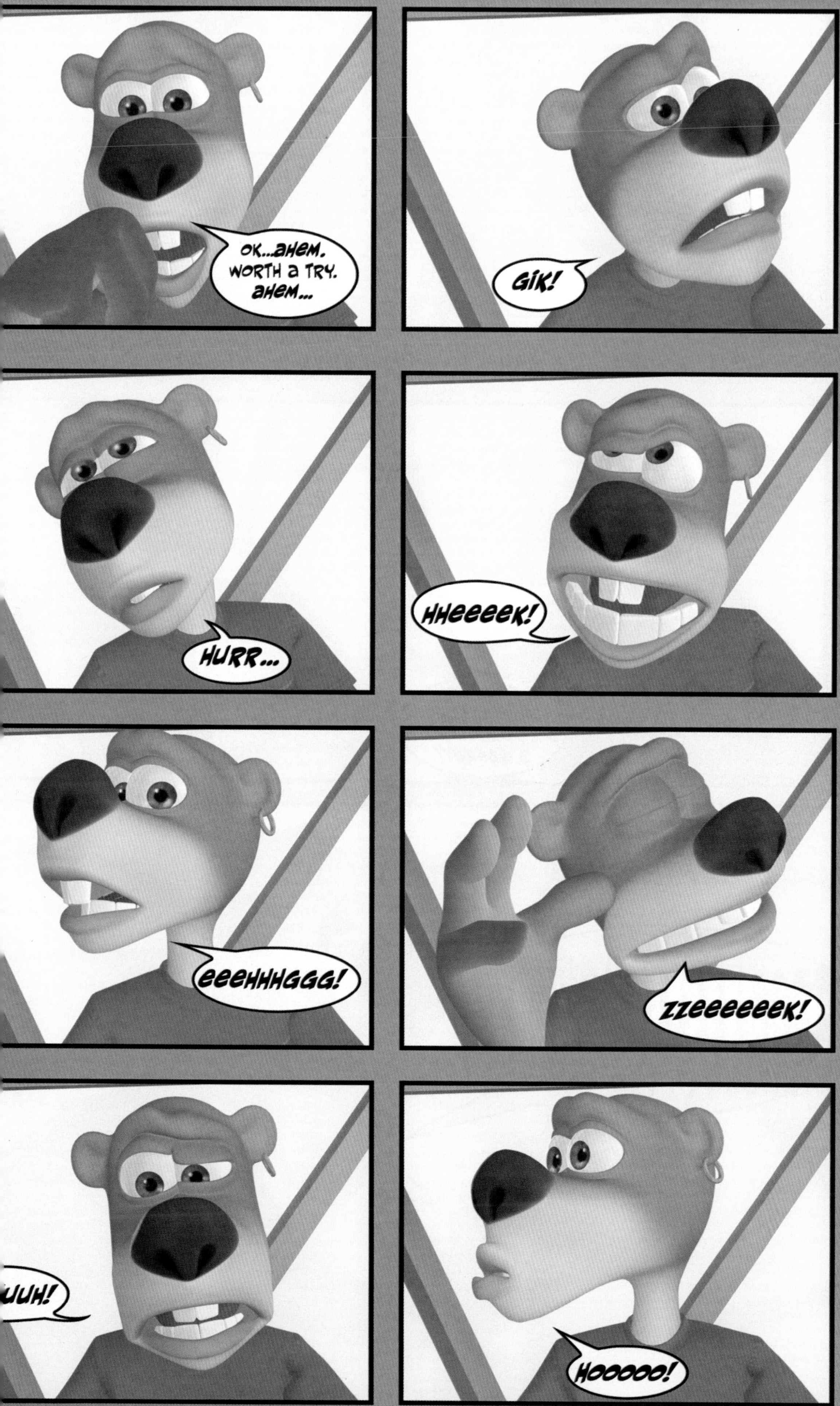
OK...AHEM. WORTH A TRY. AHEM...
GIK!
HURR...
HHEEEEK!
EEEHHHGGG!
ZZEEEEEEEK!
UUH!
HOOOOO!

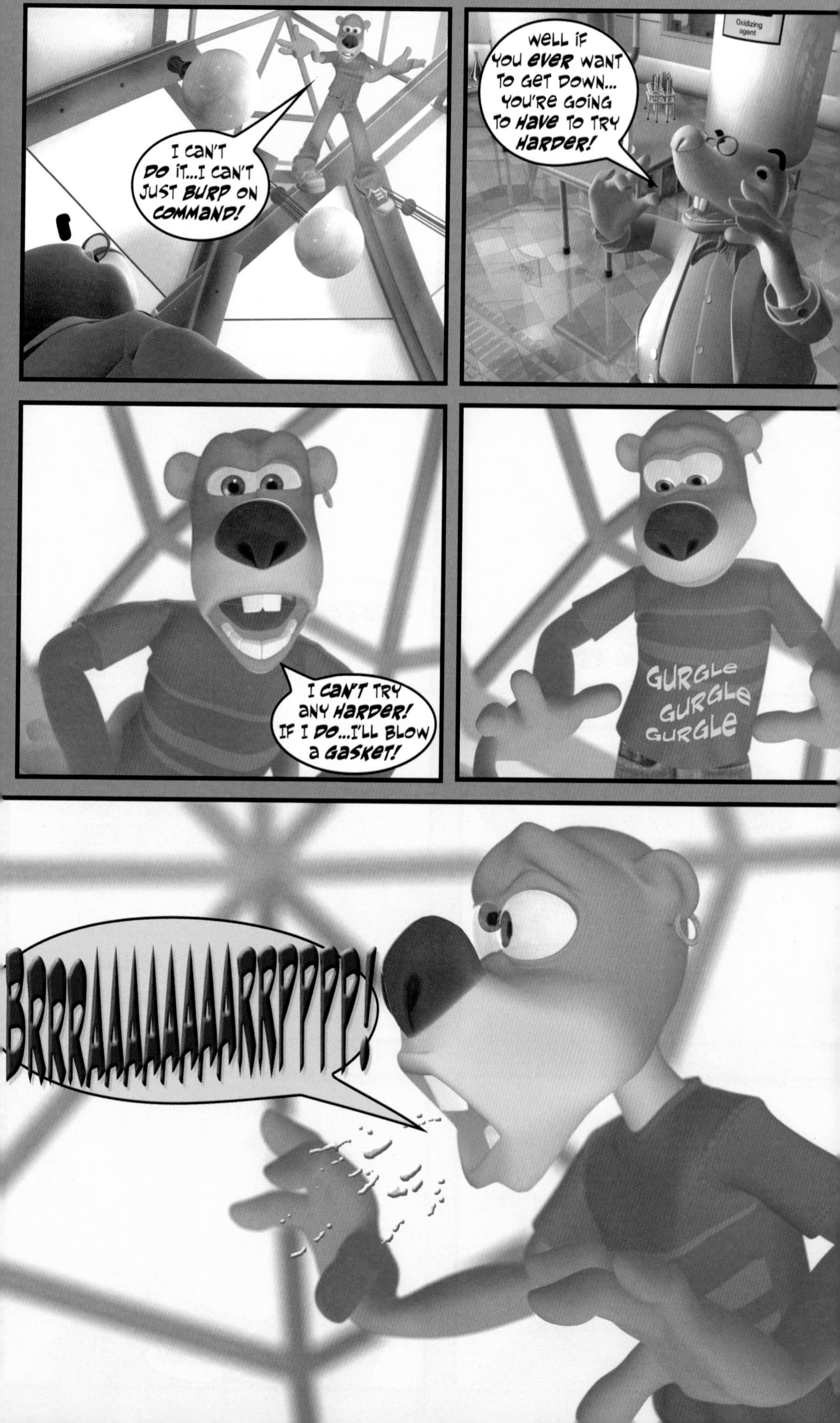
I CAN'T DO IT...I CAN'T JUST BURP ON COMMAND!
Oxidizing agent
WELL IF YOU EVER WANT TO GET DOWN... YOU'RE GOING TO HAVE TO TRY HARDER!
I CAN'T TRY ANY HARDER! IF I DO...I'LL BLOW A GASKET!
GURGLE GURGLE GURGLE GURGLE
BRRAAAAAAARRPPPP!

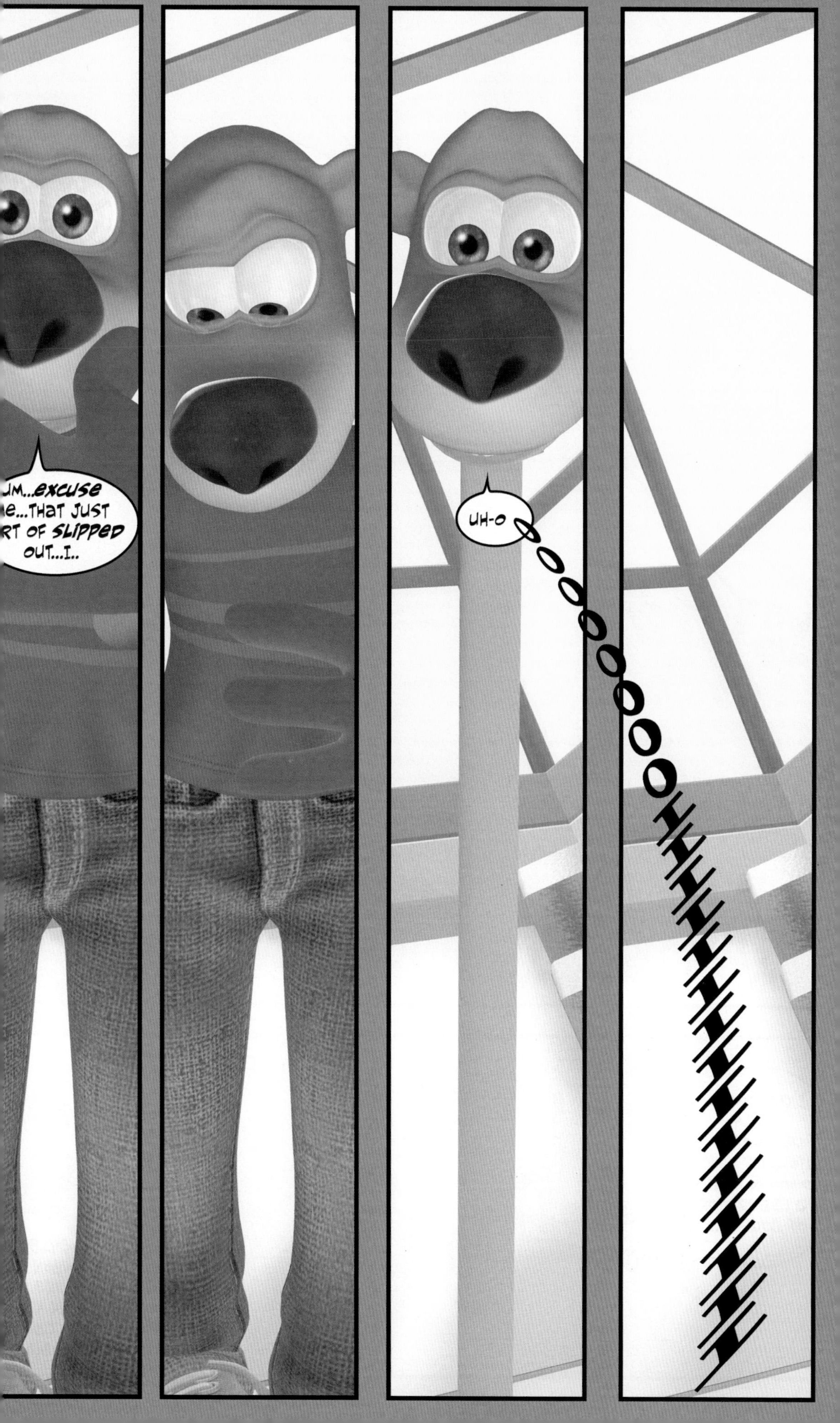
UM...EXCUSE
ME...THAT JUST
RT OF SLIPPED
OUT...I..
UH-O
OOOOOOOOHHHHHHHHHHHHHHHHHHHHH

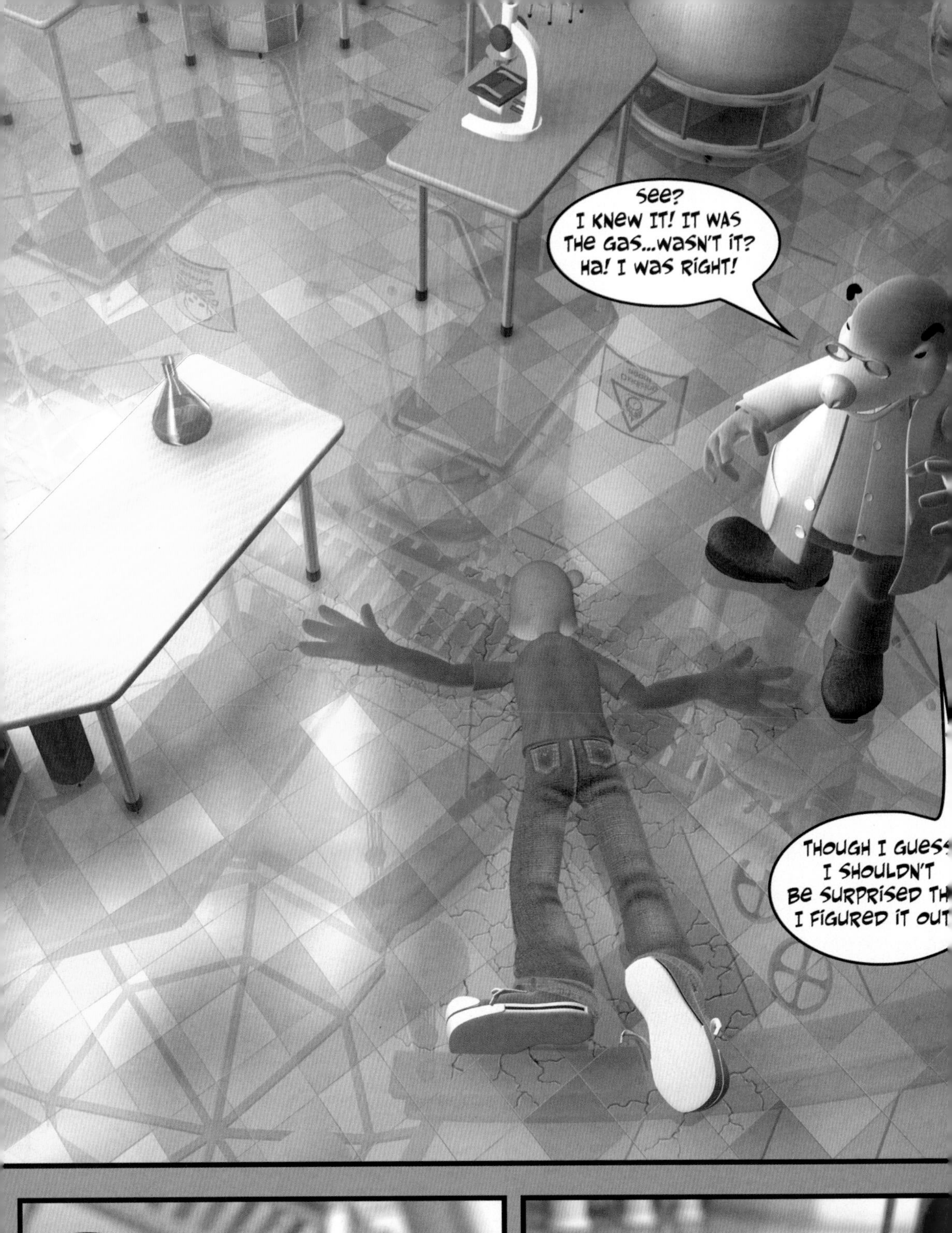
SEE?
I KNEW IT! IT WAS
THE GAS...WASN'T IT?
HA! I WAS RIGHT!
THOUGH I GUES
I SHOULDN'T
BE SURPRISED TH
I FIGURED IT OUT

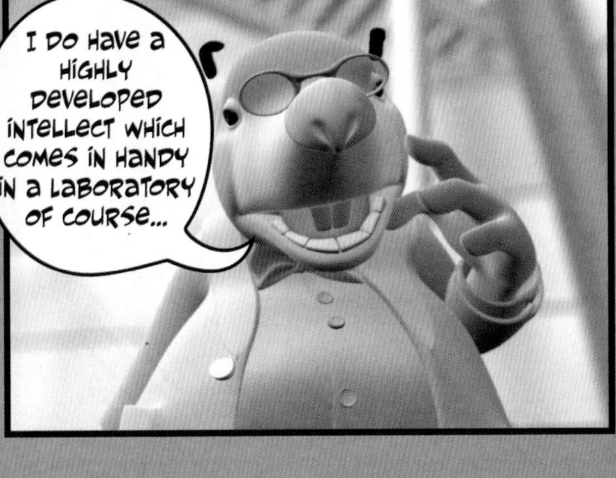
I DO HAVE A HIGHLY DEVELOPED INTELLECT WHICH COMES IN HANDY IN A LABORATORY OF COURSE...

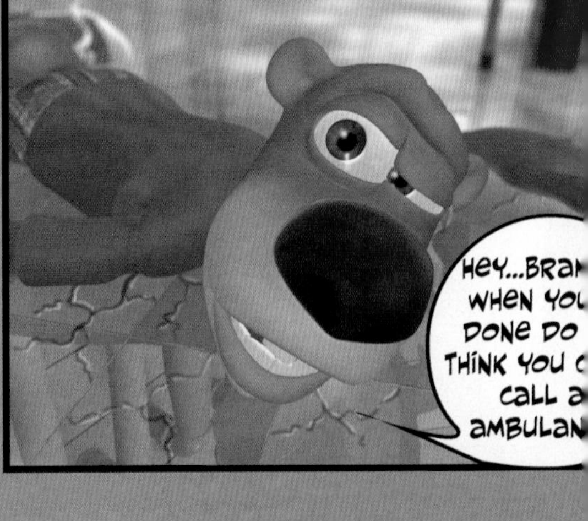
HEY...BRA
WHEN YOU
DONE DO
THINK YOU
CALL A
AMBULAN

CRAZY SCIENCE EXPERIMENTS!

TRY THIS AT HOME WITH YOUR PARENTS...

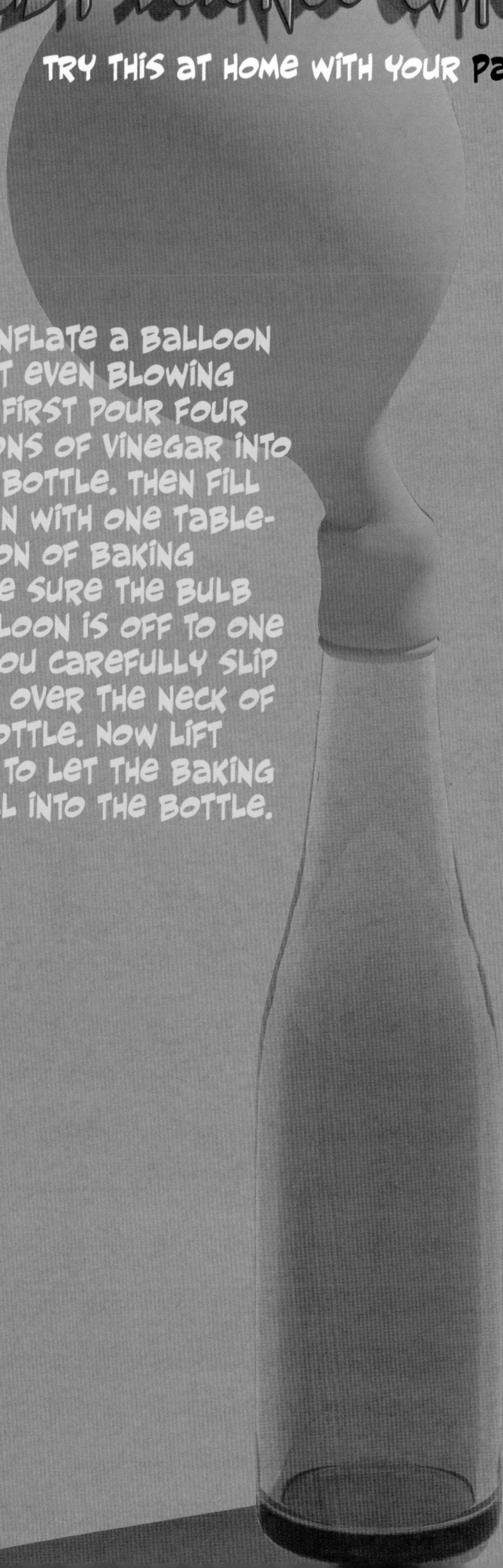

ANT TO INFLATE A BALLOON WITHOUT EVEN BLOWING NTO IT? FIRST POUR FOUR BLESPOONS OF VINEGAR INTO CLEAN BOTTLE. THEN FILL BALLOON WITH ONE TABLE-SPOON OF BAKING SODA. BE SURE THE BULB THE BALOON IS OFF TO ONE DE AS YOU CAREFULLY SLIP S MOUTH OVER THE NECK OF THE BOTTLE. NOW LIFT E BULB TO LET THE BAKING ODA FALL INTO THE BOTTLE.

DID IT WORK? OF COURSE IT DID! THE BALLOON INFLATED ALL BY ITSELF...DIDN'T IT? THAT'S BECAUSE THE BAKING SODA AND VINEGAR FORM CARBON DIOXIDE WHEN THEY TOUCH! SINCE THE GAS CAN'T GO ANYWHERE BUT UP...IT FILLS THE BALLOON! PRETTY NEAT STUFF!

The Lab

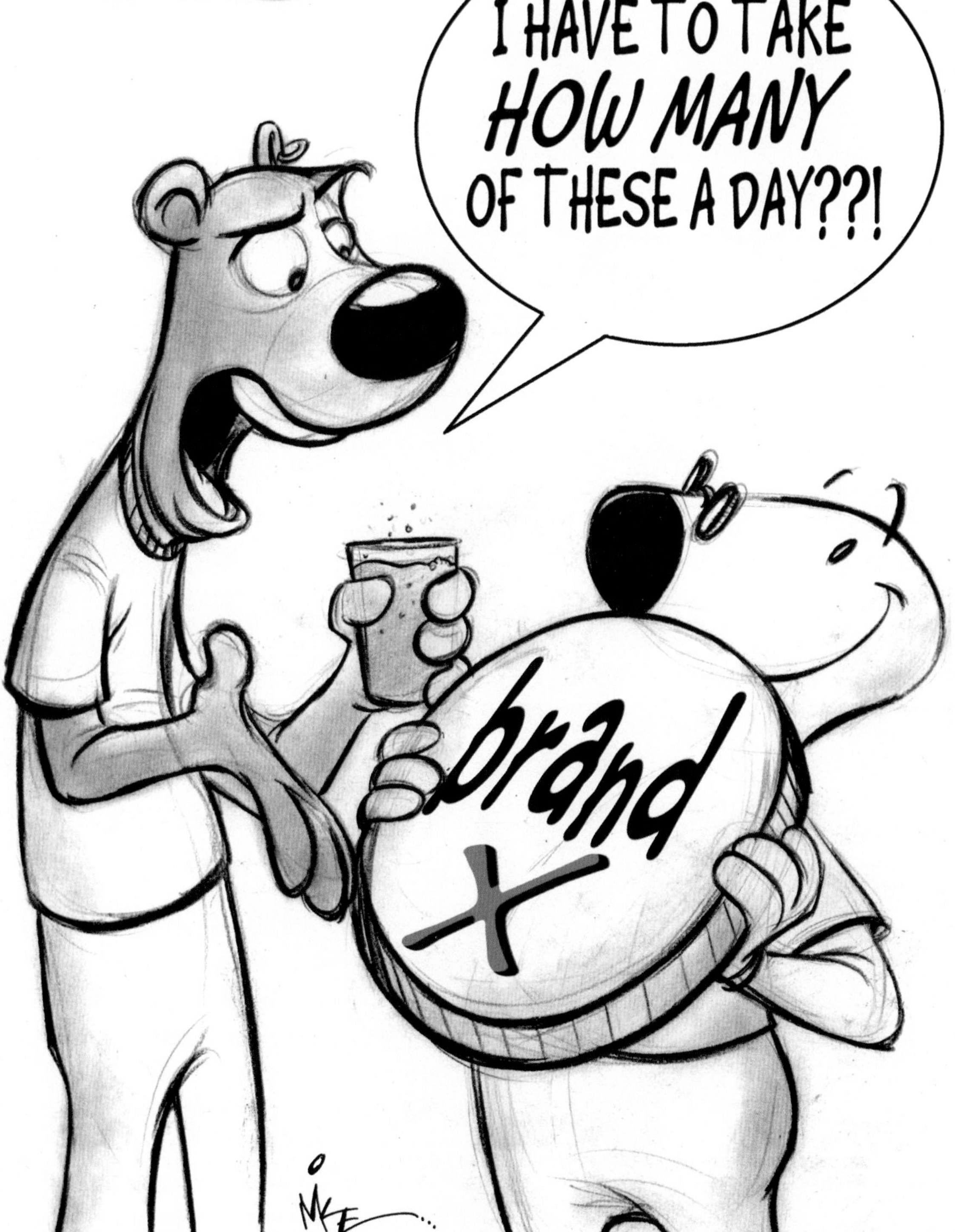
I HAVE TO TAKE *HOW MANY* OF THESE A DAY??!
brand X
MIKE...

Pin-up by Mike Kunkel

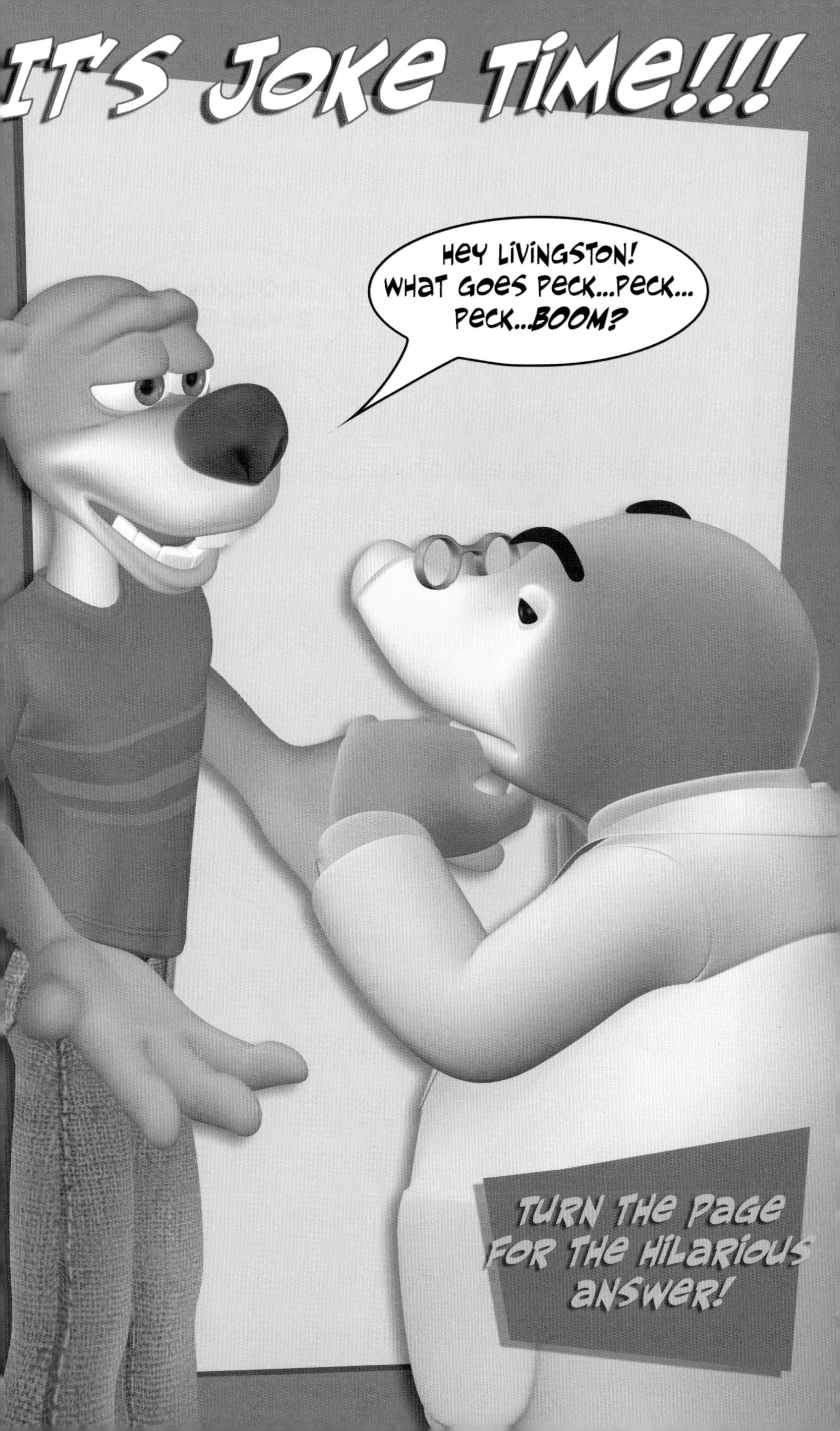
IT'S JOKE TIME!!!
HEY LIVINGSTON! WHAT GOES PECK...PECK... PECK...BOOM?
TURN THE PAGE FOR THE HILARIOUS ANSWER!

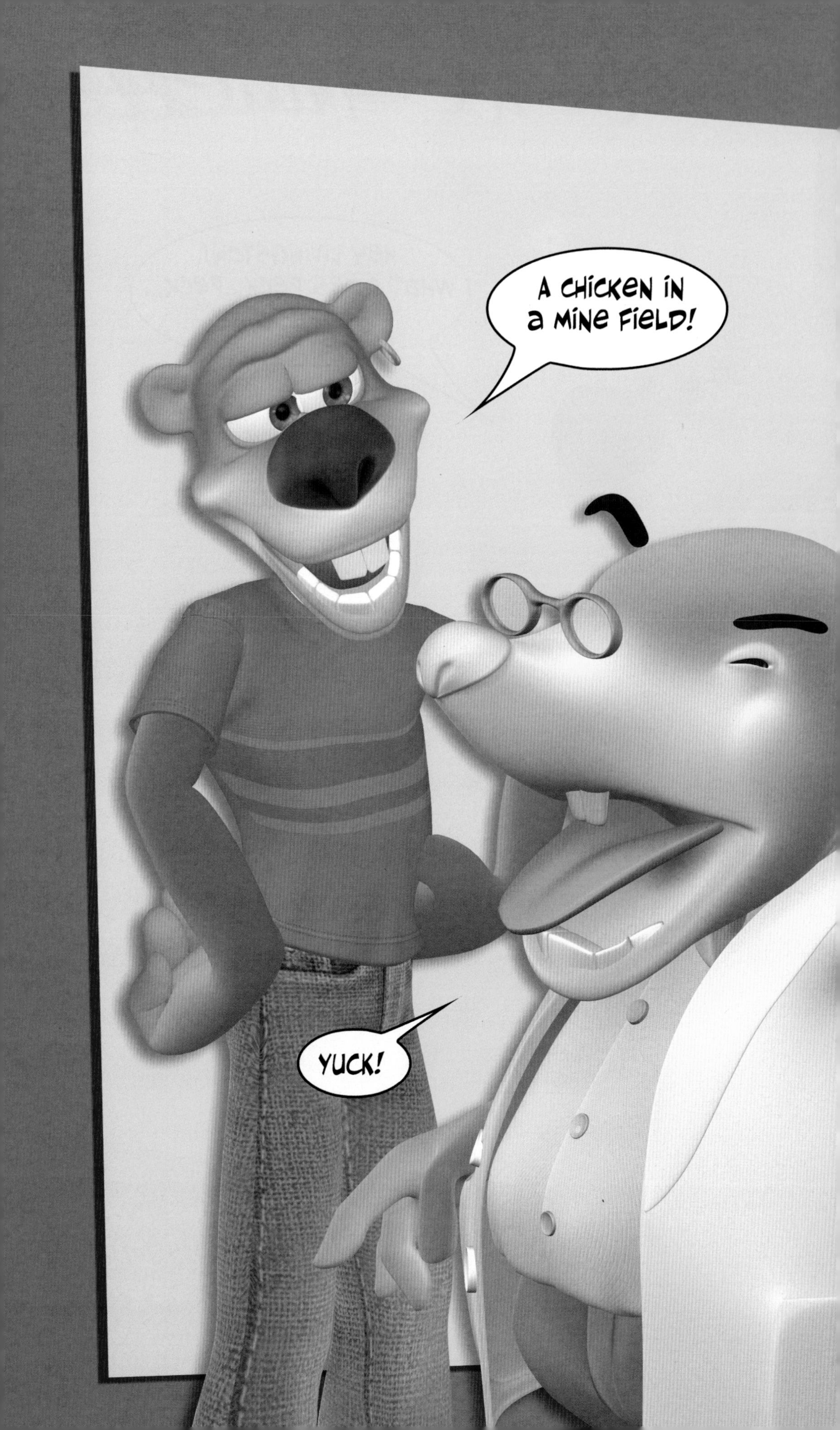
A CHICKEN IN
A MINE FIELD!
YUCK!

BEGINNINGS...

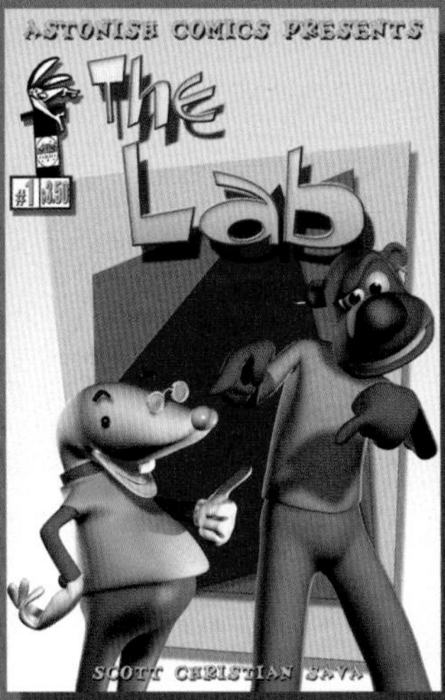
ASTONISH COMICS PRESENTS
The Lab
SCOTT CHRISTIAN SAVA

The cover for The Lab issue 1
2001

Livingston meets his new intern for the first time in this re-telling of the very first issue of The Lab!

You may notice some fun differences from the current look and feel....
Check out Esteban's funny accent....
Or dig that crazy look the guys are sporting!
Ah....memories....

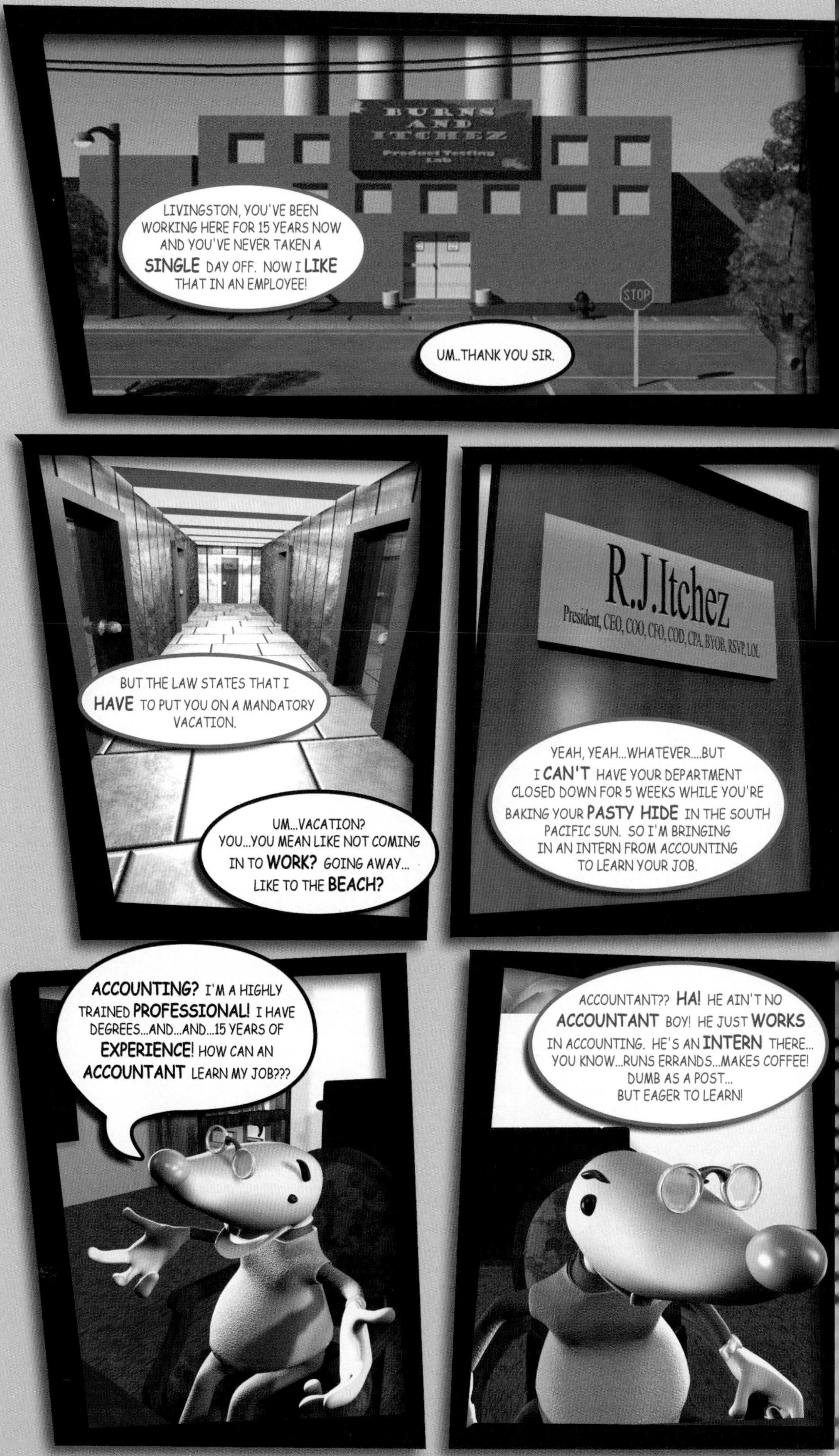
BURNS AND ITCHEZ
Product Testing Lab
LIVINGSTON, YOU'VE BEEN WORKING HERE FOR 15 YEARS NOW AND YOU'VE NEVER TAKEN A SINGLE DAY OFF. NOW I LIKE THAT IN AN EMPLOYEE!
STOP
UM..THANK YOU SIR.
BUT THE LAW STATES THAT I HAVE TO PUT YOU ON A MANDATORY VACATION.
UM...VACATION? YOU...YOU MEAN LIKE NOT COMING IN TO WORK? GOING AWAY... LIKE TO THE BEACH?
R.J.Itchez
President, CEO, COO, CFO, COD, CPA, BYOB, RSVP, LOL
YEAH, YEAH...WHATEVER....BUT I CAN'T HAVE YOUR DEPARTMENT CLOSED DOWN FOR 5 WEEKS WHILE YOU'RE BAKING YOUR PASTY HIDE IN THE SOUTH PACIFIC SUN. SO I'M BRINGING IN AN INTERN FROM ACCOUNTING TO LEARN YOUR JOB.
ACCOUNTING? I'M A HIGHLY TRAINED PROFESSIONAL! I HAVE DEGREES...AND...AND...15 YEARS OF EXPERIENCE! HOW CAN AN ACCOUNTANT LEARN MY JOB???
ACCOUNTANT?? HA! HE AIN'T NO ACCOUNTANT BOY! HE JUST WORKS IN ACCOUNTING. HE'S AN INTERN THERE... YOU KNOW...RUNS ERRANDS...MAKES COFFEE! DUMB AS A POST... BUT EAGER TO LEARN!

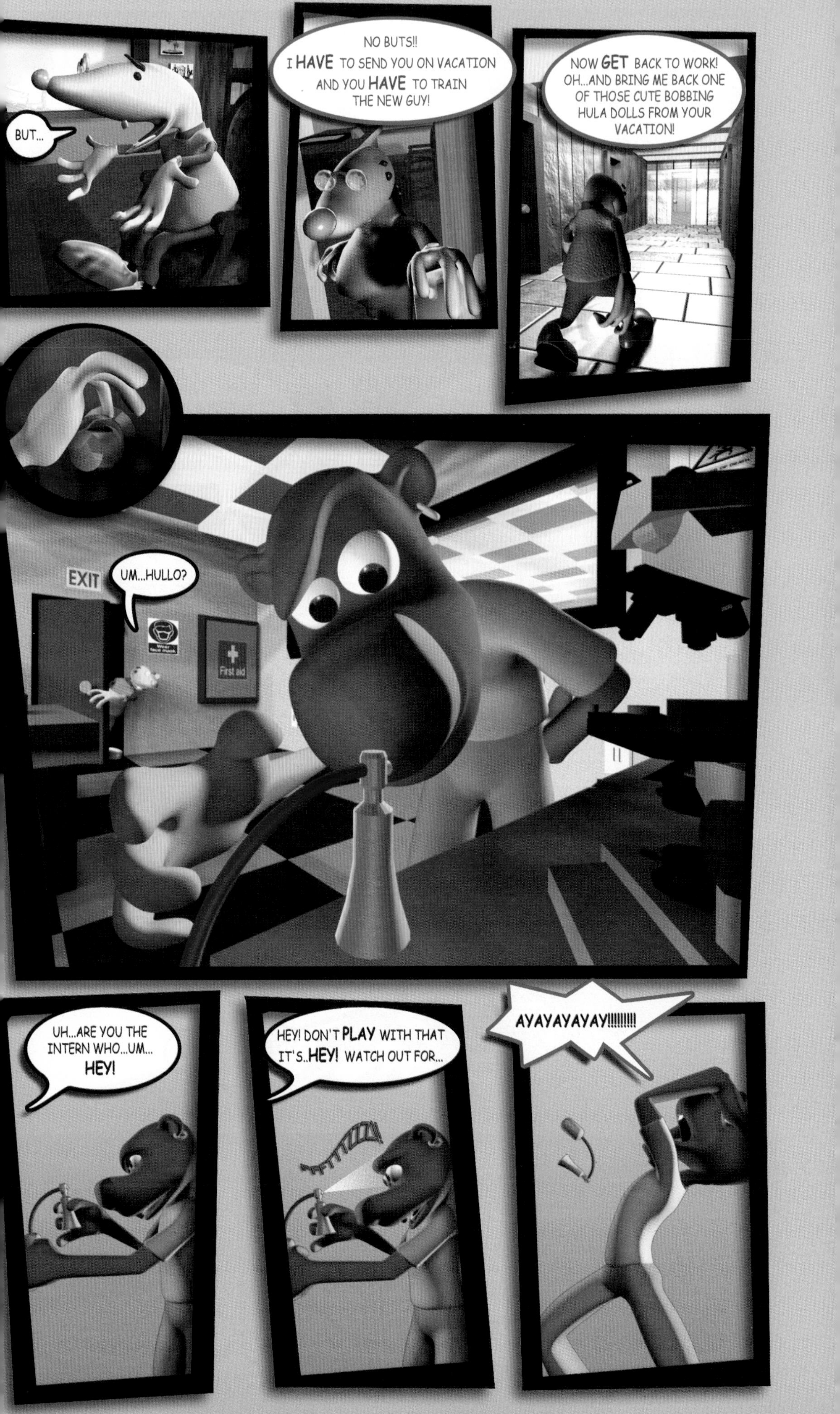

BUT...
NO BUTS!! I HAVE TO SEND YOU ON VACATION AND YOU HAVE TO TRAIN THE NEW GUY!
NOW GET BACK TO WORK! OH...AND BRING ME BACK ONE OF THOSE CUTE BOBBING HULA DOLLS FROM YOUR VACATION!
EXIT
UM...HULLO?
First aid
UH...ARE YOU THE INTERN WHO...UM... HEY!
HEY! DON'T PLAY WITH THAT IT'S..HEY! WATCH OUT FOR...
AYAYAYAYAY!!!!!!!!!

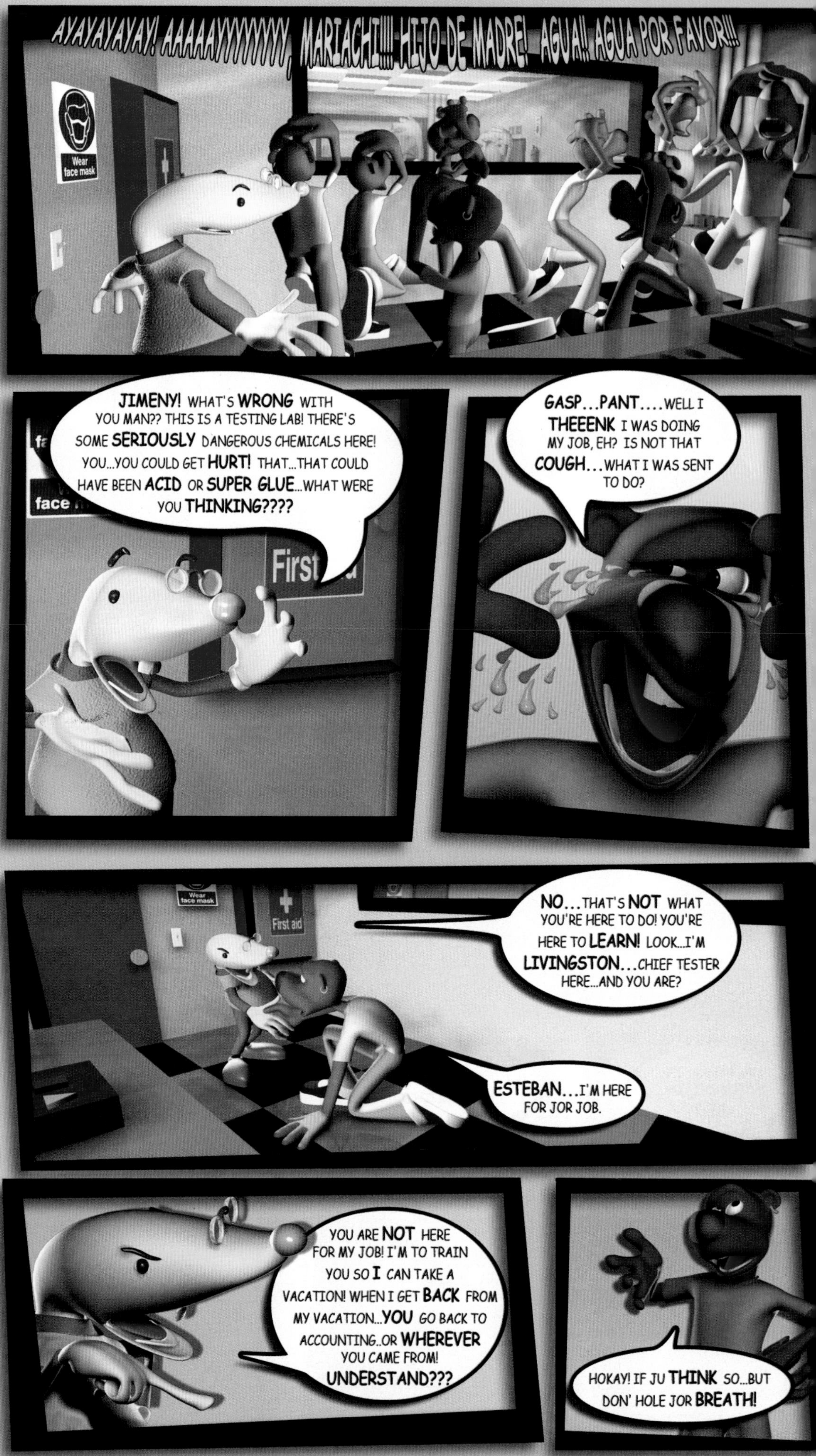
AYAYAYAYAY! AAAAAYYYYYYYY, MARIACHI!!!! HIJO DE MADRE! AGUA!! AGUA POR FAVOR!!!
Wear face mask
JIMENY! WHAT'S WRONG WITH YOU MAN?? THIS IS A TESTING LAB! THERE'S SOME SERIOUSLY DANGEROUS CHEMICALS HERE! YOU...YOU COULD GET HURT! THAT...THAT COULD HAVE BEEN ACID OR SUPER GLUE...WHAT WERE YOU THINKING????
GASP...PANT....WELL I THEEENK I WAS DOING MY JOB, EH? IS NOT THAT COUGH...WHAT I WAS SENT TO DO?
NO...THAT'S NOT WHAT YOU'RE HERE TO DO! YOU'RE HERE TO LEARN! LOOK...I'M LIVINGSTON...CHIEF TESTER HERE...AND YOU ARE?
ESTEBAN...I'M HERE FOR JOR JOB.
YOU ARE NOT HERE FOR MY JOB! I'M TO TRAIN YOU SO I CAN TAKE A VACATION! WHEN I GET BACK FROM MY VACATION...YOU GO BACK TO ACCOUNTING..OR WHEREVER YOU CAME FROM! UNDERSTAND???
HOKAY! IF JU THINK SO...BUT DON' HOLE JOR BREATH!

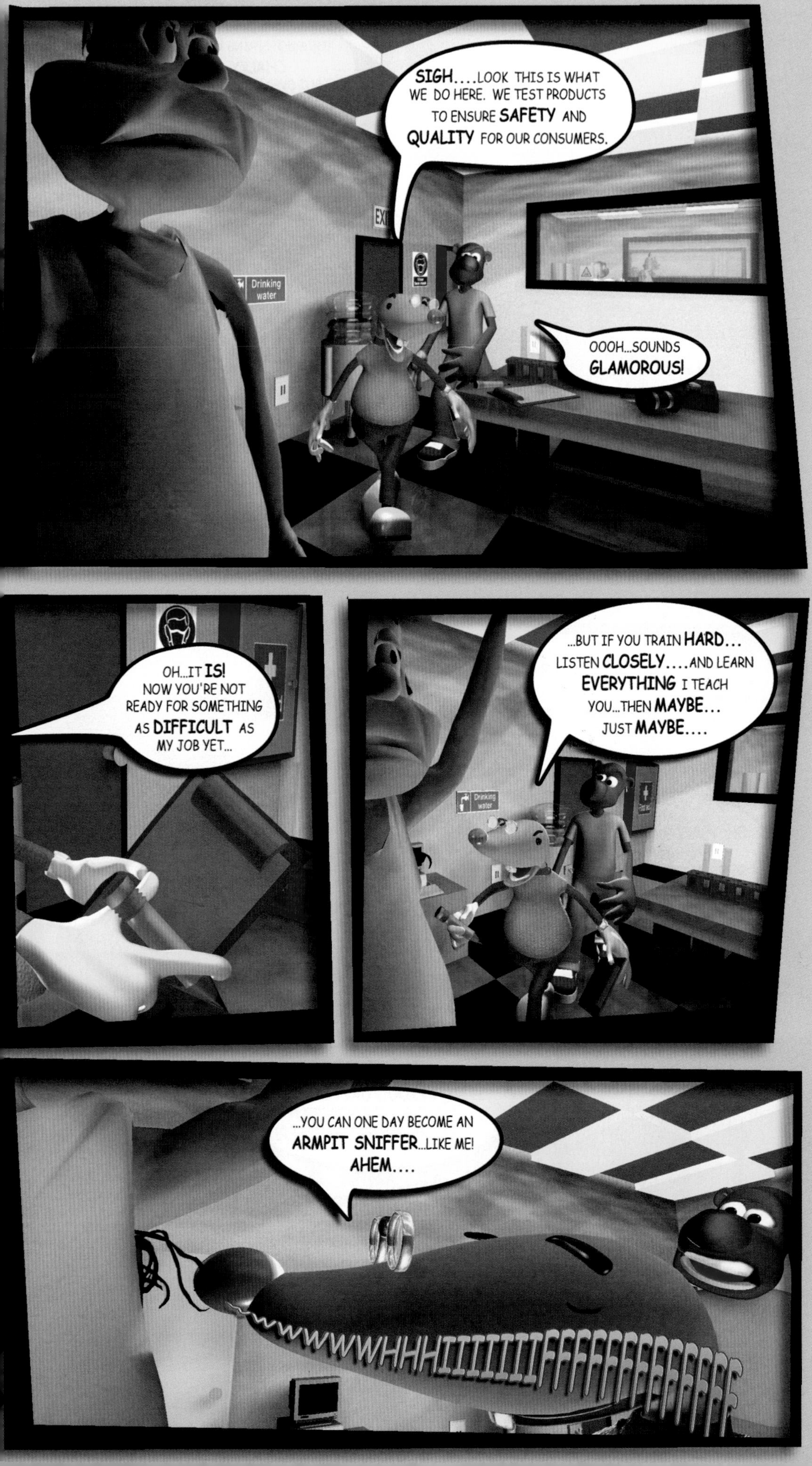
SIGH....LOOK THIS IS WHAT WE DO HERE. WE TEST PRODUCTS TO ENSURE SAFETY AND QUALITY FOR OUR CONSUMERS.
EXIT
Drinking water
OOOH...SOUNDS GLAMOROUS!
OH...IT IS! NOW YOU'RE NOT READY FOR SOMETHING AS DIFFICULT AS MY JOB YET...
...BUT IF YOU TRAIN HARD... LISTEN CLOSELY....AND LEARN EVERYTHING I TEACH YOU...THEN MAYBE... JUST MAYBE....
Drinking water
...YOU CAN ONE DAY BECOME AN ARMPIT SNIFFER...LIKE ME! AHEM....
WWWWWWWWHHHIIIIIIIIFFFFFFFFFFFFF

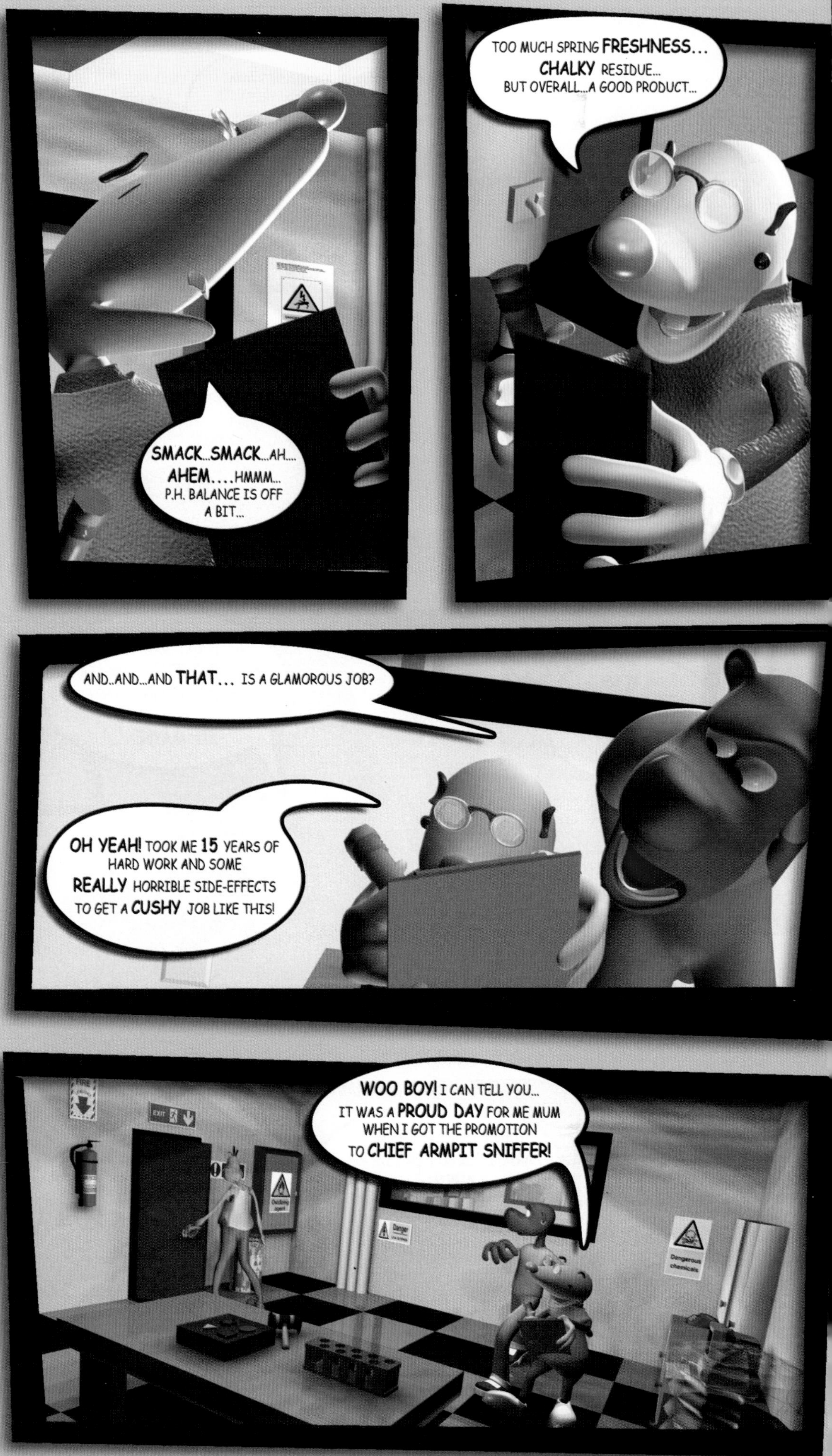
SMACK...SMACK...AH.... AHEM....HMMM... P.H. BALANCE IS OFF A BIT...
TOO MUCH SPRING FRESHNESS... CHALKY RESIDUE... BUT OVERALL...A GOOD PRODUCT...
AND..AND...AND THAT... IS A GLAMOROUS JOB?
OH YEAH! TOOK ME 15 YEARS OF HARD WORK AND SOME REALLY HORRIBLE SIDE-EFFECTS TO GET A CUSHY JOB LIKE THIS!
WOO BOY! I CAN TELL YOU... IT WAS A PROUD DAY FOR ME MUM WHEN I GOT THE PROMOTION TO CHIEF ARMPIT SNIFFER!
EXIT
Dangerous chemicals

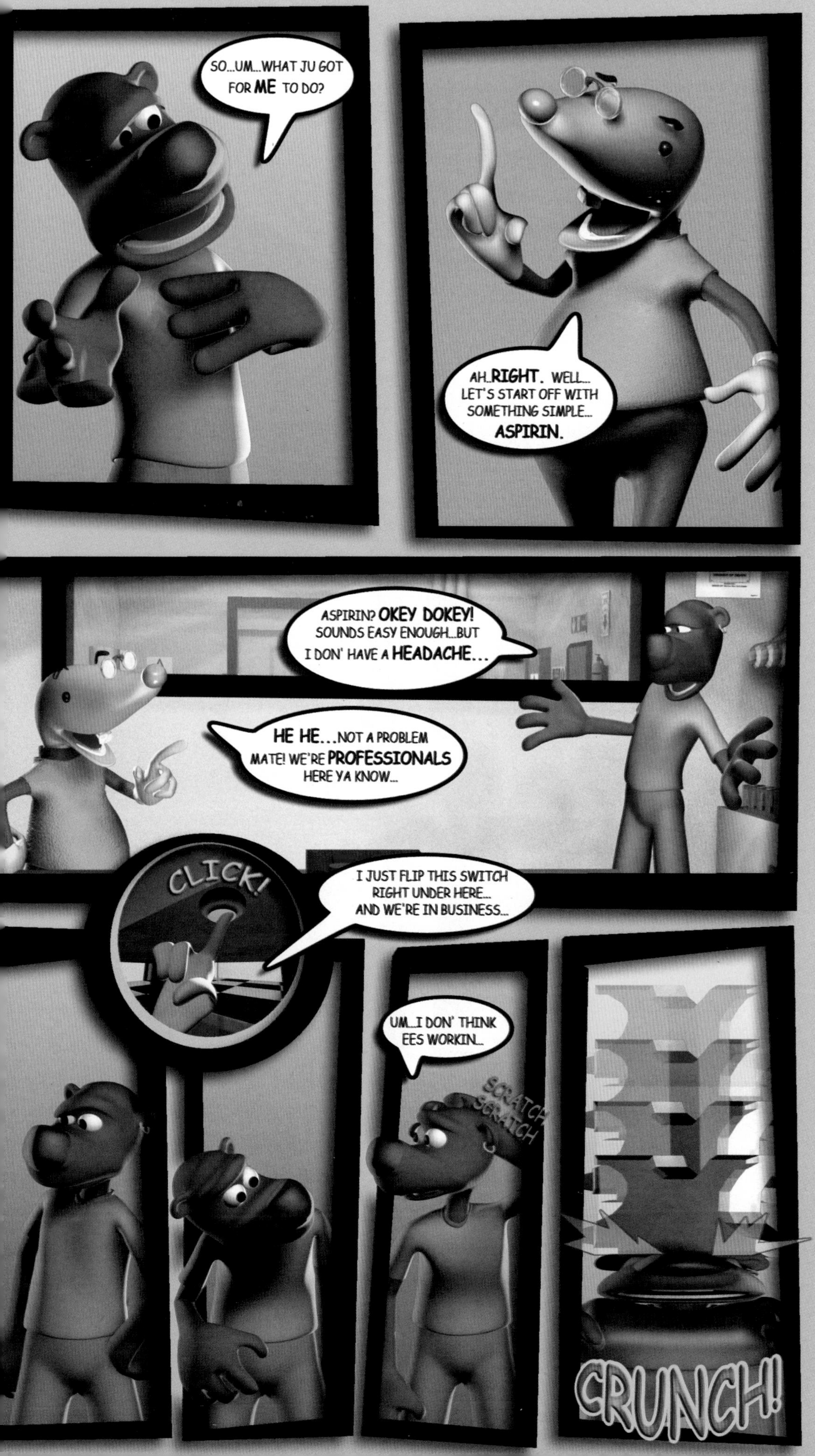
SO...UM...WHAT JU GOT FOR ME TO DO?
AH..RIGHT. WELL... LET'S START OFF WITH SOMETHING SIMPLE... ASPIRIN.
ASPIRIN? OKEY DOKEY! SOUNDS EASY ENOUGH...BUT I DON' HAVE A HEADACHE...
HE HE...NOT A PROBLEM MATE! WE'RE PROFESSIONALS HERE YA KNOW...
CLICK!
I JUST FLIP THIS SWITCH RIGHT UNDER HERE... AND WE'RE IN BUSINESS...
UM...I DON' THINK EES WORKIN...
SCRATCH SCRATCH
CRUNCH!

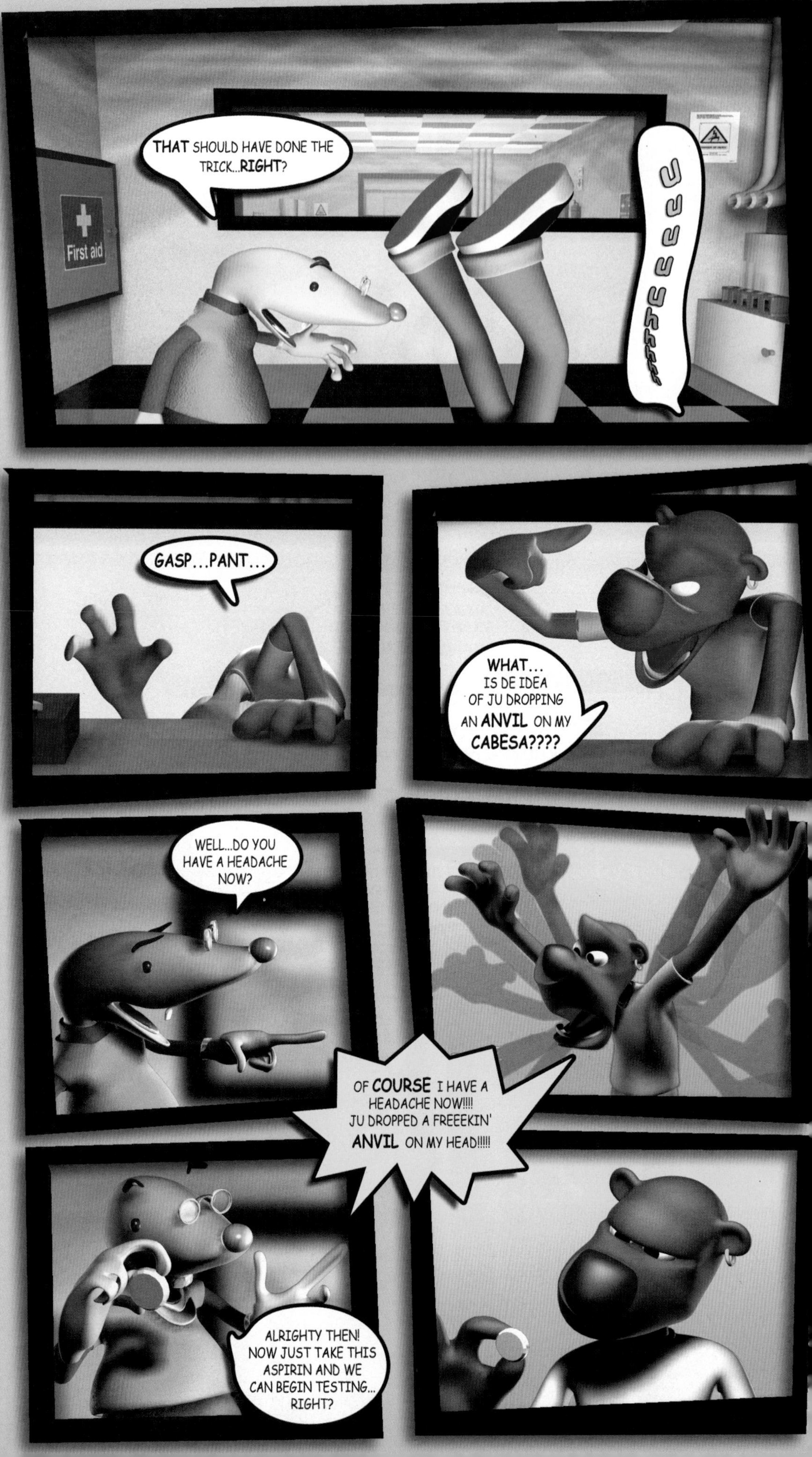

First aid
THAT SHOULD HAVE DONE THE TRICK...RIGHT?
UUUUUUUU
GASP...PANT...
WHAT... IS DE IDEA OF JU DROPPING AN ANVIL ON MY CABESA????
WELL...DO YOU HAVE A HEADACHE NOW?
OF COURSE I HAVE A HEADACHE NOW!!!! JU DROPPED A FREEEKIN' ANVIL ON MY HEAD!!!!!
ALRIGHTY THEN! NOW JUST TAKE THIS ASPIRIN AND WE CAN BEGIN TESTING... RIGHT?

AND SO...MOMENTS LATER...

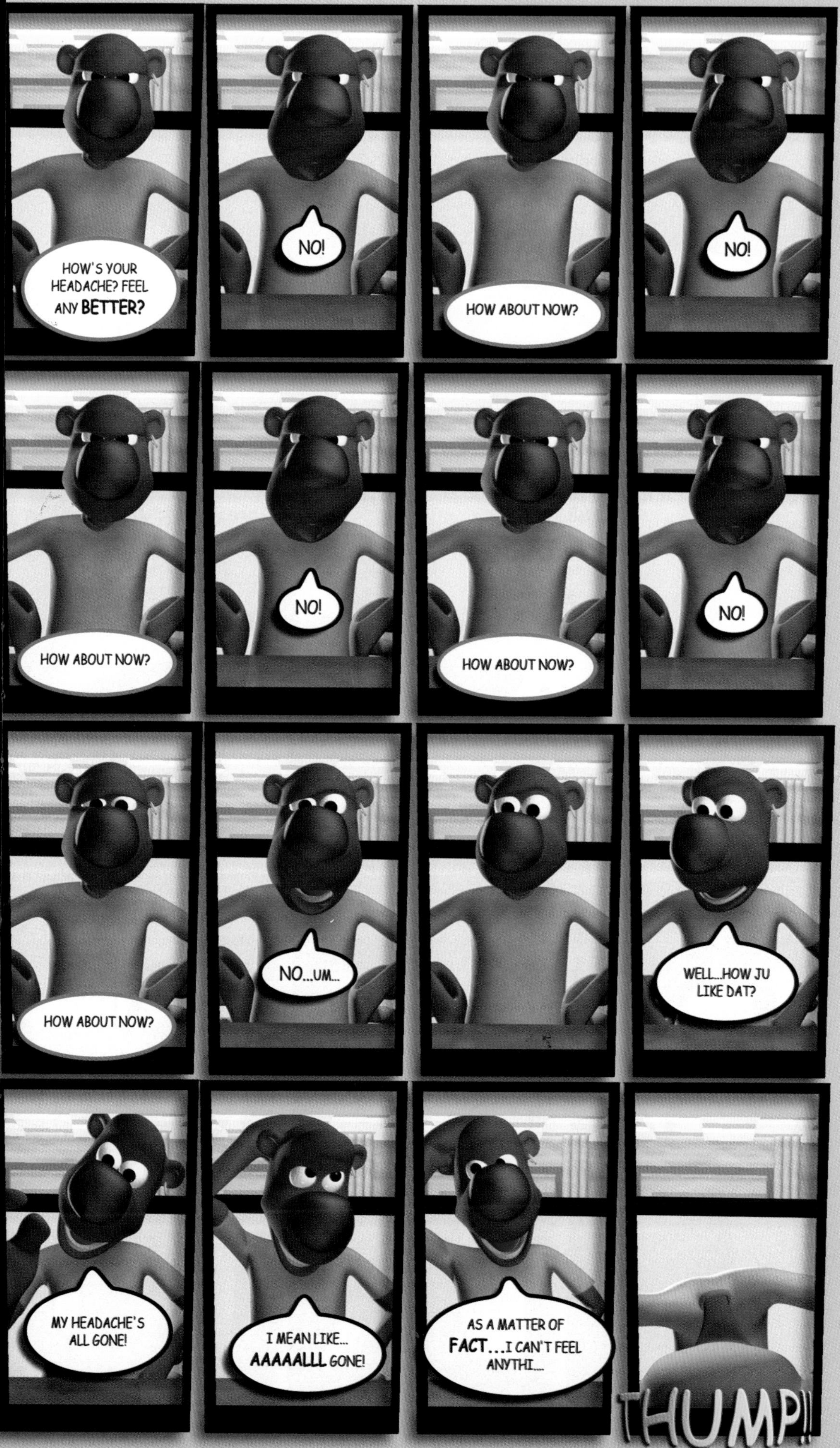

HOW'S YOUR HEADACHE? FEEL ANY BETTER?
NO!
HOW ABOUT NOW?
NO!
HOW ABOUT NOW?
NO!
HOW ABOUT NOW?
NO!
HOW ABOUT NOW?
NO...UM...
WELL...HOW JU LIKE DAT?
MY HEADACHE'S ALL GONE!
I MEAN LIKE... AAAAALLL GONE!
AS A MATTER OF FACT...I CAN'T FEEL ANYTHI....
THUMP!!

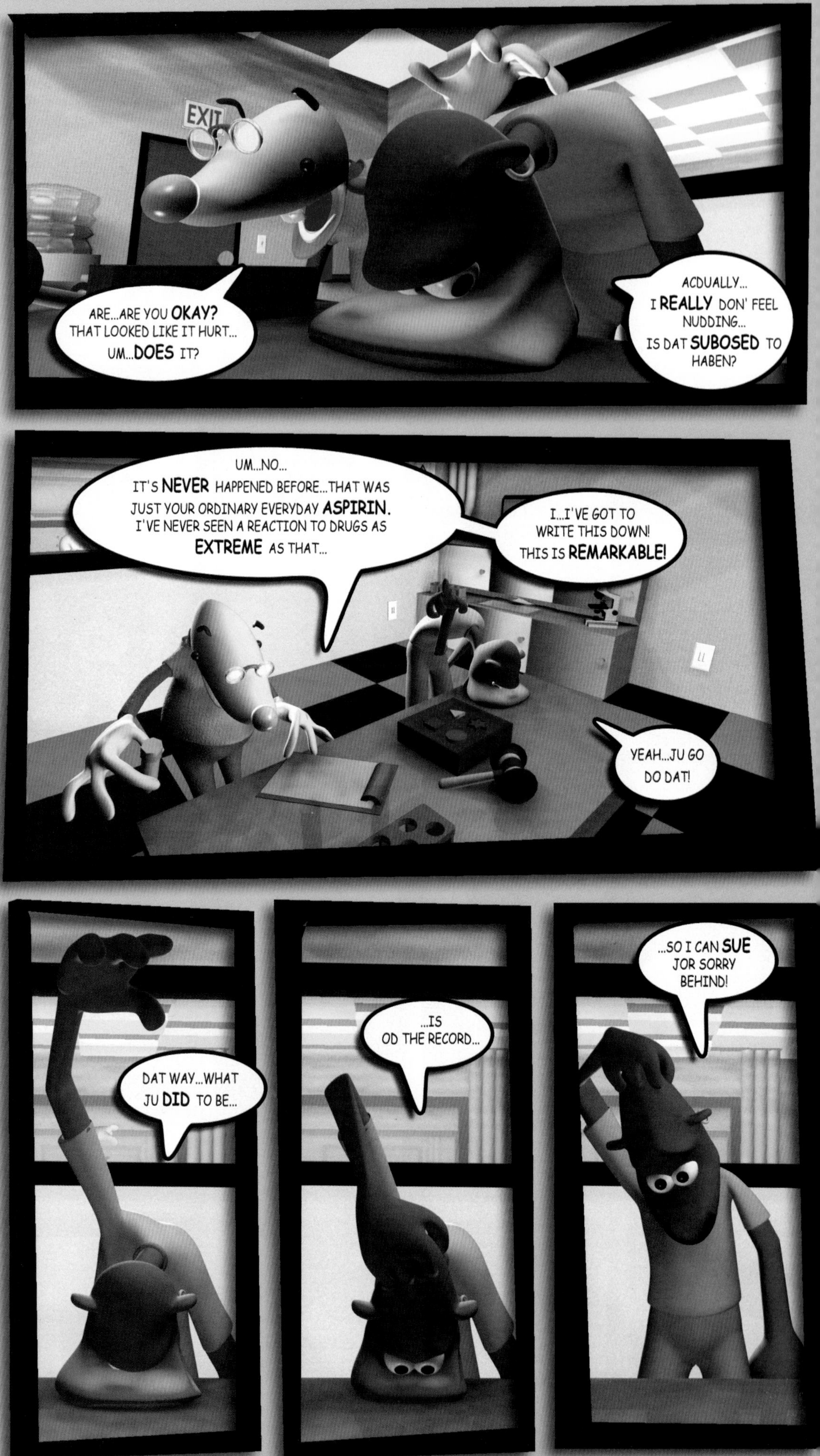
ARE...ARE YOU OKAY? THAT LOOKED LIKE IT HURT... UM...DOES IT?
ACDUALLY... I REALLY DON' FEEL NUDDING... IS DAT SUBOSED TO HABEN?
UM...NO... IT'S NEVER HAPPENED BEFORE...THAT WAS JUST YOUR ORDINARY EVERYDAY ASPIRIN. I'VE NEVER SEEN A REACTION TO DRUGS AS EXTREME AS THAT...
I...I'VE GOT TO WRITE THIS DOWN! THIS IS REMARKABLE!
YEAH...JU GO DO DAT!
DAT WAY...WHAT JU DID TO BE...
...IS OD THE RECORD...
...SO I CAN SUE JOR SORRY BEHIND!

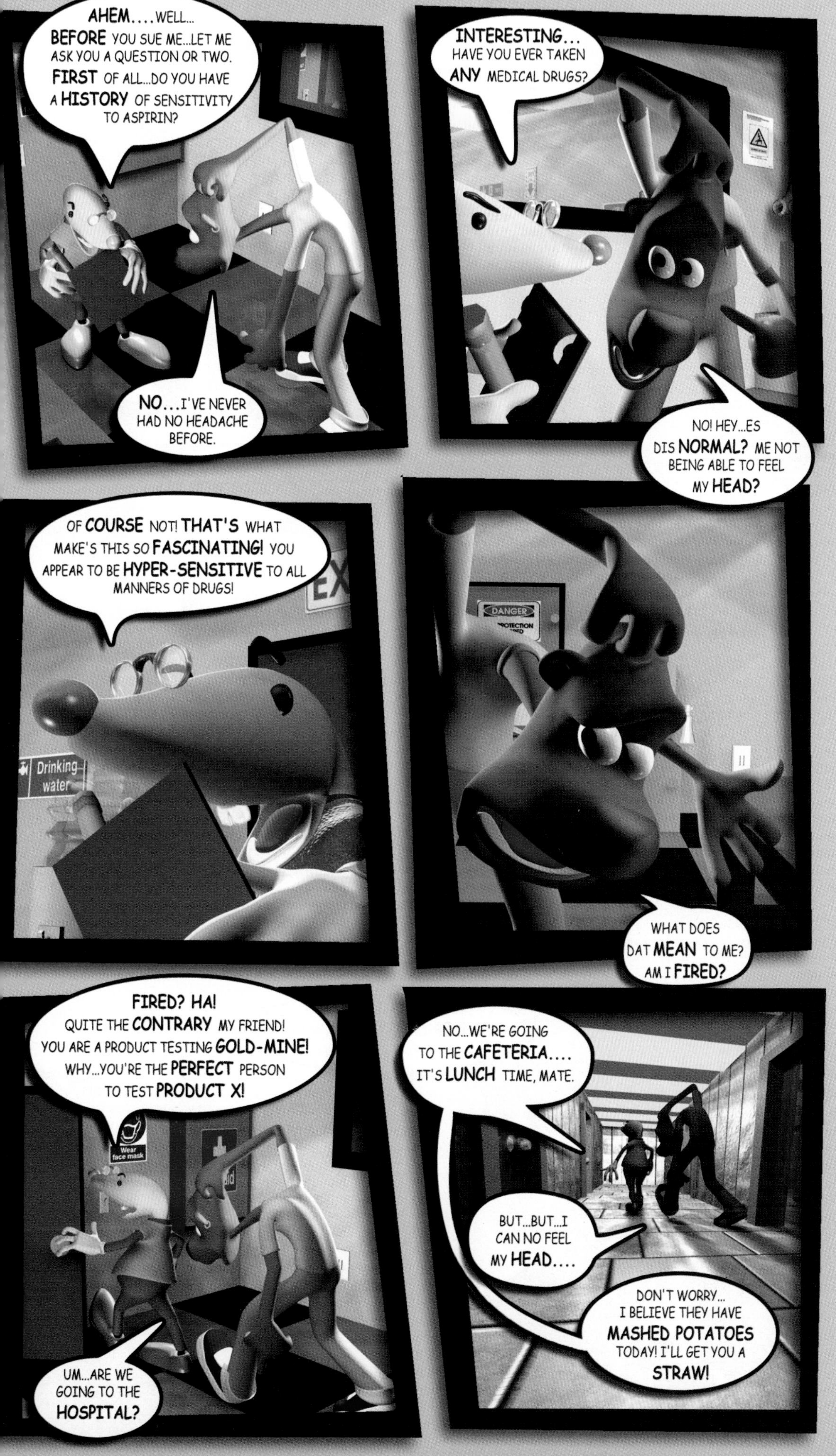
AHEM.... WELL... BEFORE YOU SUE ME...LET ME ASK YOU A QUESTION OR TWO. FIRST OF ALL...DO YOU HAVE A HISTORY OF SENSITIVITY TO ASPIRIN?
NO...I'VE NEVER HAD NO HEADACHE BEFORE.
INTERESTING... HAVE YOU EVER TAKEN ANY MEDICAL DRUGS?
NO! HEY...ES DIS NORMAL? ME NOT BEING ABLE TO FEEL MY HEAD?
OF COURSE NOT! THAT'S WHAT MAKE'S THIS SO FASCINATING! YOU APPEAR TO BE HYPER-SENSITIVE TO ALL MANNERS OF DRUGS!
Drinking water
DANGER
WHAT DOES DAT MEAN TO ME? AM I FIRED?
FIRED? HA! QUITE THE CONTRARY MY FRIEND! YOU ARE A PRODUCT TESTING GOLD-MINE! WHY...YOU'RE THE PERFECT PERSON TO TEST PRODUCT X!
Wear face mask
UM...ARE WE GOING TO THE HOSPITAL?
NO...WE'RE GOING TO THE CAFETERIA.... IT'S LUNCH TIME, MATE.
BUT...BUT...I CAN NO FEEL MY HEAD....
DON'T WORRY... I BELIEVE THEY HAVE MASHED POTATOES TODAY! I'LL GET YOU A STRAW!

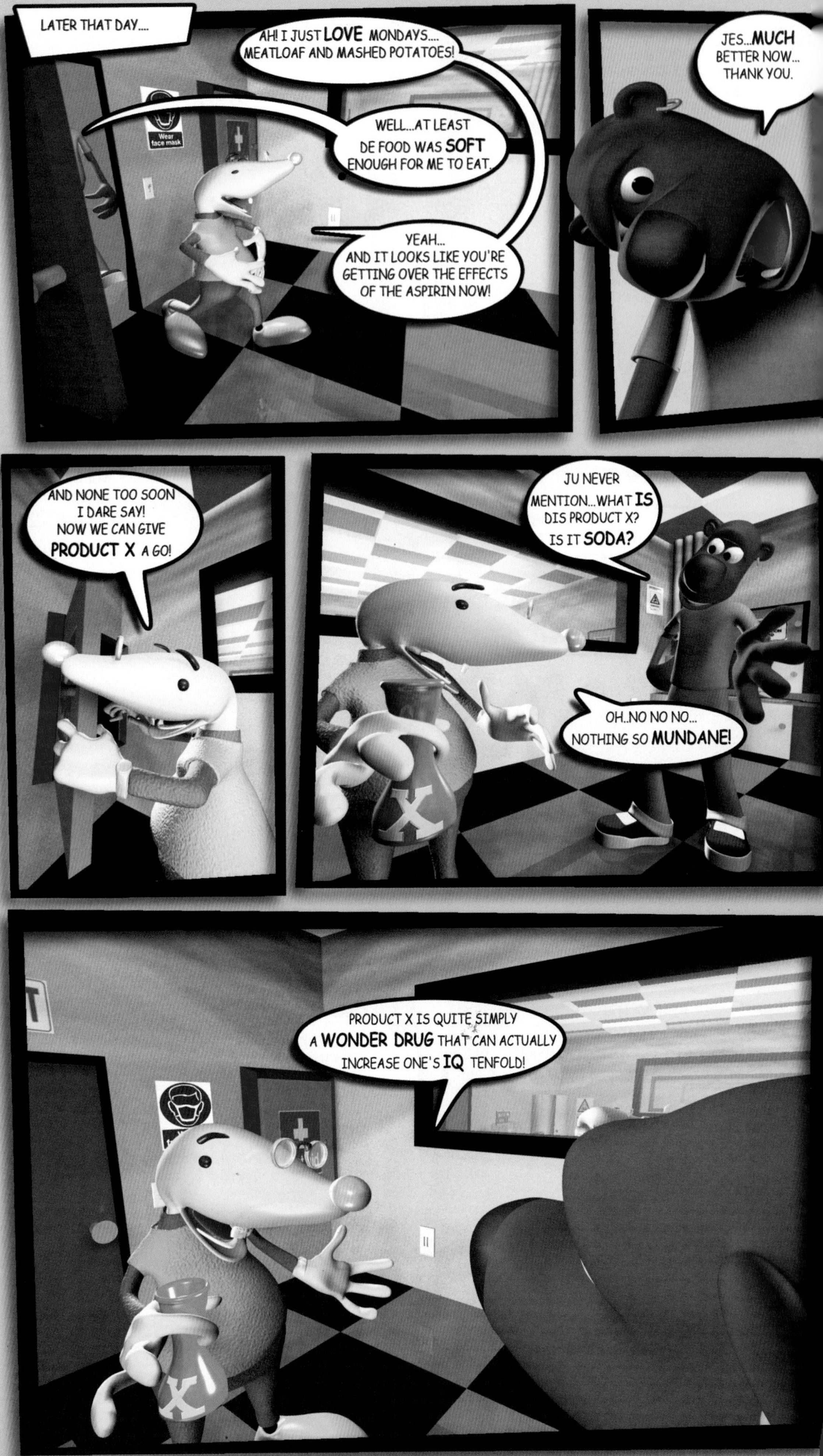
LATER THAT DAY....
AH! I JUST LOVE MONDAYS.... MEATLOAF AND MASHED POTATOES!
WELL...AT LEAST DE FOOD WAS SOFT ENOUGH FOR ME TO EAT.
YEAH... AND IT LOOKS LIKE YOU'RE GETTING OVER THE EFFECTS OF THE ASPIRIN NOW!
JES...MUCH BETTER NOW... THANK YOU.
AND NONE TOO SOON I DARE SAY! NOW WE CAN GIVE PRODUCT X A GO!
JU NEVER MENTION...WHAT IS DIS PRODUCT X? IS IT SODA?
OH..NO NO NO... NOTHING SO MUNDANE!
PRODUCT X IS QUITE SIMPLY A WONDER DRUG THAT CAN ACTUALLY INCREASE ONE'S IQ TENFOLD!

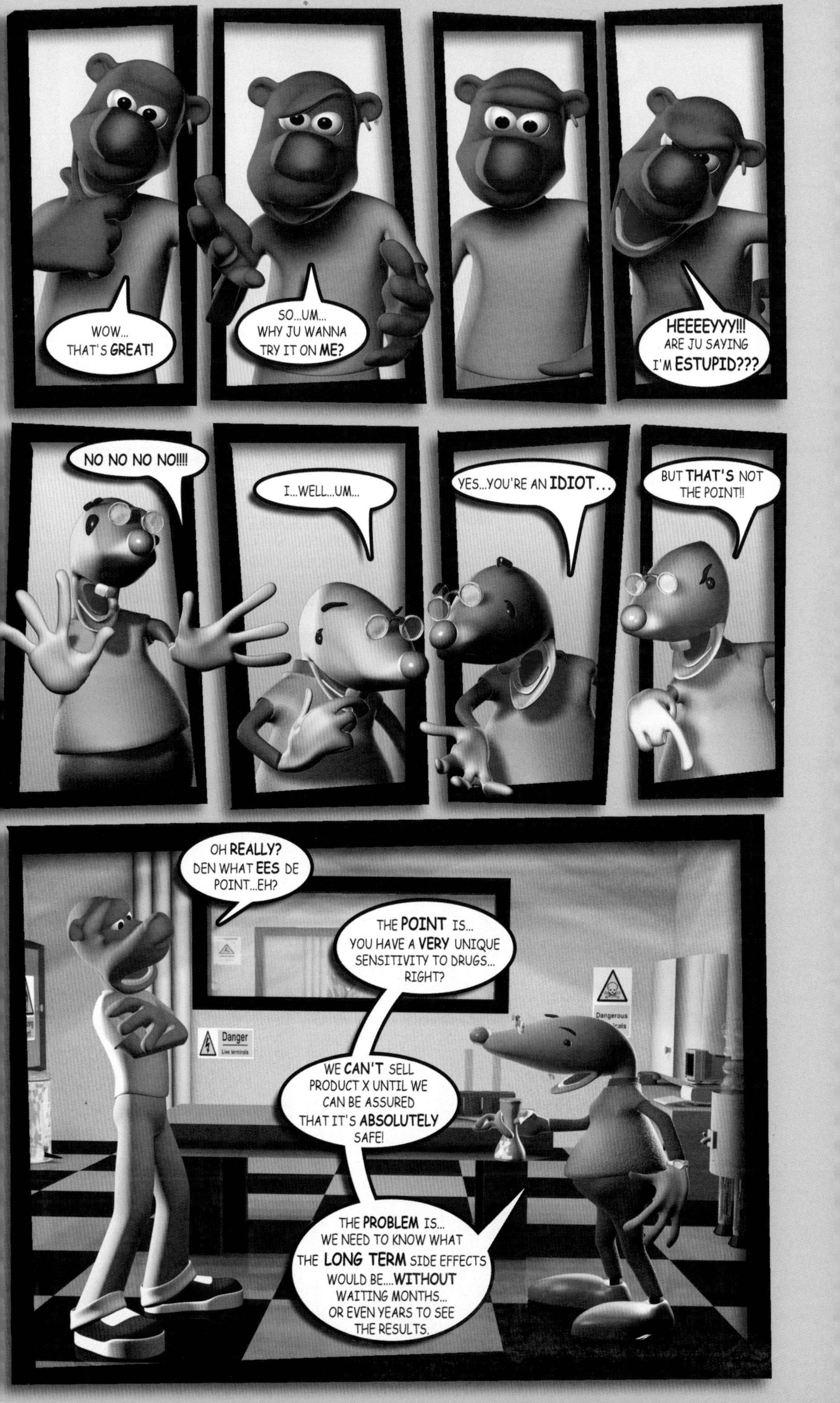
WOW...
THAT'S GREAT!
SO...UM...
WHY JU WANNA
TRY IT ON ME?
HEEEEYYY!!!
ARE JU SAYING
I'M ESTUPID???
NO NO NO NO!!!!
I...WELL...UM...
YES...YOU'RE AN IDIOT...
BUT THAT'S NOT
THE POINT!!
OH REALLY?
DEN WHAT EES DE
POINT...EH?
THE POINT IS...
YOU HAVE A VERY UNIQUE
SENSITIVITY TO DRUGS...
RIGHT?
WE CAN'T SELL
PRODUCT X UNTIL WE
CAN BE ASSURED
THAT IT'S ABSOLUTELY
SAFE!
THE PROBLEM IS...
WE NEED TO KNOW WHAT
THE LONG TERM SIDE EFFECTS
WOULD BE....WITHOUT
WAITING MONTHS...
OR EVEN YEARS TO SEE
THE RESULTS.
Danger
Dangerous

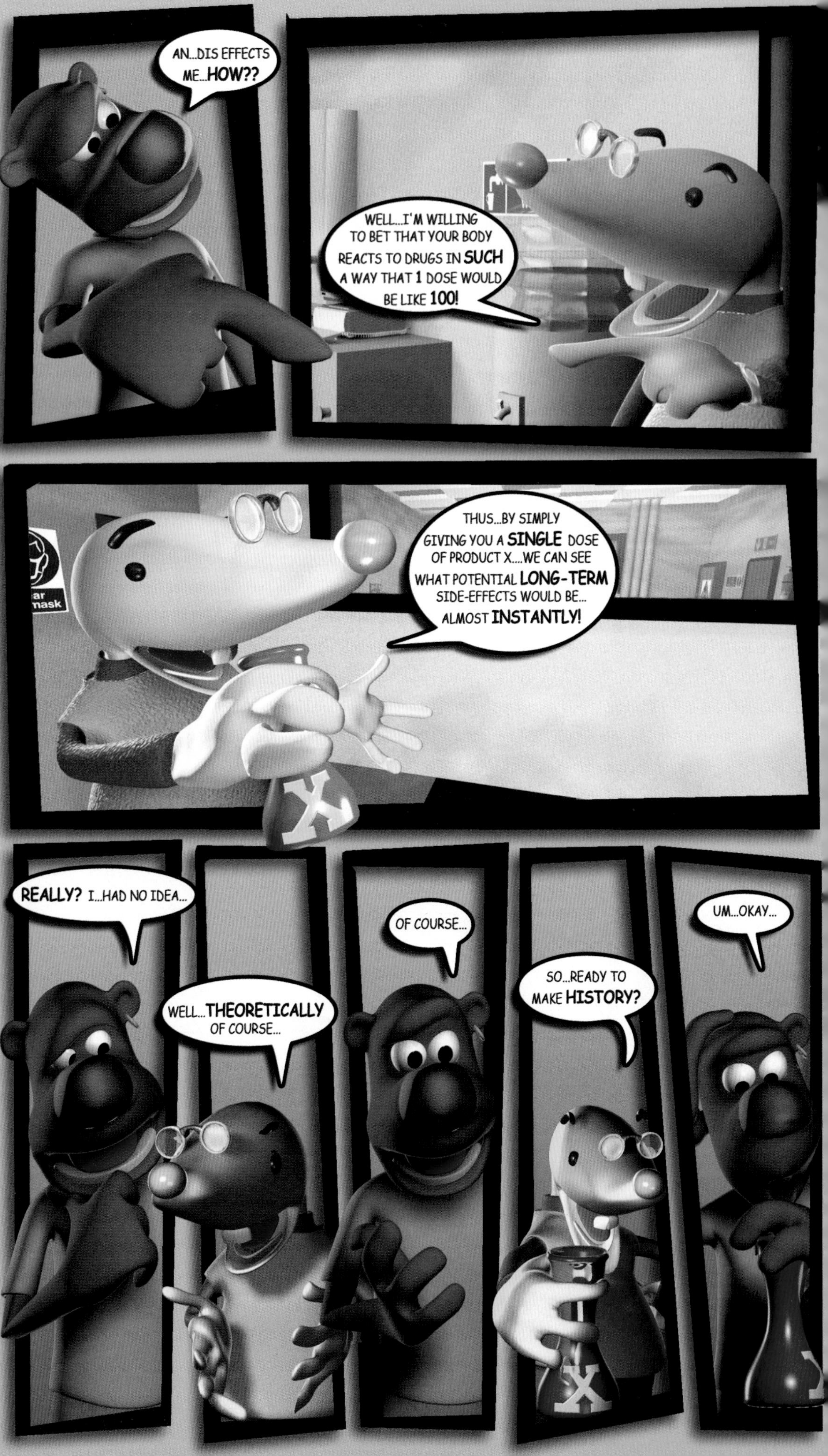
AN...DIS EFFECTS ME...HOW??
WELL...I'M WILLING TO BET THAT YOUR BODY REACTS TO DRUGS IN SUCH A WAY THAT 1 DOSE WOULD BE LIKE 100!
THUS...BY SIMPLY GIVING YOU A SINGLE DOSE OF PRODUCT X....WE CAN SEE WHAT POTENTIAL LONG-TERM SIDE-EFFECTS WOULD BE... ALMOST INSTANTLY!
REALLY? I...HAD NO IDEA...
WELL...THEORETICALLY OF COURSE...
OF COURSE...
SO...READY TO MAKE HISTORY?
UM...OKAY...

BLEEEAAAHHH!!
NOW WHAT?
UM...DO YOU FEEL ANY SMARTER?
NOT AT THIS PARTICULAR MOMENT... NO...

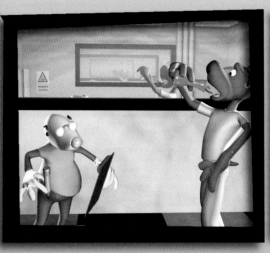

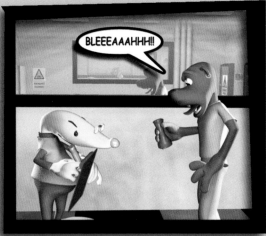

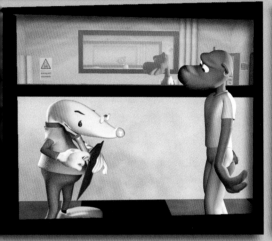

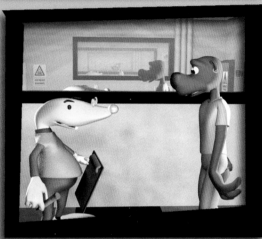

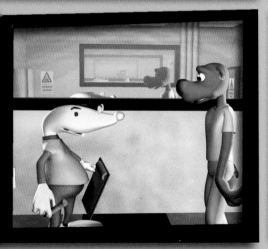

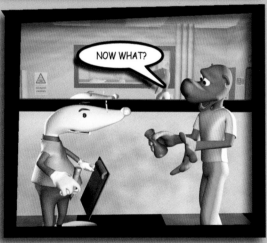

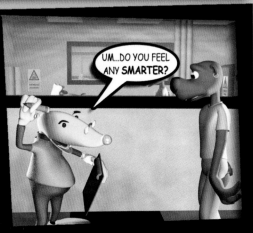

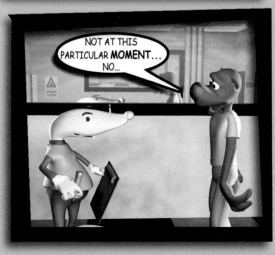

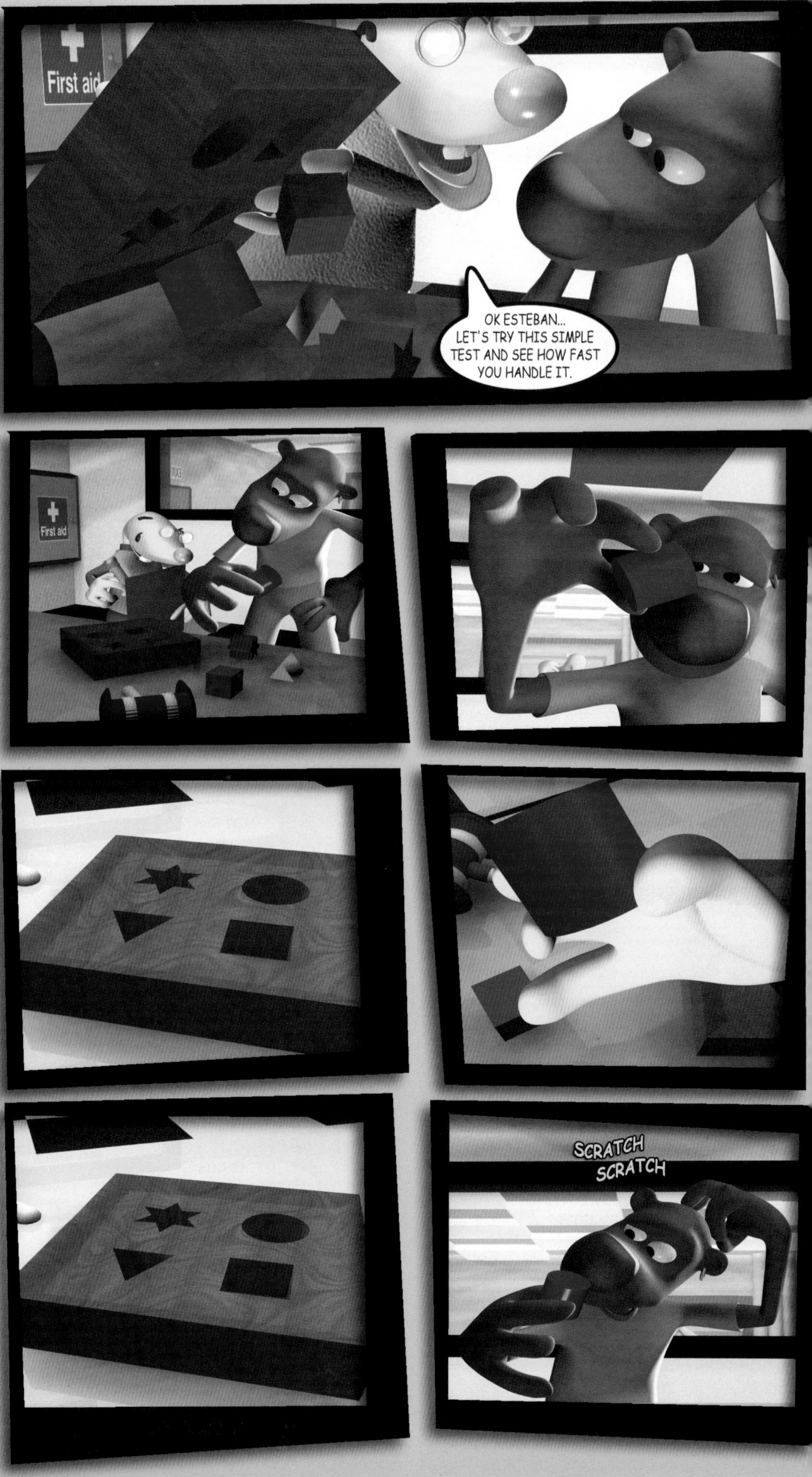
First aid
OK ESTEBAN... LET'S TRY THIS SIMPLE TEST AND SEE HOW FAST YOU HANDLE IT.
First aid
SCRATCH SCRATCH

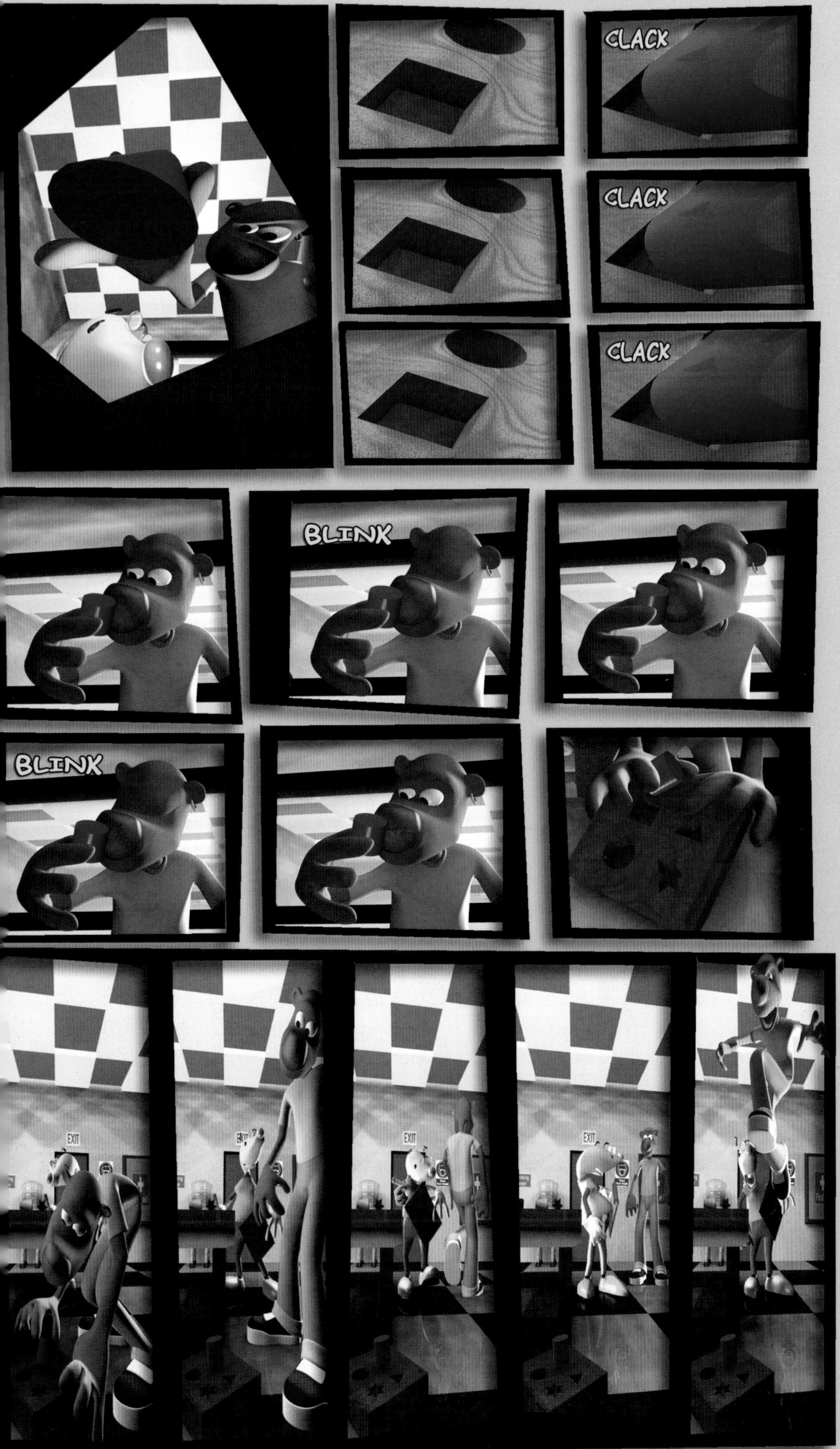
CLACK
CLACK
CLACK
BLINK
BLINK
EXIT
EXIT
EXIT
EXIT

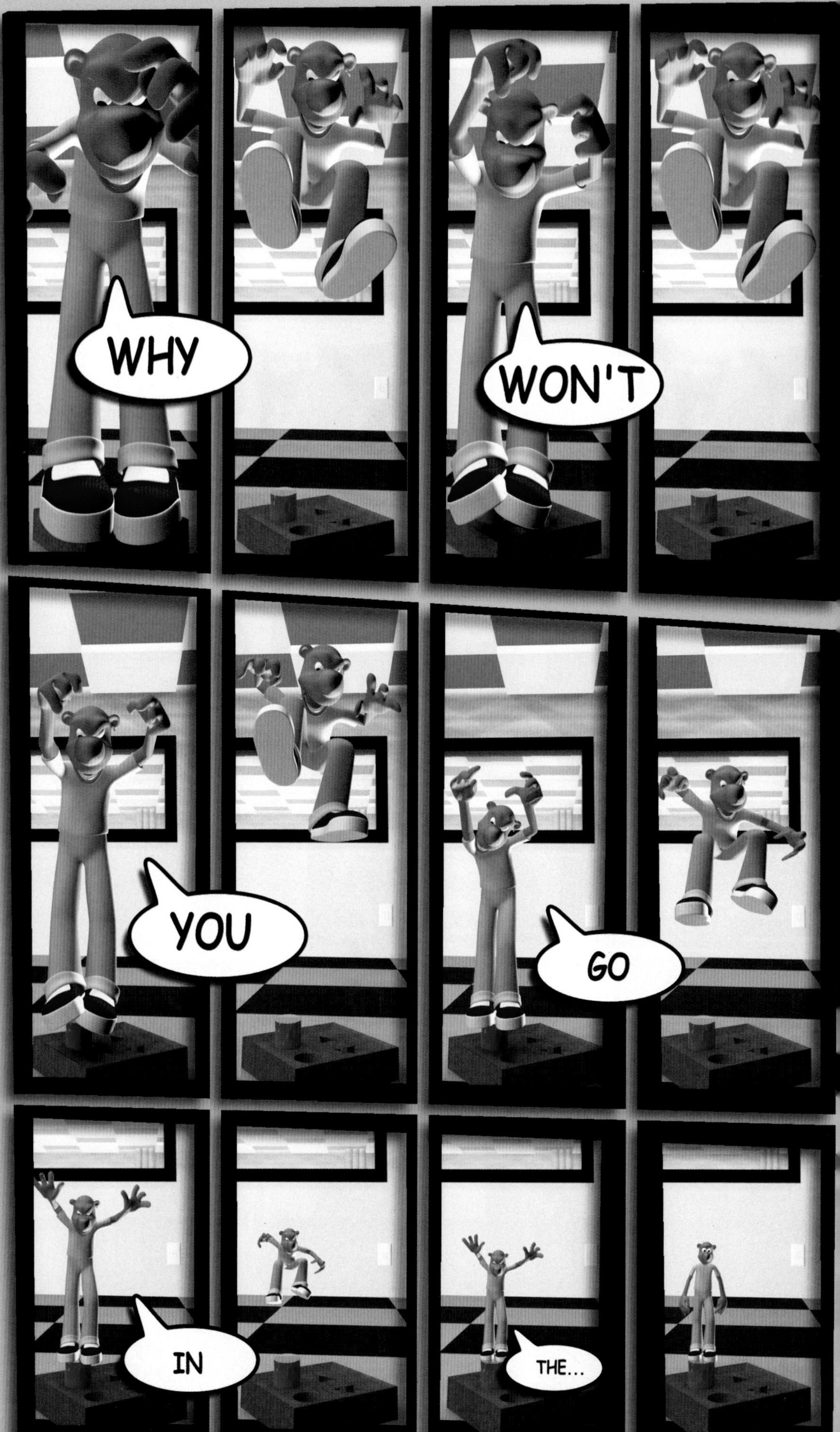

WHY
WON'T
YOU
GO
IN
THE...

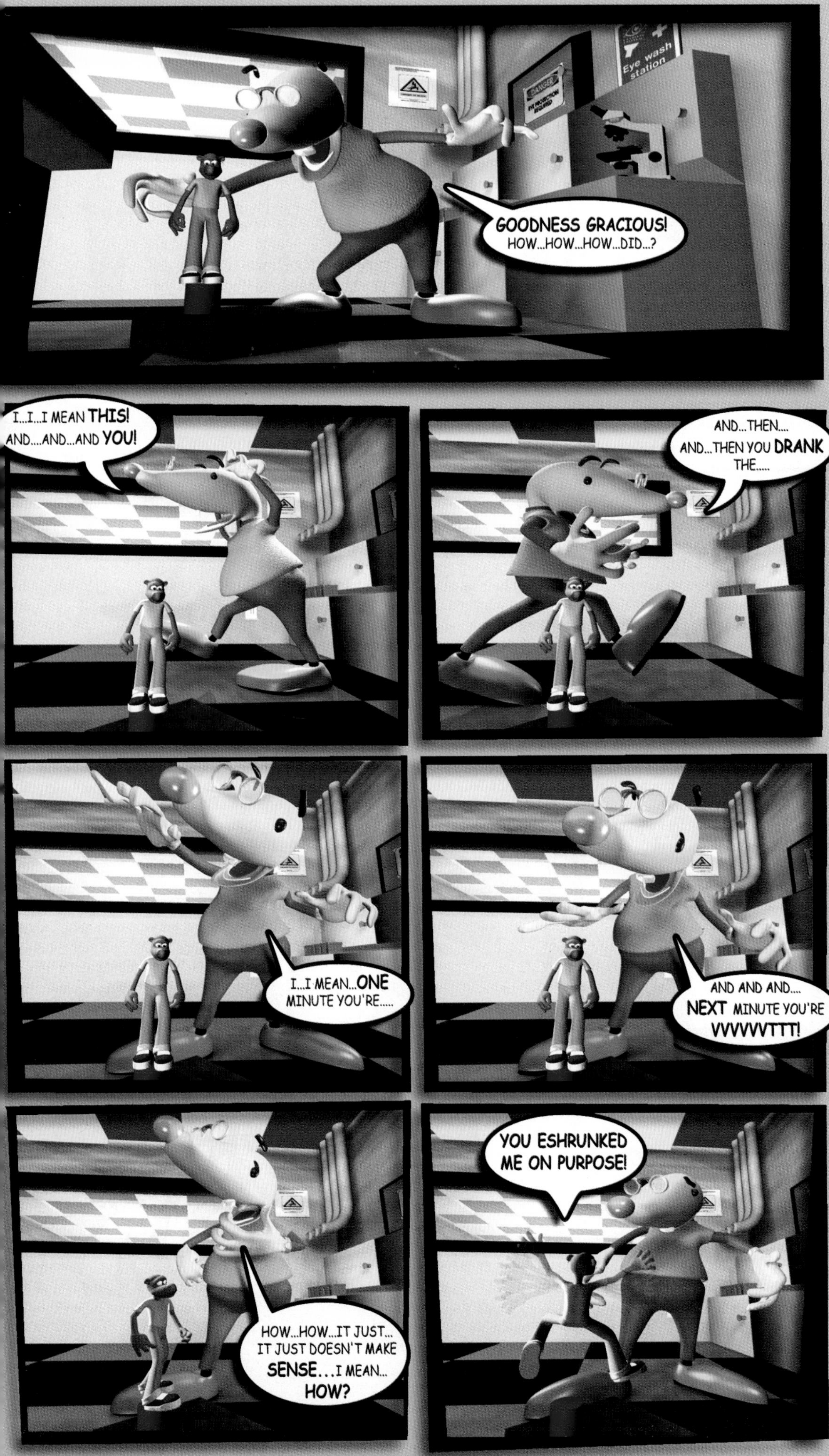

Eye wash station
GOODNESS GRACIOUS!
HOW...HOW...HOW...DID...?
I...I...I MEAN THIS!
AND....AND...AND YOU!
AND...THEN....
AND...THEN YOU DRANK THE.....
I...I MEAN...ONE MINUTE YOU'RE.....
AND AND AND....
NEXT MINUTE YOU'RE VVVVVVTTT!
HOW...HOW...IT JUST...
IT JUST DOESN'T MAKE SENSE...I MEAN...
HOW?
YOU ESHRUNKED ME ON PURPOSE!

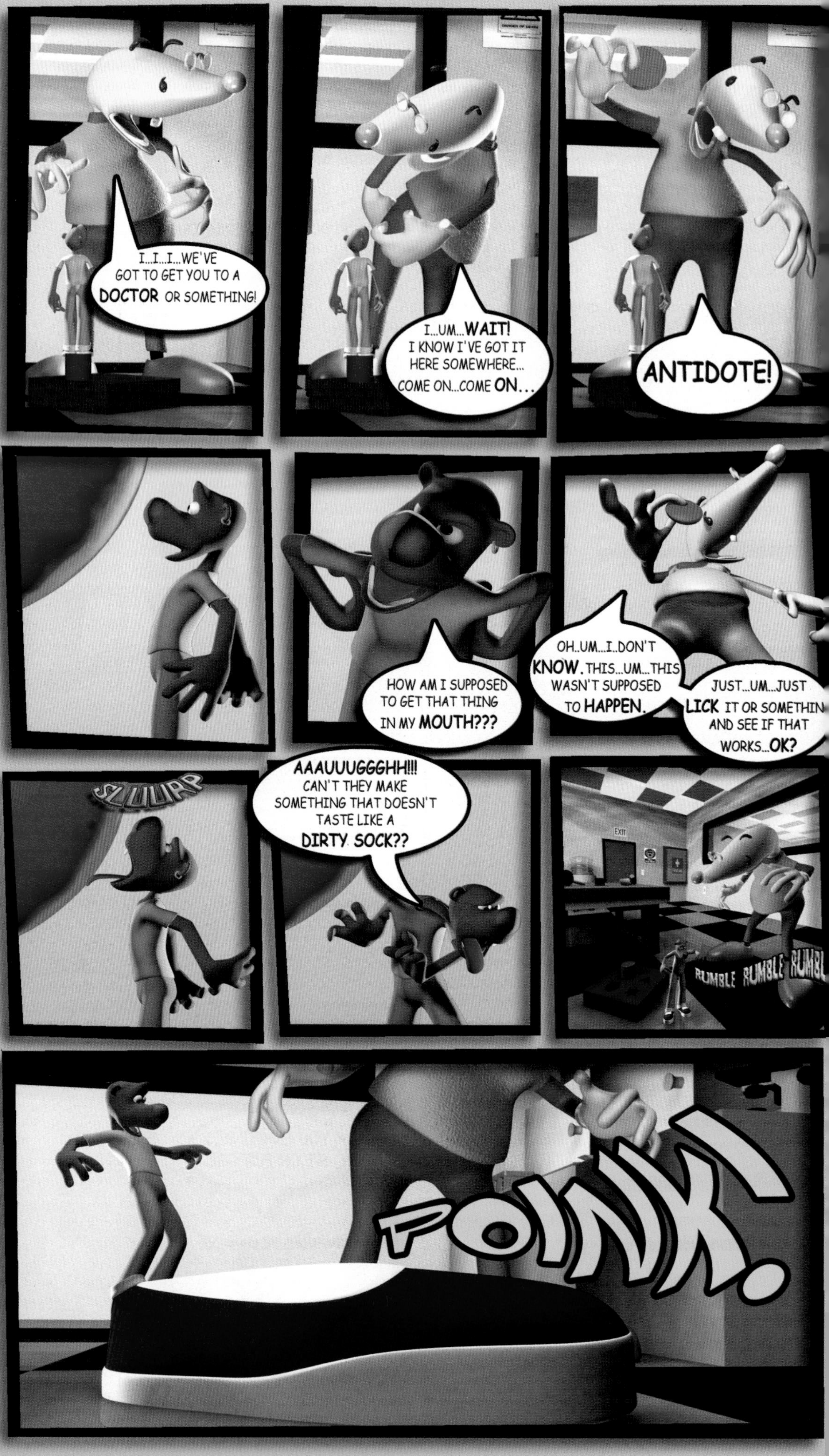

I...I...I...WE'VE GOT TO GET YOU TO A DOCTOR OR SOMETHING!
I...UM...WAIT! I KNOW I'VE GOT IT HERE SOMEWHERE... COME ON...COME ON...
ANTIDOTE!
HOW AM I SUPPOSED TO GET THAT THING IN MY MOUTH???
OH..UM...I..DON'T KNOW. THIS...UM...THIS WASN'T SUPPOSED TO HAPPEN.
JUST...UM...JUST LICK IT OR SOMETHIN AND SEE IF THAT WORKS...OK?
SLUURP
AAAUUUGGGHH!!! CAN'T THEY MAKE SOMETHING THAT DOESN'T TASTE LIKE A DIRTY SOCK??
EXIT
RUMBLE RUMBLE RUMBL
POINK!

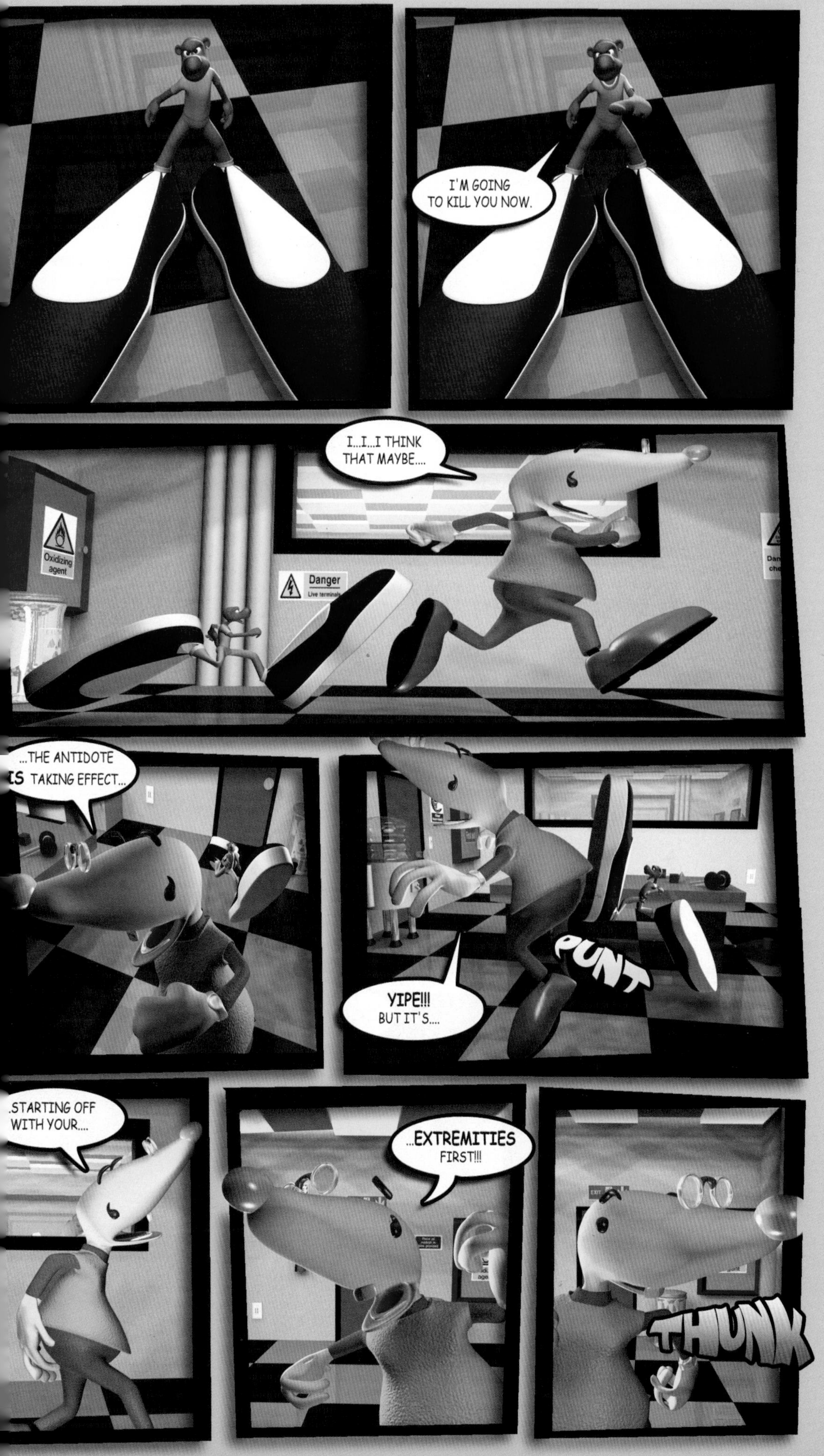
I'M GOING
TO KILL YOU NOW.
I...I...I THINK
THAT MAYBE....
Oxidizing agent
Danger
Live terminals
...THE ANTIDOTE
IS TAKING EFFECT...
YIPE!!!
BUT IT'S....
PUNT
.STARTING OFF
WITH YOUR....
...EXTREMITIES
FIRST!!!
THUNK

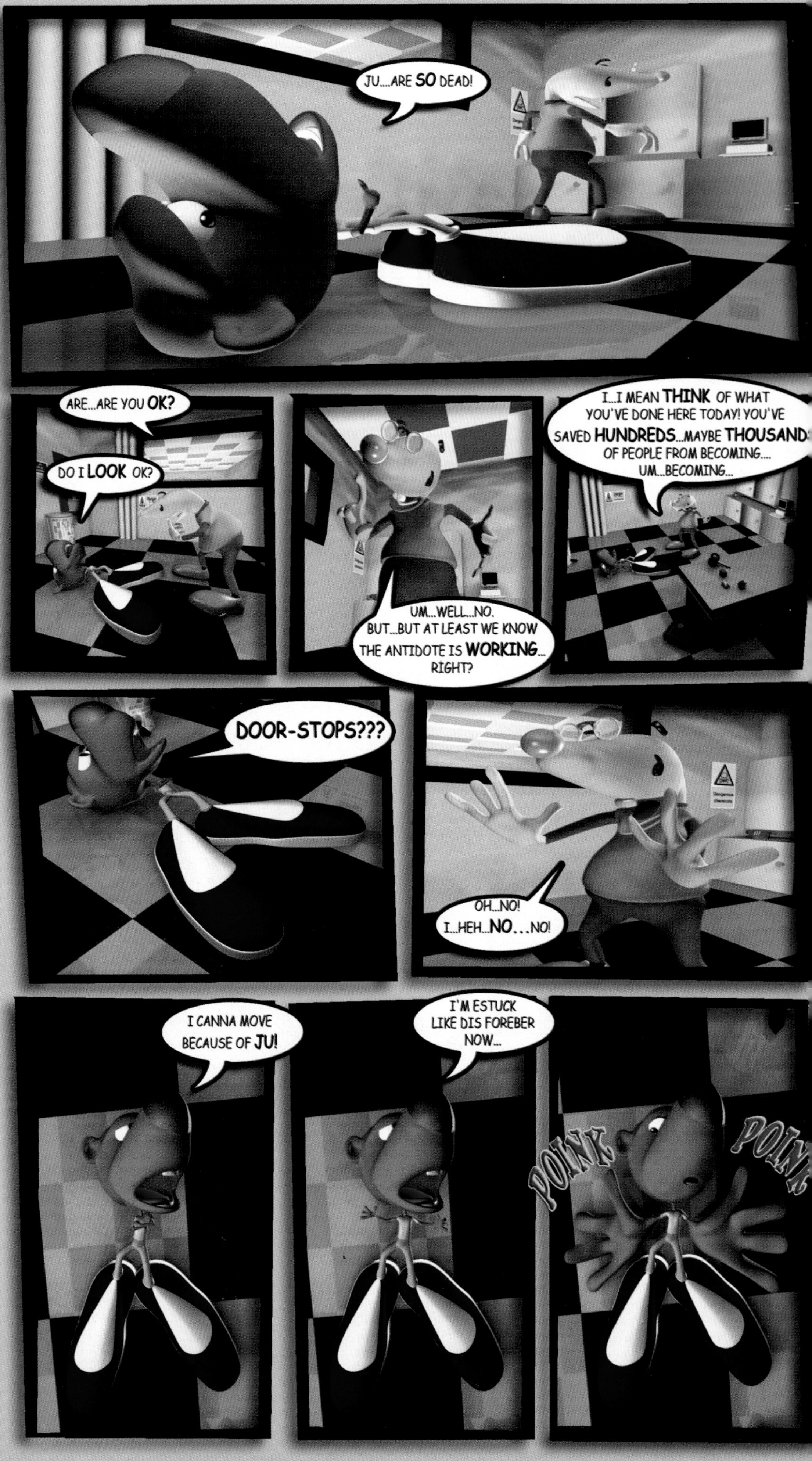
JU....ARE SO DEAD!
ARE...ARE YOU OK?
DO I LOOK OK?
UM...WELL...NO.
BUT...BUT AT LEAST WE KNOW
THE ANTIDOTE IS WORKING...
RIGHT?
I...I MEAN THINK OF WHAT
YOU'VE DONE HERE TODAY! YOU'VE
SAVED HUNDREDS...MAYBE THOUSANDS
OF PEOPLE FROM BECOMING....
UM...BECOMING...
DOOR-STOPS???
OH...NO!
I...HEH...NO...NO!
I CANNA MOVE
BECAUSE OF JU!
I'M ESTUCK
LIKE DIS FOREBER
NOW...
POINK
POINK

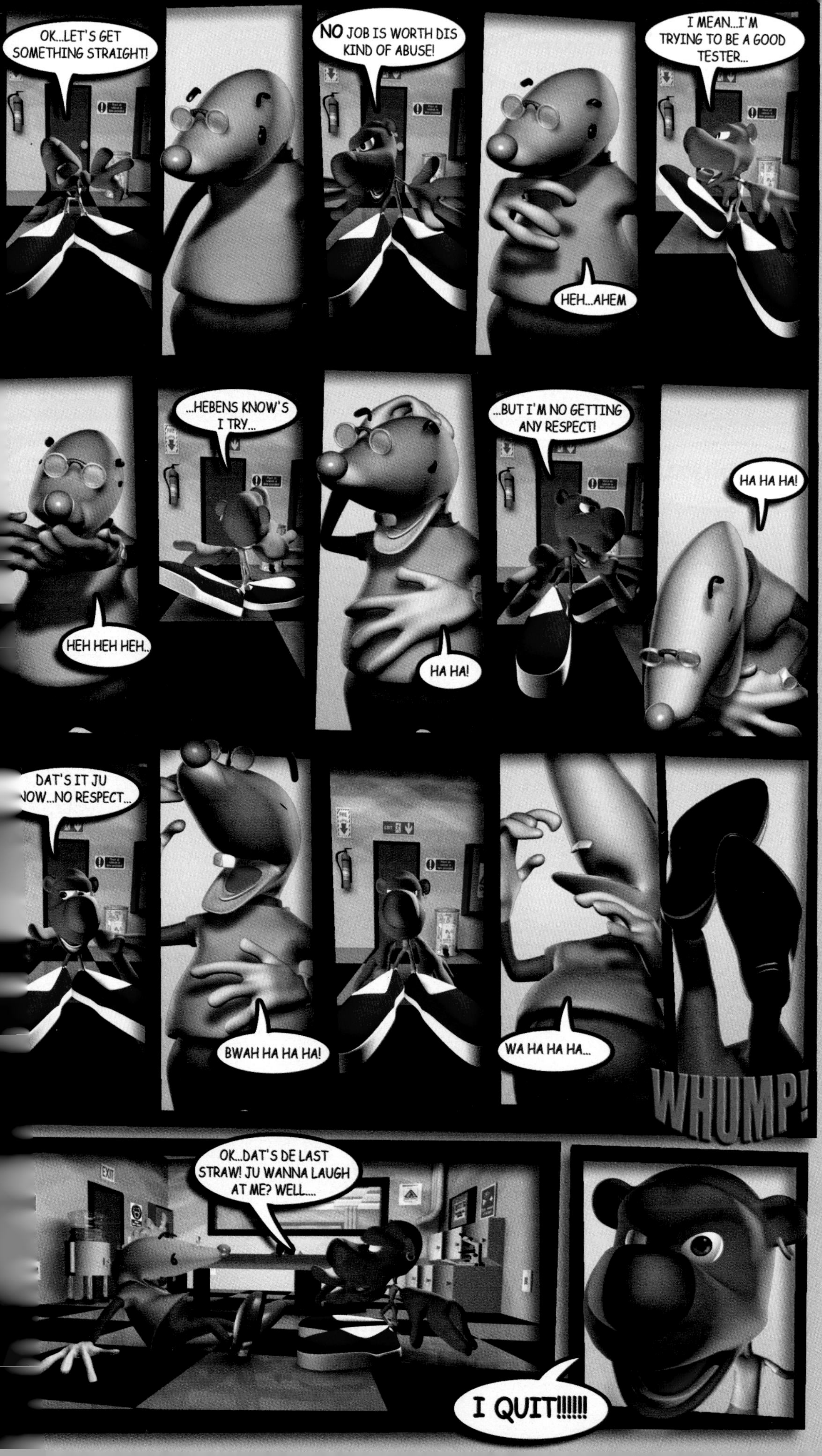
OK...LET'S GET SOMETHING STRAIGHT!
NO JOB IS WORTH DIS KIND OF ABUSE!
HEH...AHEM
I MEAN...I'M TRYING TO BE A GOOD TESTER...
HEH HEH HEH..
...HEBENS KNOW'S I TRY...
HA HA!
...BUT I'M NO GETTING ANY RESPECT!
HA HA HA!
DAT'S IT JU NOW...NO RESPECT...
BWAH HA HA HA!
WA HA HA HA...
WHUMP!
OK...DAT'S DE LAST STRAW! JU WANNA LAUGH AT ME? WELL....
I QUIT!!!!!!

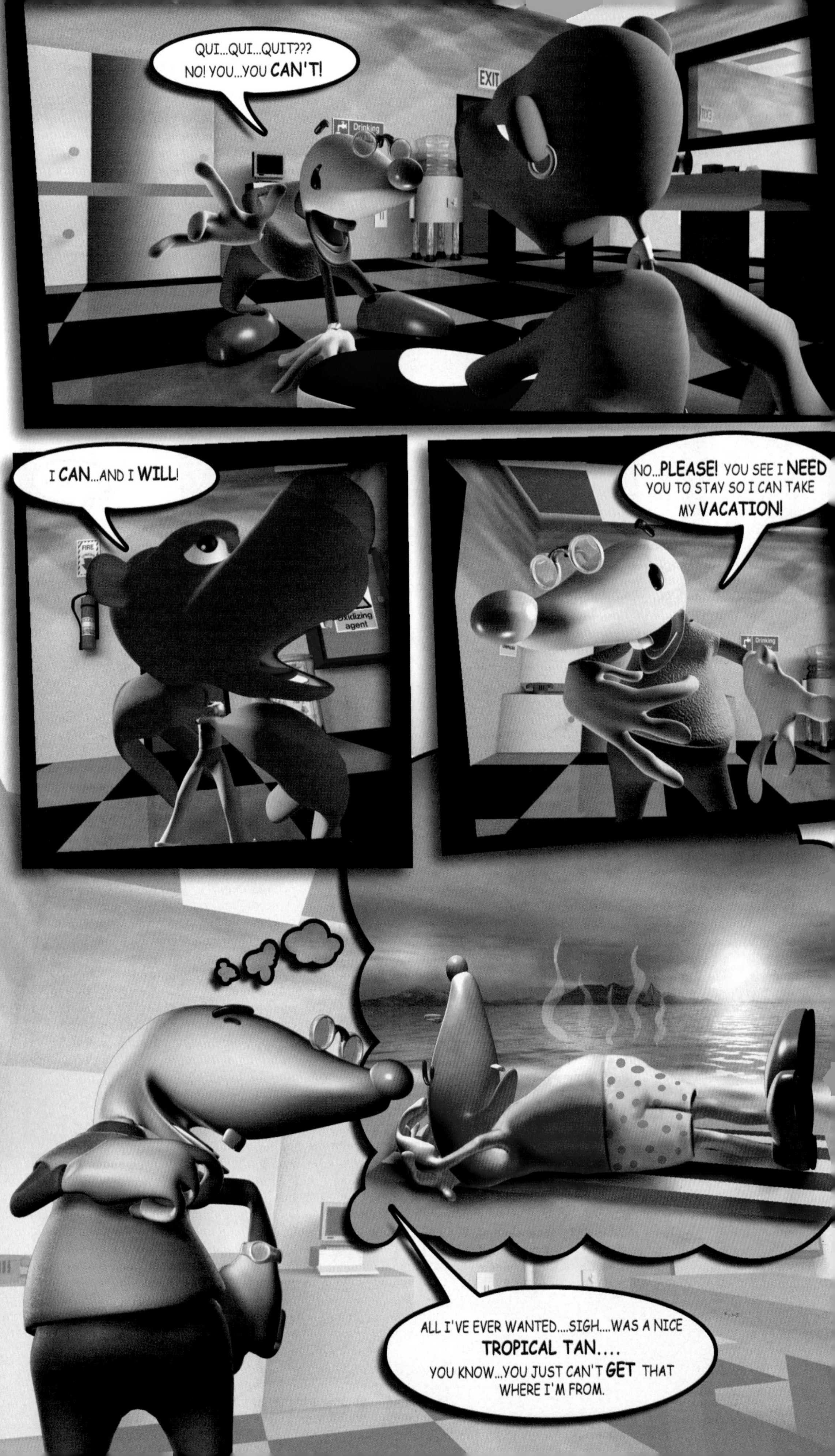
QUI...QUI...QUIT???
NO! YOU...YOU CAN'T!
EXIT
I CAN...AND I WILL!
Oxidizing agent
NO...PLEASE! YOU SEE I NEED YOU TO STAY SO I CAN TAKE MY VACATION!
ALL I'VE EVER WANTED....SIGH....WAS A NICE TROPICAL TAN....
YOU KNOW...YOU JUST CAN'T GET THAT WHERE I'M FROM.

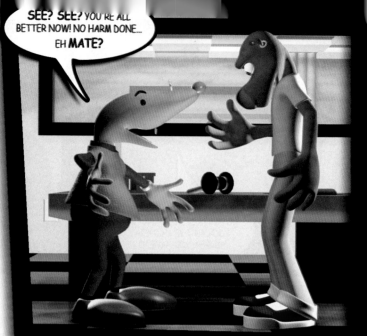

SEE? SEE? YOU'RE ALL BETTER NOW! NO HARM DONE... EH **MATE?**

LOOK **IF** I STAY...ES CAUSE I HAVE A DREAM TOO!

OF **COURSE!** OF **COURSE!** WHAT IS IT? YOUR OWN **HOUSE?** A NEW **CAR? TRAVELLING?**

Drinking water

NO NO NO..... I'VE **ALWAYS** WANTED TO BE.... AN **OPERA SINGER!**

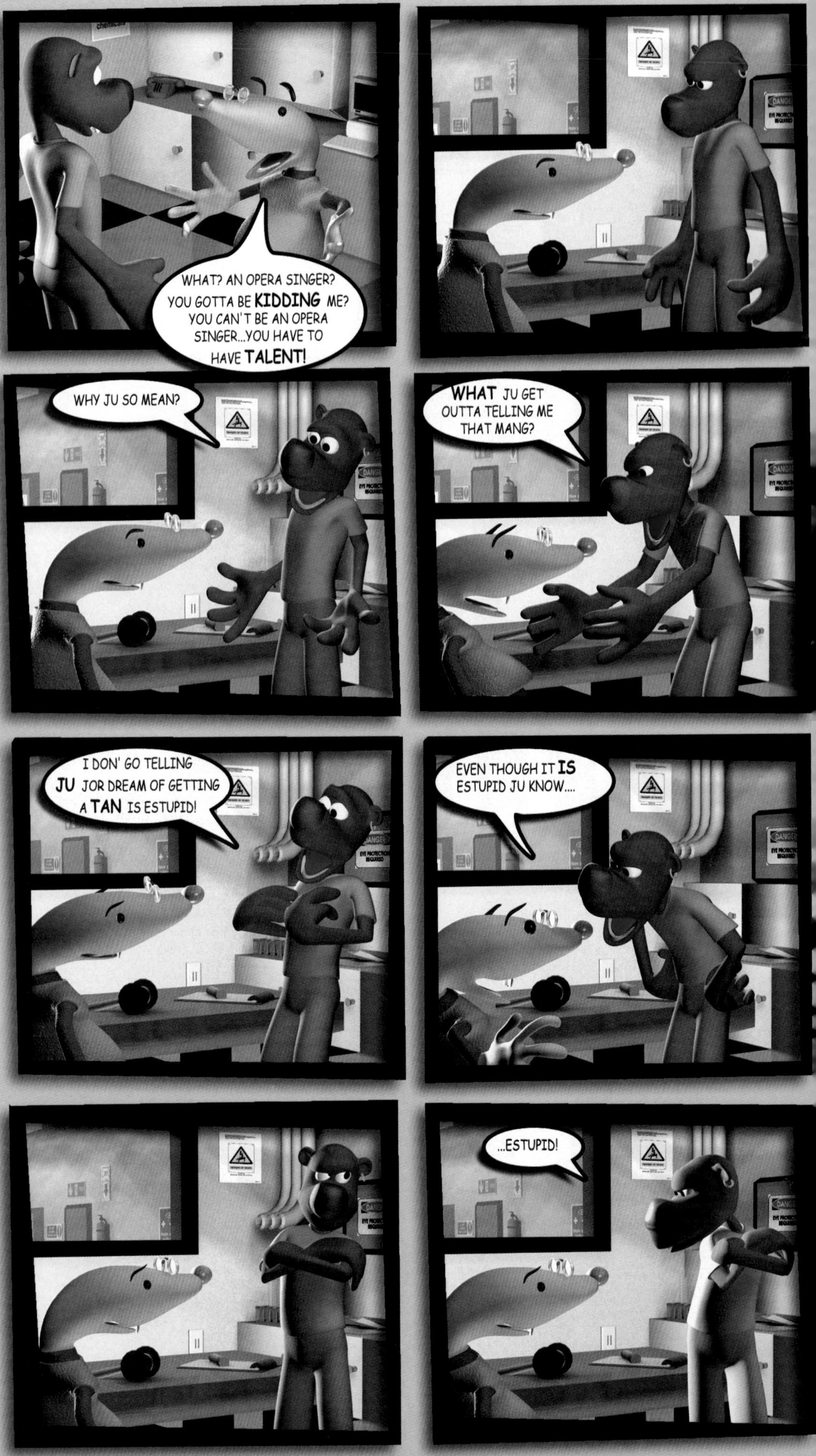
chemicals
WHAT? AN OPERA SINGER? YOU GOTTA BE KIDDING ME? YOU CAN'T BE AN OPERA SINGER...YOU HAVE TO HAVE TALENT!
WHY JU SO MEAN?
WHAT JU GET OUTTA TELLING ME THAT MANG?
I DON' GO TELLING JU JOR DREAM OF GETTING A TAN IS ESTUPID!
EVEN THOUGH IT IS ESTUPID JU KNOW....
...ESTUPID!

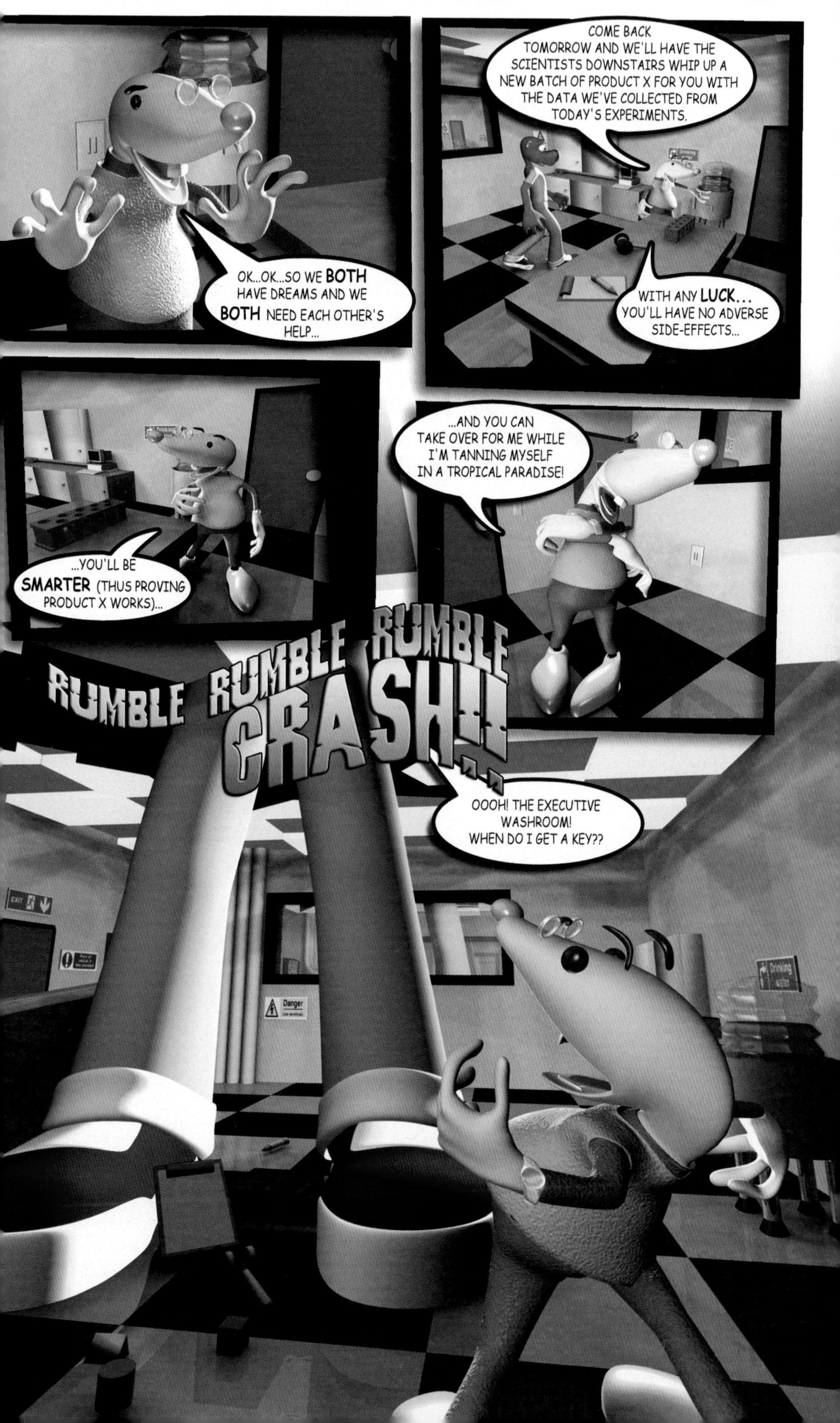
OK...OK...SO WE BOTH HAVE DREAMS AND WE BOTH NEED EACH OTHER'S HELP...
COME BACK TOMORROW AND WE'LL HAVE THE SCIENTISTS DOWNSTAIRS WHIP UP A NEW BATCH OF PRODUCT X FOR YOU WITH THE DATA WE'VE COLLECTED FROM TODAY'S EXPERIMENTS.
WITH ANY LUCK... YOU'LL HAVE NO ADVERSE SIDE-EFFECTS...
...YOU'LL BE SMARTER (THUS PROVING PRODUCT X WORKS)...
...AND YOU CAN TAKE OVER FOR ME WHILE I'M TANNING MYSELF IN A TROPICAL PARADISE!
RUMBLE RUMBLE RUMBLE RUMBLE
CRASH!!
OOOH! THE EXECUTIVE WASHROOM! WHEN DO I GET A KEY??
EXIT
Danger
Drinking water

CRAZY SCIENCE EXPERIMENTS!

PARENTS...

FILL TWO CLEAN JARS WITH WATER.
NOW TAKE A DRY HANDKERCHIEF MADE OF COTTON, SILK, OR LINEN AND PLACE ONE END IN EACH JAR.
NOW LET YOUR EXPERIMENT SIT OVERNIGHT...TRUST US.
WHEN YOU WAKE UP...SOME OF THE WATER WILL HAVE TRAVELED THROUGH THE HANDKERCHIEF TO THE OTHER JAR! WOW!

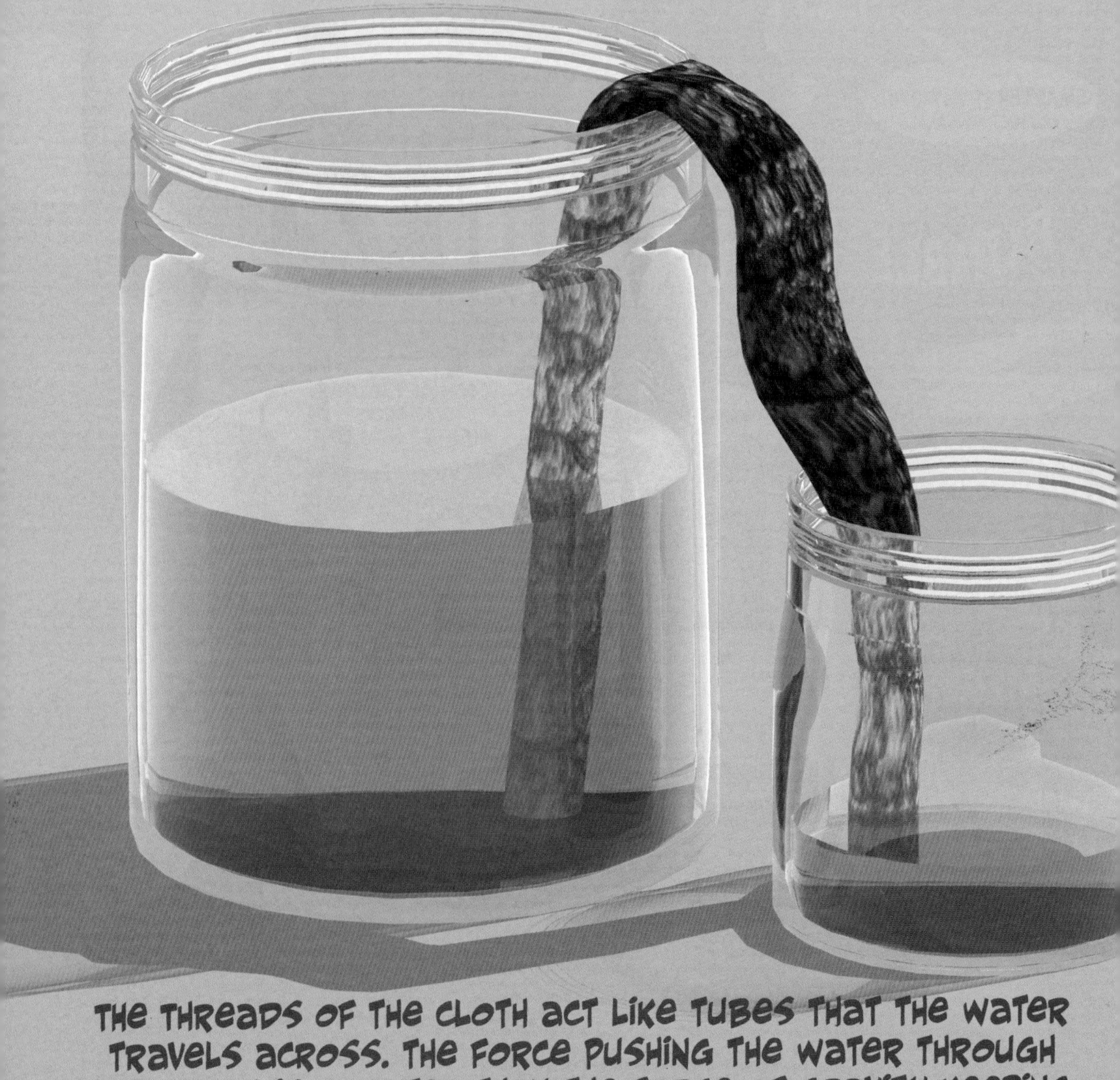

THE THREADS OF THE CLOTH ACT LIKE TUBES THAT THE WATER TRAVELS ACROSS. THE FORCE PUSHING THE WATER THROUGH THE TUBES IS GREATER THAN THE FORCE OF GRAVITY KEEPING IT DOWN...SO IT RISES UP AND OVER INTO THE OTHER GLASS....

IT'S JOKE TIME!!!
WHY SHOULD YOU WALK CAREFULLY WHEN IT'S RAINING CATS AND DOGS?
TURN THE PAGE FOR THE SIDE SPLITTING ANSWER!

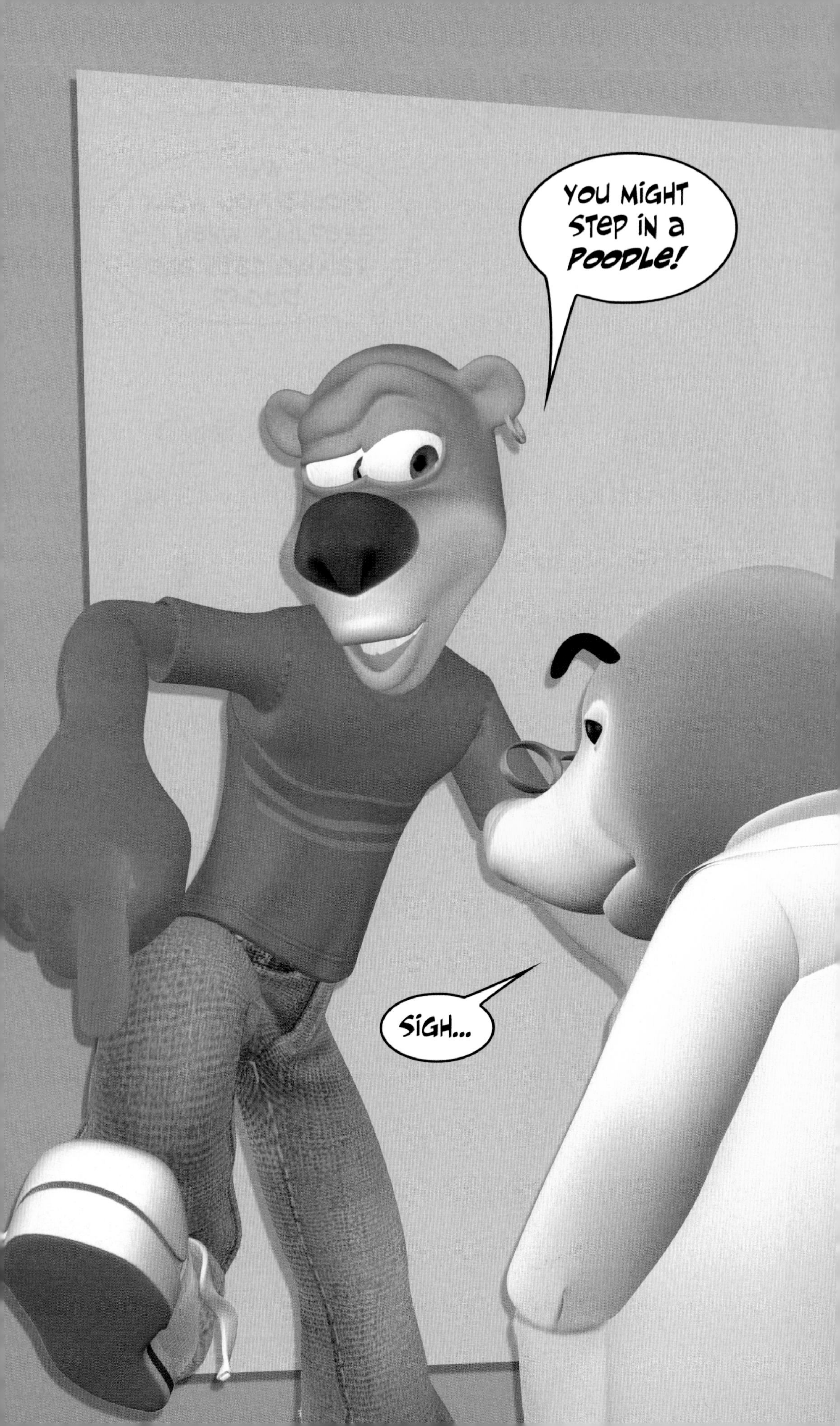
YOU MIGHT STEP IN A POODLE!
SIGH...

Black and White

ESTEBAN AND LIVINGSTON
DID A GUEST APPEARANCE
IN THE NEW FUND BOOK IN
2003.
SINCE THE BOOK WAS IN BLACK
AND WHITE ONLY...WE HAD TO
FIND A WAY TO "TURN OFF THE
COLOR".
OF COURSE...IN A LAB...THERE'S
ALWAYS A BUTTON THAT CAN
DO THAT....RIGHT?

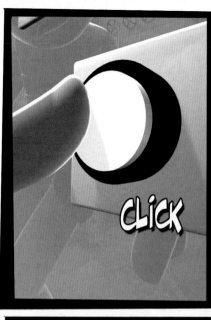

CLICK

GAAH! WHAT HAPPENED TO ALL THE COLOR???

OH GOD! OH GOD!

I'M...I'M HAVING AN ANEURYSM...

I'M TOO YOUNG TO DIE!!!

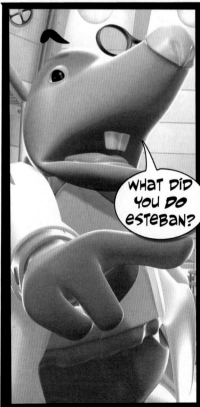

WHAT DID YOU DO ESTEBAN?

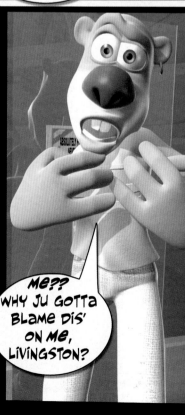

ME?? WHY JU GOTTA BLAME DIS' ON ME, LIVINGSTON?

BECAUSE... YOU ARE TH SOURCE OF EV THING THAT EXPL IMPLODES, OR ISN'T RIGHT H IN THE LAB

WHAT DID YOU DO?

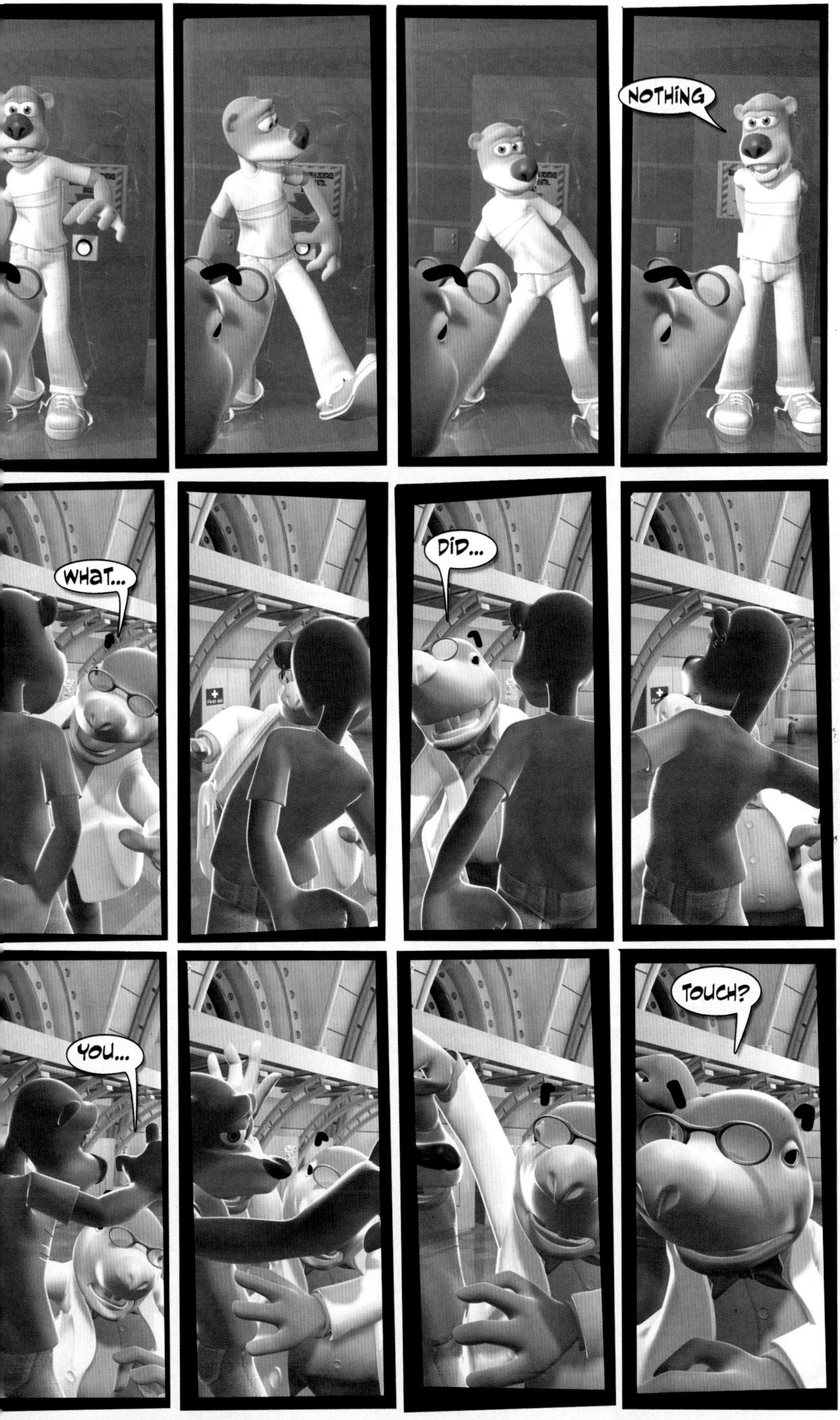
NOTHING
WHAT...
DID...
YOU...
TOUCH?

ABSOLUTELY POSITIVELY UNDER NO CIRCUMSTANCES NEVER EVER EVER PUSH THIS BUTTON..... SERIOUSLY!

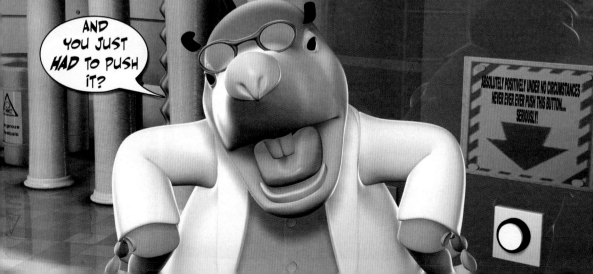

AND YOU JUST *HAD* TO PUSH IT?

ABSOLUTELY POSITIVELY UNDER NO CIRCUMSTANCES NEVER EVER EVER PUSH THIS BUTTON..... SERIOUSLY!

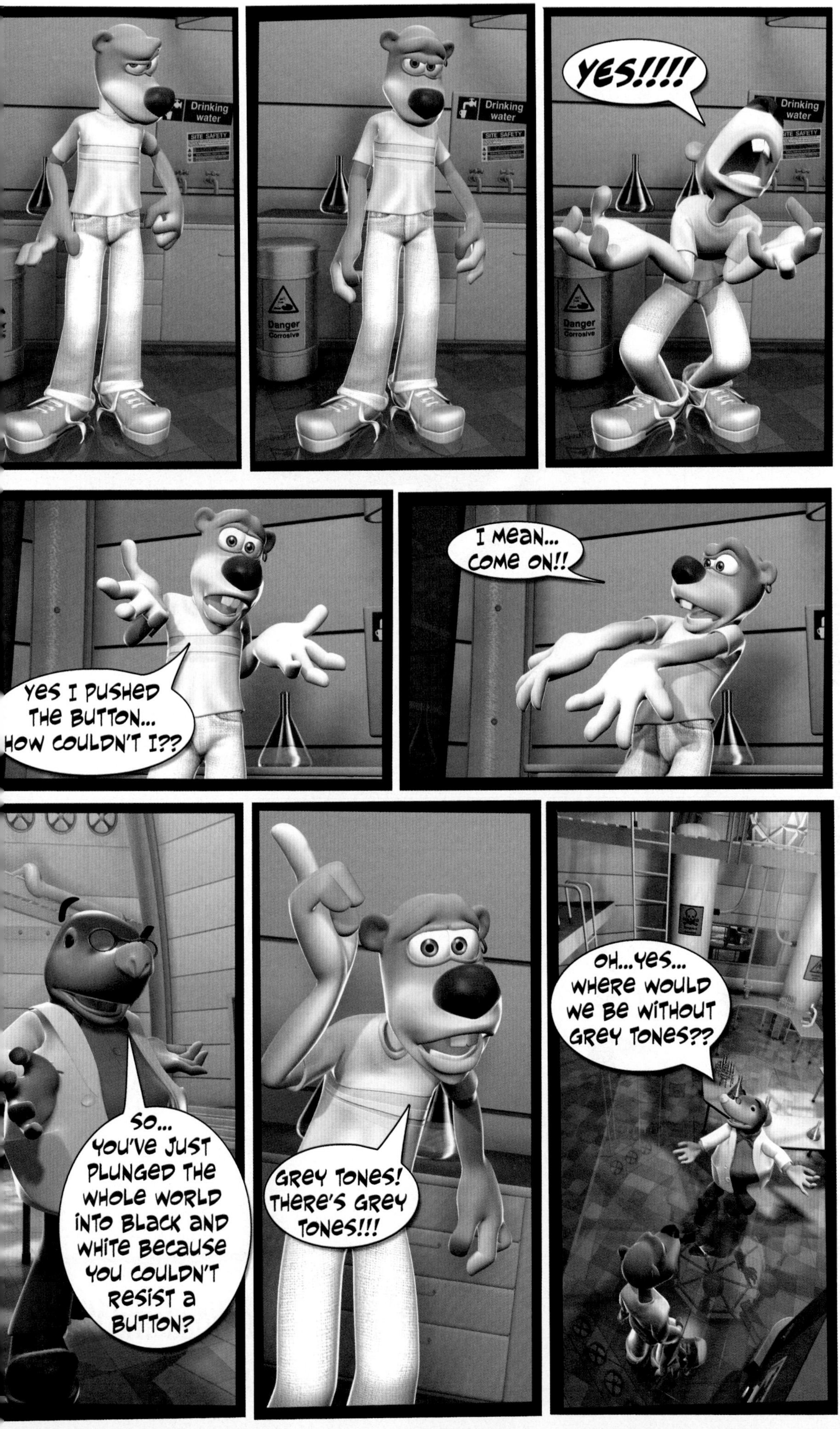
Drinking water
Drinking water
YES!!!!
Drinking water
Danger Corrosive
YES I PUSHED THE BUTTON... HOW COULDN'T I??
I MEAN... COME ON!!
SO... YOU'VE JUST PLUNGED THE WHOLE WORLD INTO BLACK AND WHITE BECAUSE YOU COULDN'T RESIST A BUTTON?
GREY TONES! THERE'S GREY TONES!!!
OH...YES... WHERE WOULD WE BE WITHOUT GREY TONES??

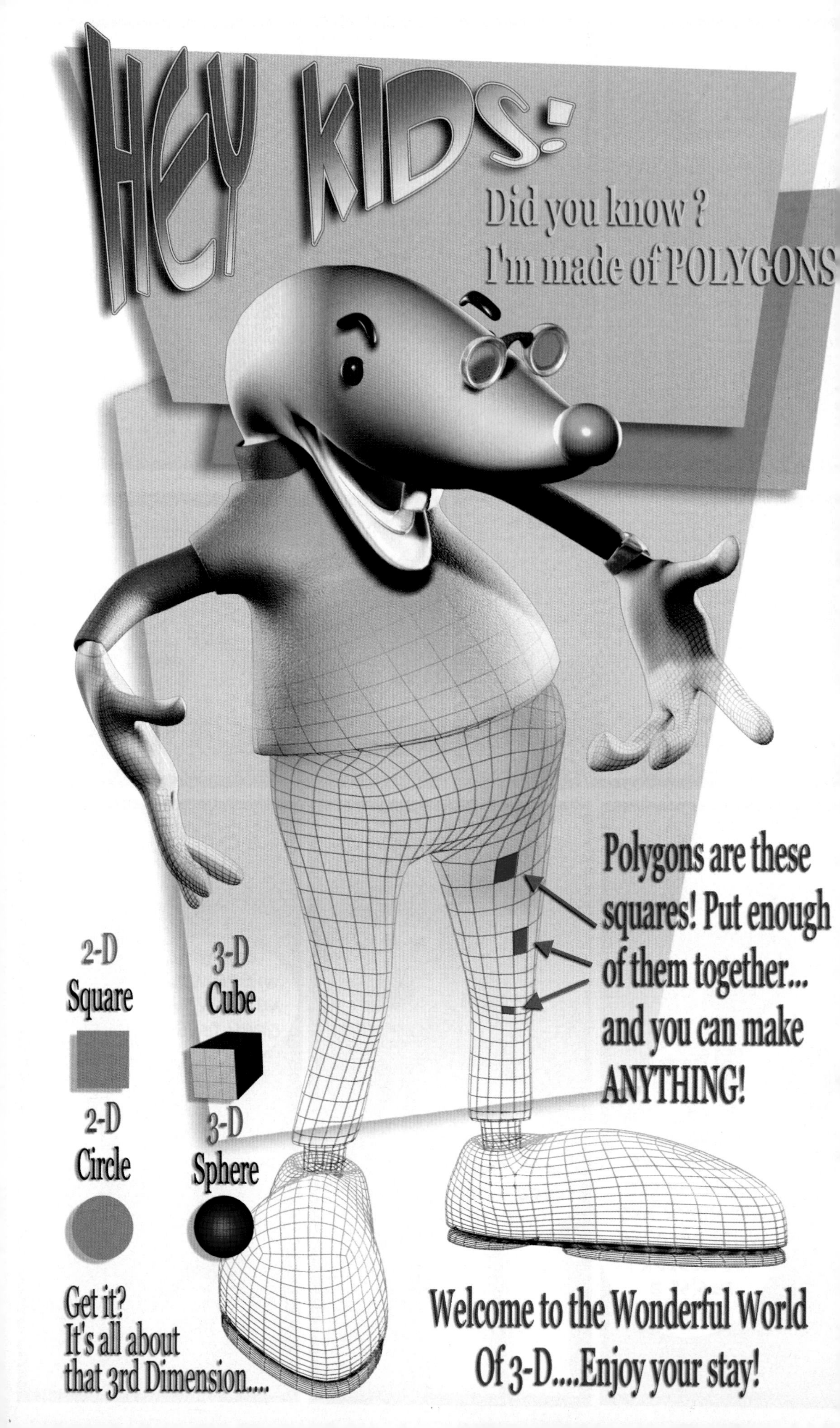
HEY KIDS!
Did you know ?
I'm made of POLYGONS
Polygons are these squares! Put enough of them together... and you can make ANYTHING!
2-D
Square
3-D
Cube
2-D
Circle
3-D
Sphere
Get it?
It's all about that 3rd Dimension....
Welcome to the Wonderful World Of 3-D....Enjoy your stay!

CRAZY SCIENCE EXPERIMENTS!

TRY THIS AT HOME WITH YOUR PARENTS...

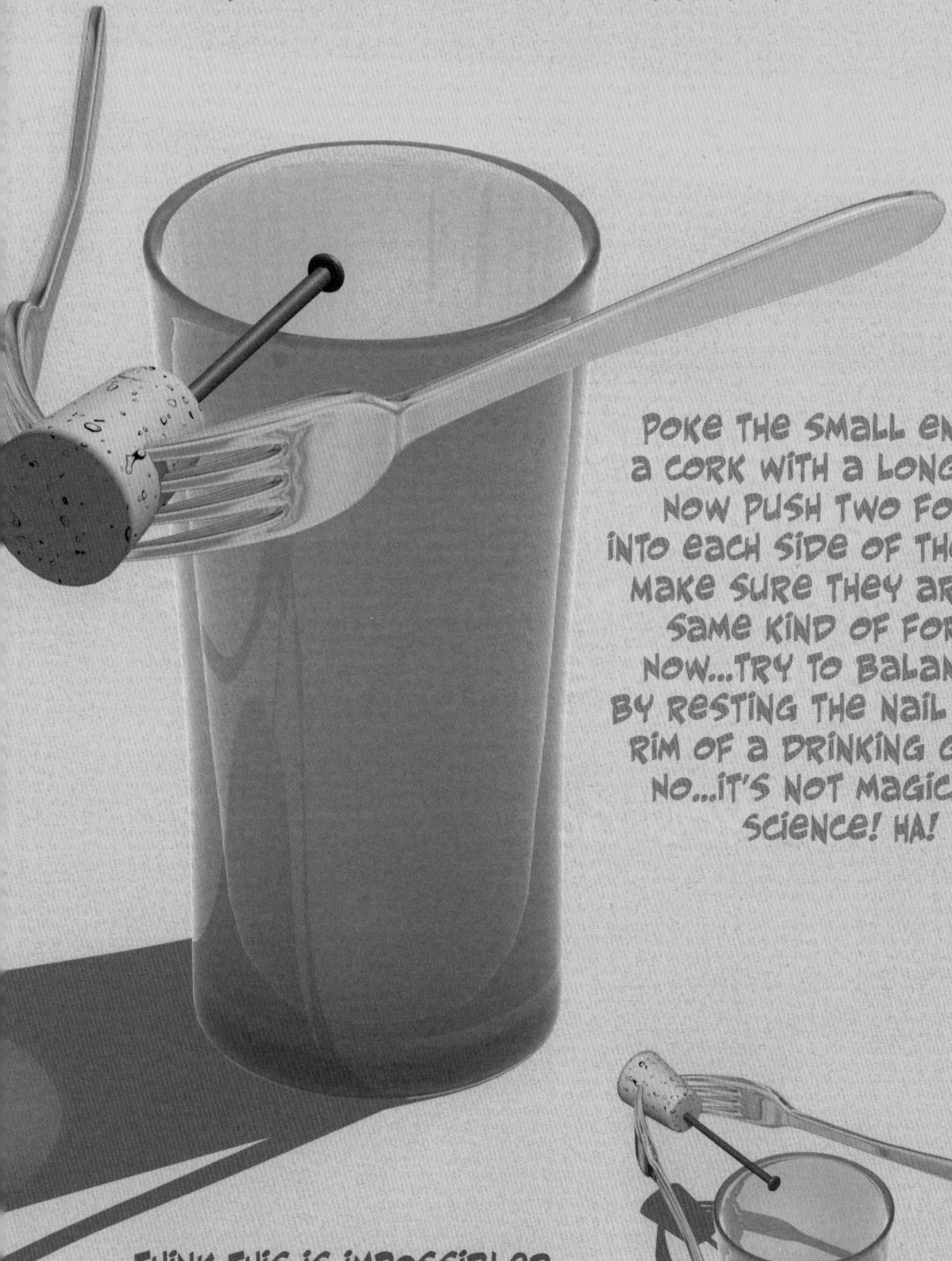

POKE THE SMALL END OF A CORK WITH A LONG NAIL. NOW PUSH TWO FORKS INTO EACH SIDE OF THE CORK. MAKE SURE THEY ARE THE SAME KIND OF FORKS. NOW...TRY TO BALANCE IT BY RESTING THE NAIL ON THE RIM OF A DRINKING GLASS. NO...IT'S NOT MAGIC...IT'S SCIENCE! HA!

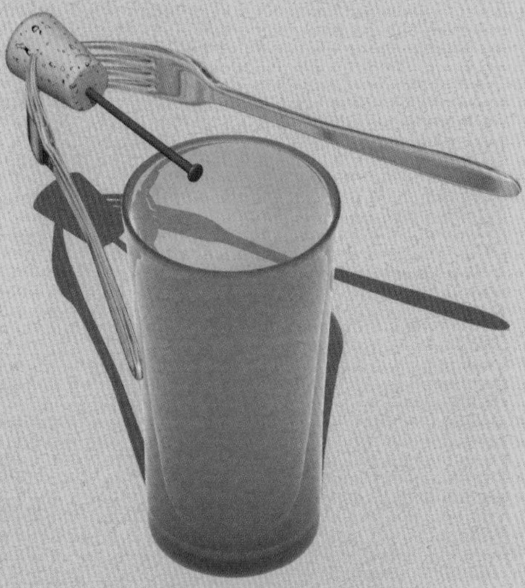

THINK THIS IS IMPOSSIBLE? WELL OBVIOUSLY IT'S NOT SILLY. SEE...THE FORKS HELP BALANCE THE WEIGHT OF YOUR NEW GRAVITY DEFYING DEVICE EVENLY SO IT'S PERFECTLY BALANCED. COOL...HUH?

THE STARING CONTEST

AT THE BURNS AND ITCHEZ LAB,
ESTEBAN IS THE KING OF
STARING! NO ONE YET HAS
BEEN ABLE TO BEAT HIM.

ARE YOU GOOD ENOUGH?

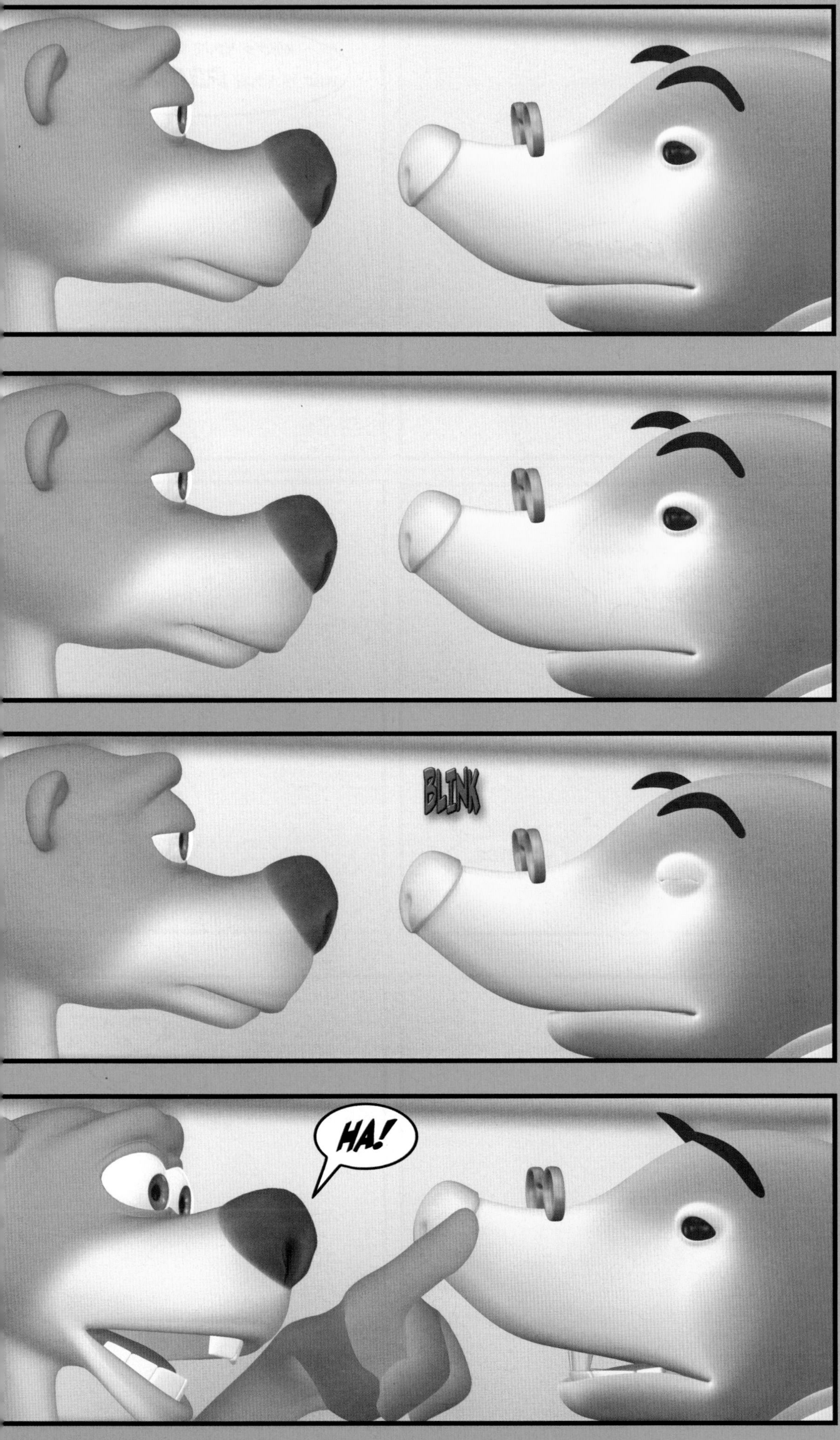
BLINK
HA!

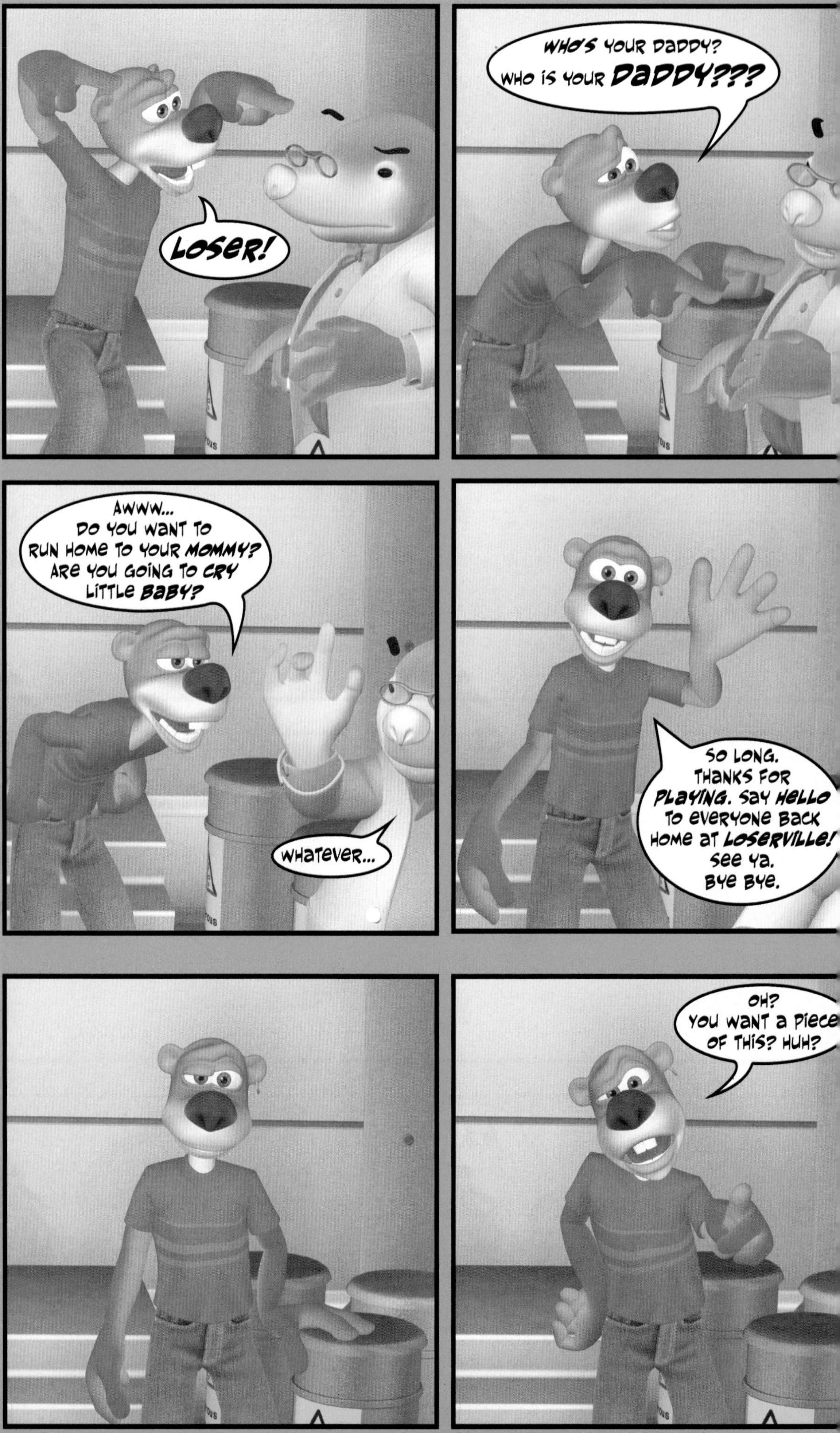
LOSER!
WHO'S YOUR DADDY?
WHO IS YOUR DADDY???
AWWW...
DO YOU WANT TO
RUN HOME TO YOUR MOMMY?
ARE YOU GOING TO CRY
LITTLE BABY?
WHATEVER...
SO LONG.
THANKS FOR
PLAYING. SAY HELLO
TO EVERYONE BACK
HOME AT LOSERVILLE!
SEE YA.
BYE BYE.
OH?
YOU WANT A PIECE
OF THIS? HUH?

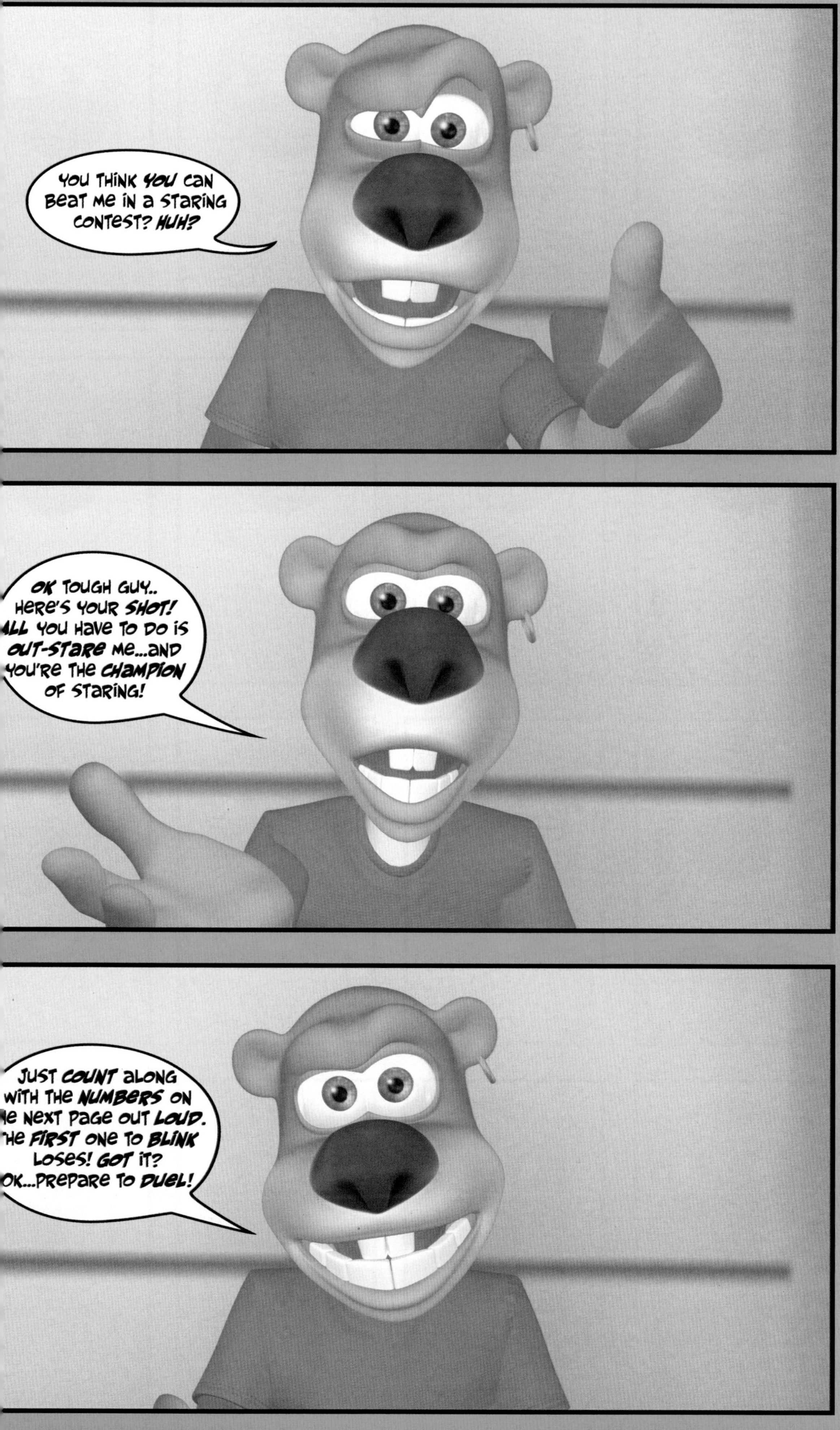
YOU THINK YOU CAN BEAT ME IN A STARING CONTEST? HUH?
OK TOUGH GUY.. HERE'S YOUR SHOT! LL YOU HAVE TO DO IS OUT-STARE ME...AND YOU'RE THE CHAMPION OF STARING!
JUST COUNT ALONG WITH THE NUMBERS ON E NEXT PAGE OUT LOUD. HE FIRST ONE TO BLINK LOSES! GOT IT? OK...PREPARE TO DUEL!

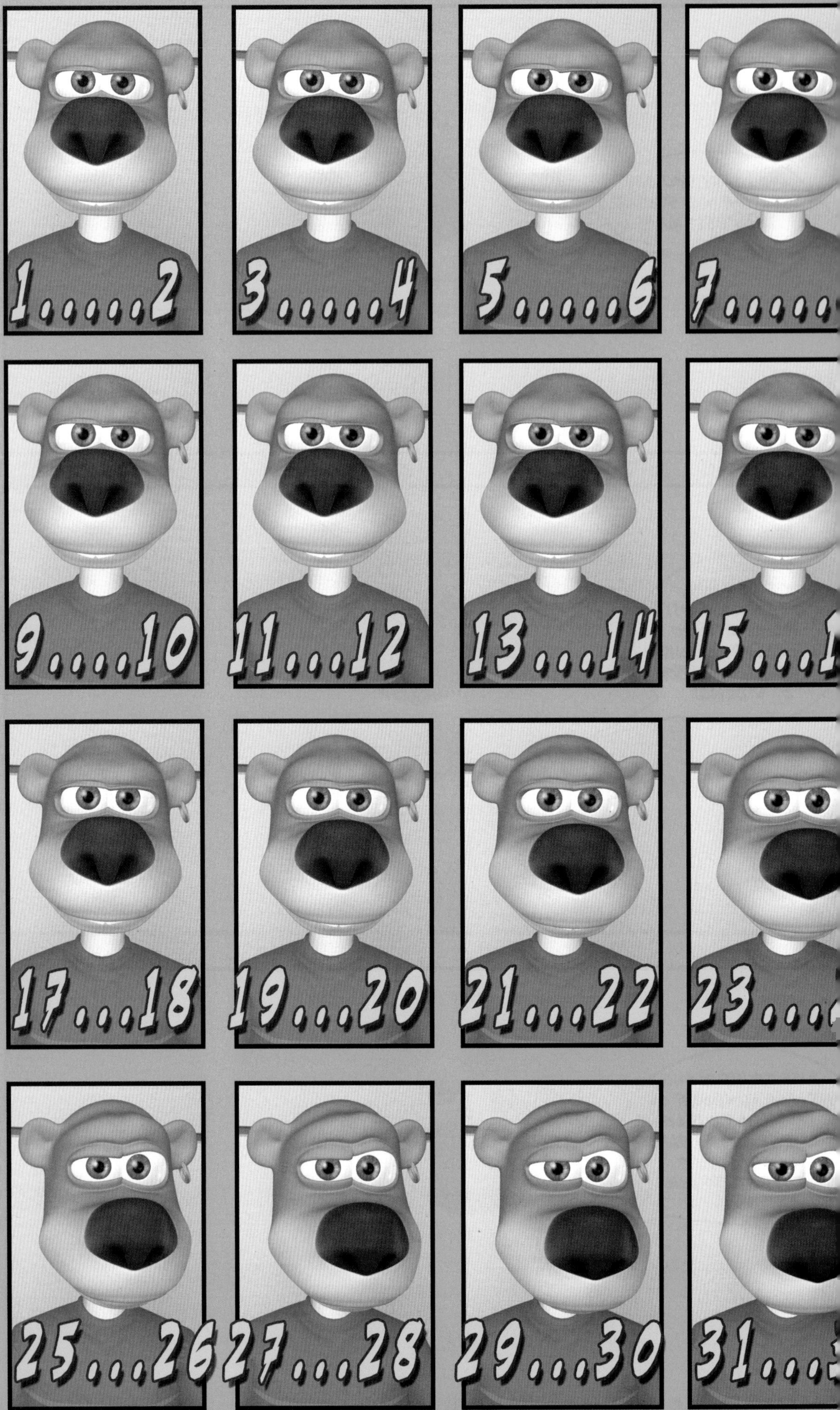
1......2
3......4
5......6
7.....
9.....10
11....12
13....14
15....
17....18
19....20
21....22
23....
25....26
27....28
29....30
31....

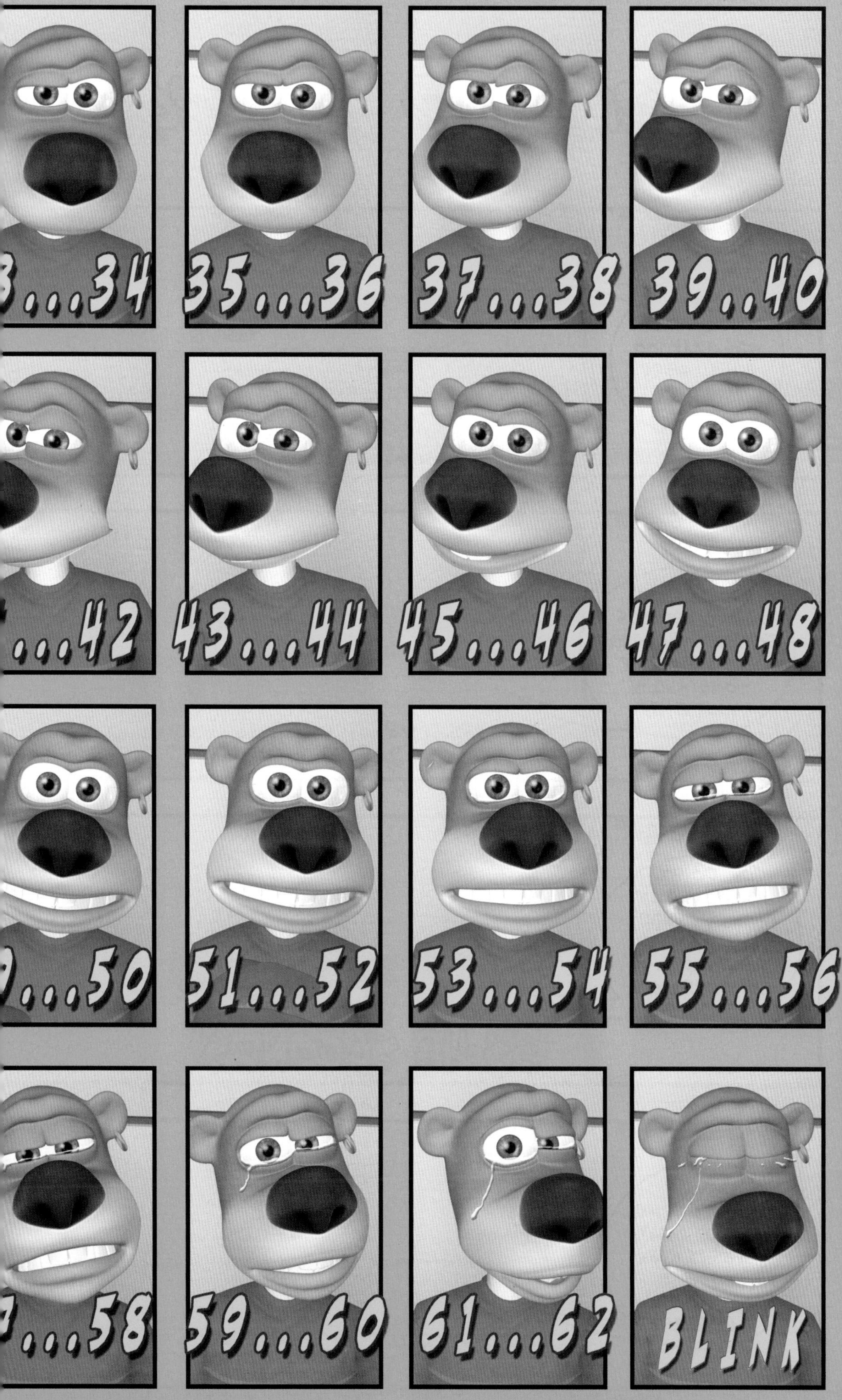
...34
35...36
37...38
39..40
...42
43...44
45...46
47...48
...50
51...52
53...54
55...56
...58
59...60
61...62
BLINK

HOW DID YOU DO?

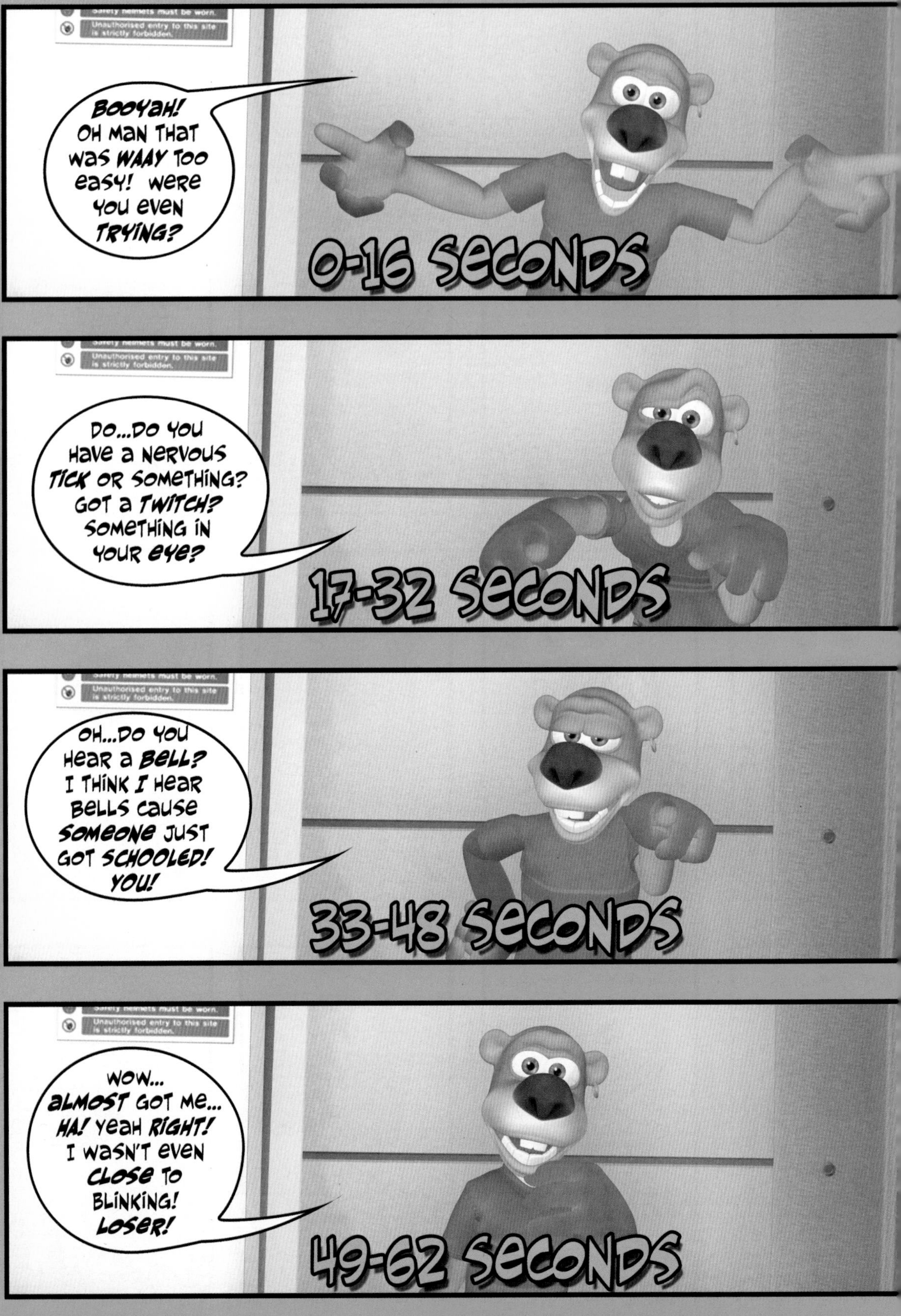
Safety helmets must be worn.
Unauthorised entry to this site is strictly forbidden.
BOOYAH! OH MAN THAT WAS WAAY TOO EASY! WERE YOU EVEN TRYING?
0-16 SECONDS
DO...DO YOU HAVE A NERVOUS TICK OR SOMETHING? GOT A TWITCH? SOMETHING IN YOUR EYE?
17-32 SECONDS
OH...DO YOU HEAR A BELL? I THINK I HEAR BELLS CAUSE SOMEONE JUST GOT SCHOOLED! YOU!
33-48 SECONDS
WOW... ALMOST GOT ME... HA! YEAH RIGHT! I WASN'T EVEN CLOSE TO BLINKING! LOSER!
49-62 SECONDS

63 OR MORE SECONDS
YOU WIN!!!

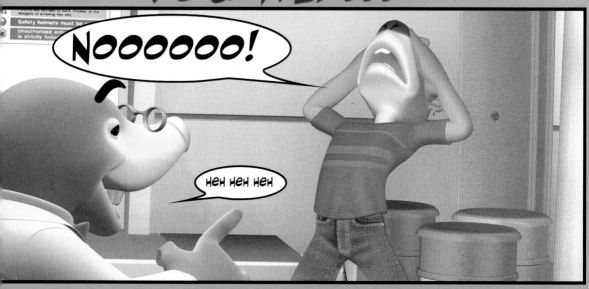

NOOOOOO!
HEH HEH HEH
Safety helmets must be worn.
Unauthorised entry to this site is strictly forbidden.
WOW! WAY TO GO THERE! THANKS...NOW I DON'T HAVE TO HEAR HIS BRAGGING ALL DAY LONG!
THUMP!
THOUGH I WILL HAVE TO WATCH HIM SULK IN THE CORNER NOW... SIGH.

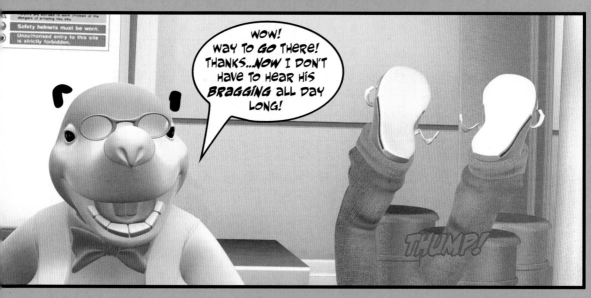

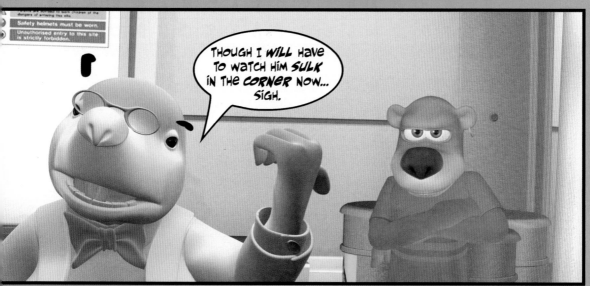

TRY THIS FUN WORD SEARCH!

LOOK UP, DOWN, FRONT, BACKWARDS, AND EVEN DIAGONAL!

W	A	R	Q	P	M	T	A	N	X	L	B	Y	G	D	O	F	O
S	E	M	K	U	B	Z	R	F	N	V	A	I	L	R	Z	A	P
H	X	A	O	T	X	E	M	G	B	O	O	M	B	O	X	E	E
O	P	S	S	O	U	A	P	D	P	E	B	L	X	C	U	L	R
W	L	S	H	E	L	Q	I	A	C	D	H	Y	O	H	I	E	A
T	O	I	U	B	L	M	T	H	E	L	A	B	J	Q	R	C	S
U	S	S	I	X	Q	O	K	L	A	I	I	D	R	E	K	T	I
N	I	T	V	D	Y	B	H	B	A	V	C	E	O	N	F	R	N
E	O	A	U	X	Q	T	O	M	K	I	T	U	I	P	S	I	G
S	N	N	H	D	I	R	B	G	H	N	Q	R	V	W	A	C	E
R	P	T	N	W	A	A	W	O	R	G	H	X	J	V	C	B	R
O	Y	E	M	T	N	N	L	K	Z	S	G	D	C	X	T	O	D
W	F	U	O	S	V	A	C	U	I	T	C	B	H	V	R	O	S
T	A	R	L	D	I	K	T	I	J	O	H	G	I	A	K	G	F
N	Y	N	E	S	L	K	H	J	N	N	Y	D	V	C	E	A	P
E	B	R	Q	B	R	A	Q	I	P	G	J	C	J	A	O	L	N
M	Z	O	S	P	G	N	S	N	Z	E	N	L	O	T	L	O	X
I	F	J	E	W	A	T	O	P	A	V	M	I	F	I	G	O	M
R	T	P	K	B	D	I	X	U	I	X	B	W	G	O	Y	C	Z
E	V	Z	E	F	L	D	M	Z	W	R	C	T	D	N	L	M	A
P	A	T	Z	N	I	O	H	Q	F	J	I	V	Z	D	I	N	O
X	S	C	O	A	F	T	T	D	I	A	D	N	A	B	X	S	O
E	F	D	Q	N	L	E	G	Z	A	X	T	C	U	D	O	R	P

FIND THESE WORDS...

ESTEBAN	MOLE	SHRINK	ELECTRIC BOOGALOO
LIVINGSTON	WEASEL	GROW	BOOM BOX
THE LAB	LABORATORY	DANCING	EXPLOSION
ANTIDOTE	EXPERIMENT	SINGING	ARMPIT
PRODUCT X	BAND AID	SHOWTUNES	ASPRIN
ANVIL	ASSISTANT	TAN	
VACATION	OPERA SINGER		

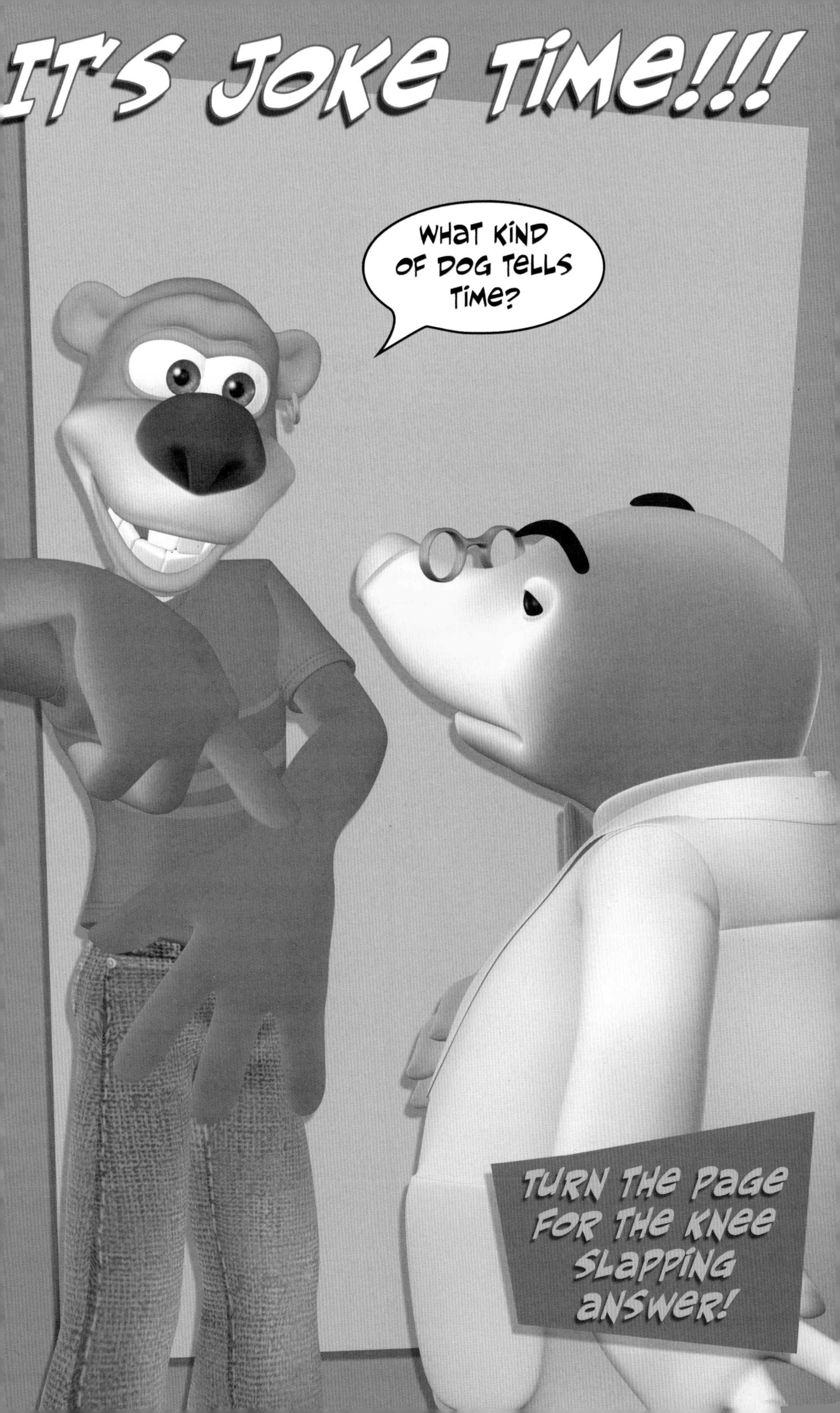
IT'S JOKE TIME!!!
WHAT KIND OF DOG TELLS TIME?
TURN THE PAGE FOR THE KNEE SLAPPING ANSWER!

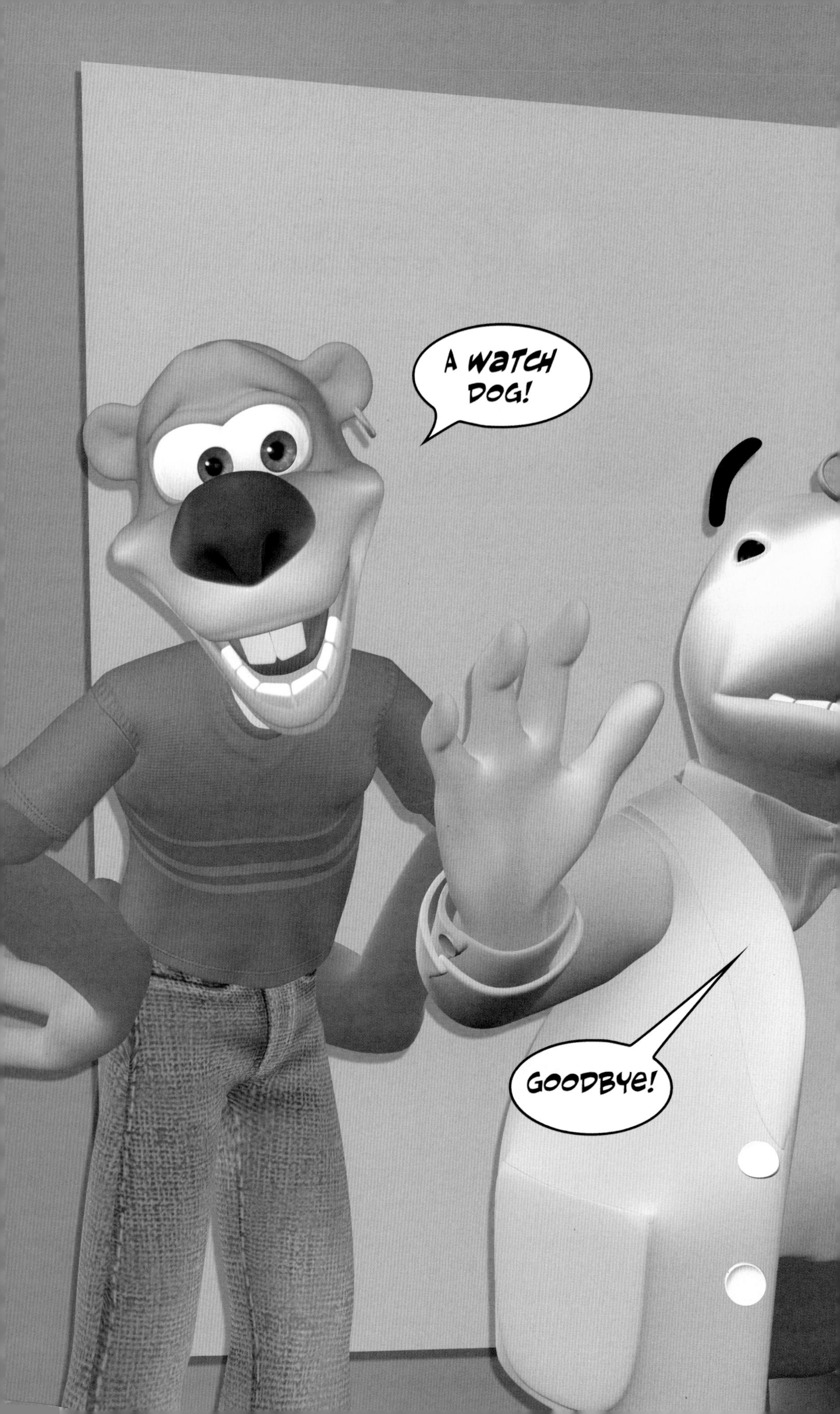
A WATCH DOG!
GOODBYE!

CRAZY SCIENCE EXPERIMENTS!

TRY THIS AT HOME WITH YOUR PARENTS...

HERE'S A FUN ONE...
FIND A SALT SHAKER WITH
FLAT SIDES LIKE YOU SEE
HERE. SPRINKLE A HILL OF
SALT ON A HARD SURFACE.
NOW STAND THE SALT
SHAKER ON IT'S EDGE.
KEEP TRYING UNTIL YOU
GOT IT. NOW THAT IT'S
BALANCED...GENTLY BLOW
THE SALT AWAY!
VOILA! STANDING SALT
SHAKER!

THE GRAINS OF SALT HAVE FLAT SIDES JUST LIKE THE SALT
SHAKER. THIS HELPS THE SHAKER STAND UP...JUST A COUPLE OF
WELL PLACED SALT GRAINS CAN SUPPORT THE WHOLE
SHAKER! THAT'S SOME TOUGH LITTLE SALT GRAINS...EH?

ELECTRIC BOOGALOO

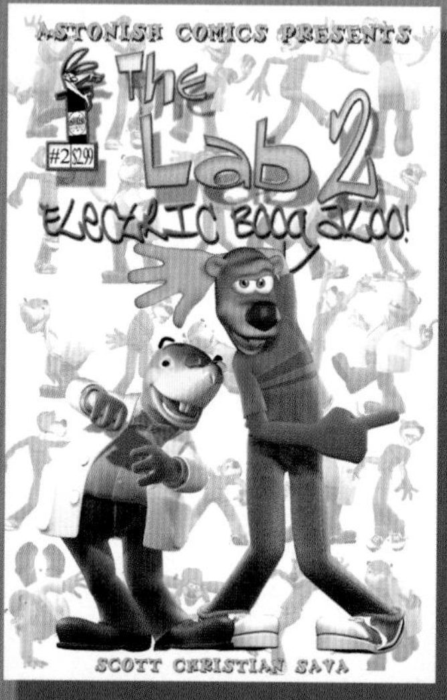

ASTONISH COMICS PRESENTS
The Lab 2
ELECTRIC BOOGALOO!
#2 $2.99
SCOTT CHRISTIAN SAVA

THE COVER FOR THE LAB 2 ELECTRIC BOOGALOO
2003

LAUGH ALONG WITH ESTEBAN AND LIVINGSTON WHILE THEY DANCE AND GROOVE IN THEIR SECOND BIG COMIC BOOK ISSUE!

PRODUCT X BRINGS OUT SOME GROOVY SIDE EFFECTS THIS TIME WHEN IT MAKES ESTEBAN AND LIVINGSTON DANCE UNCONTROLLABLY!
JUST HOW DOES IT TURN OUT?
TURN THE PAGE AND SEE....

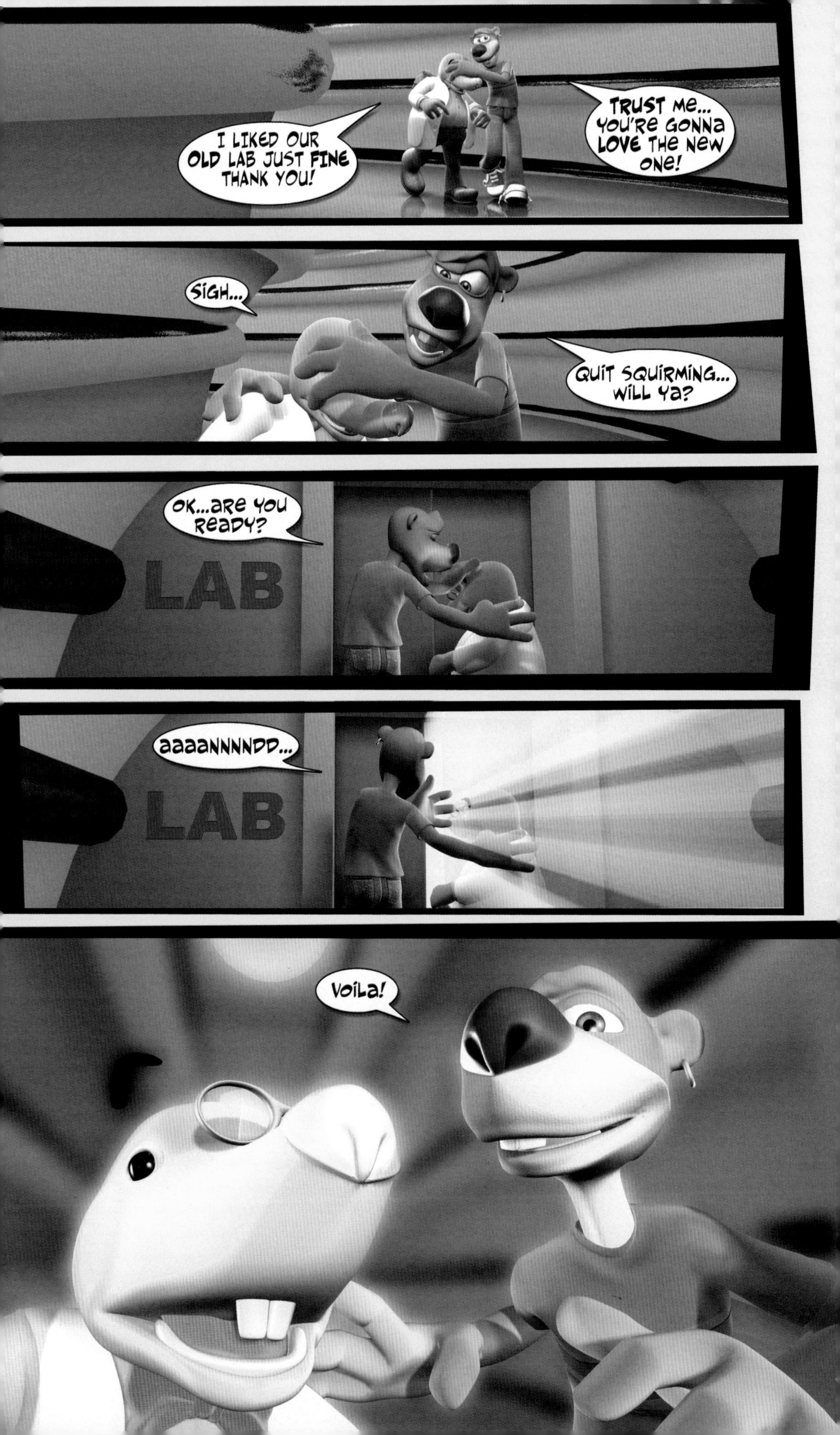

I LIKED OUR OLD LAB JUST FINE THANK YOU!
TRUST ME... YOU'RE GONNA LOVE THE NEW ONE!
SIGH...
QUIT SQUIRMING... WILL YA?
OK...ARE YOU READY?
LAB
AAAANNNNDD...
LAB
VOILA!

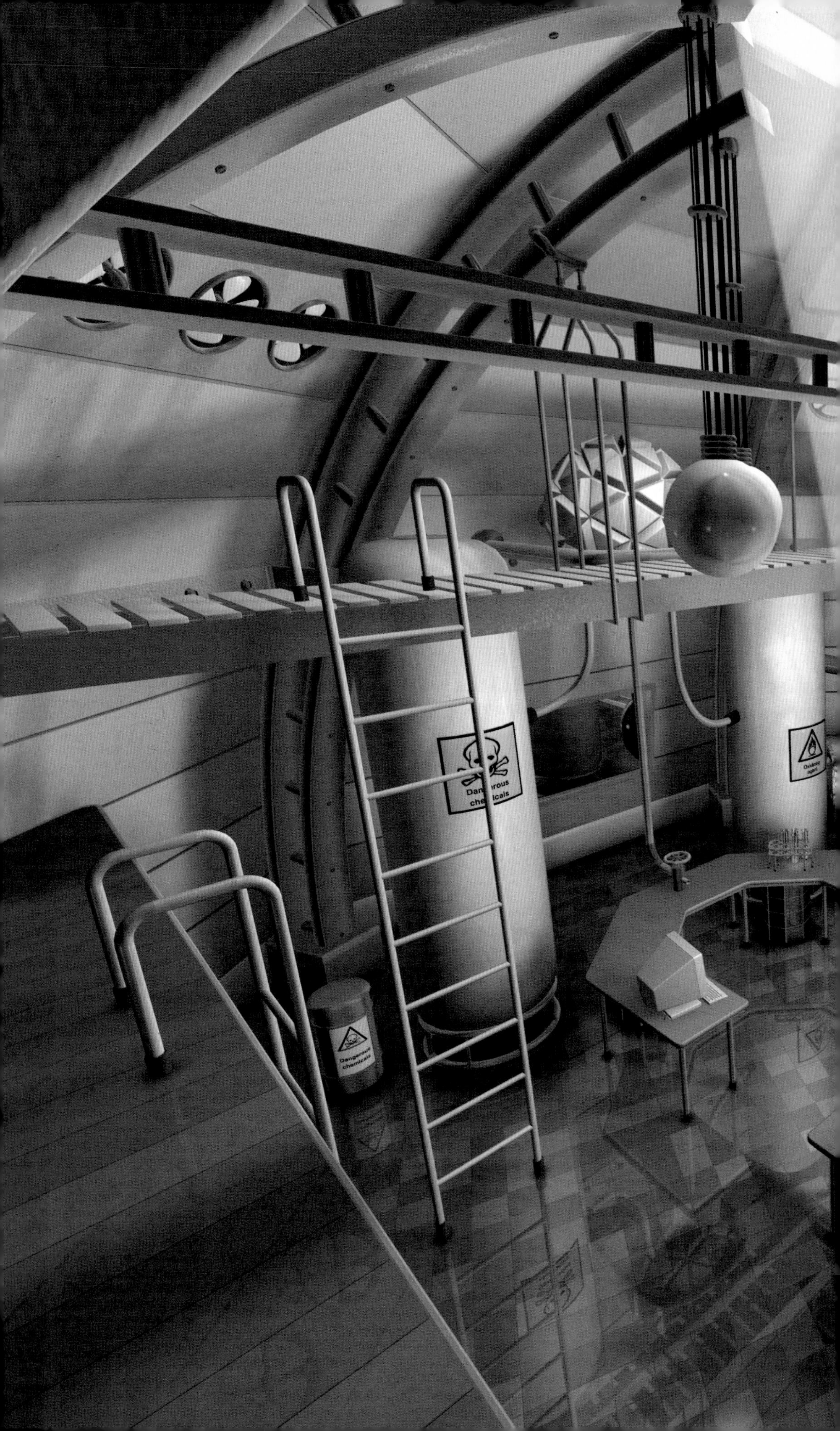
Dangerous chemicals

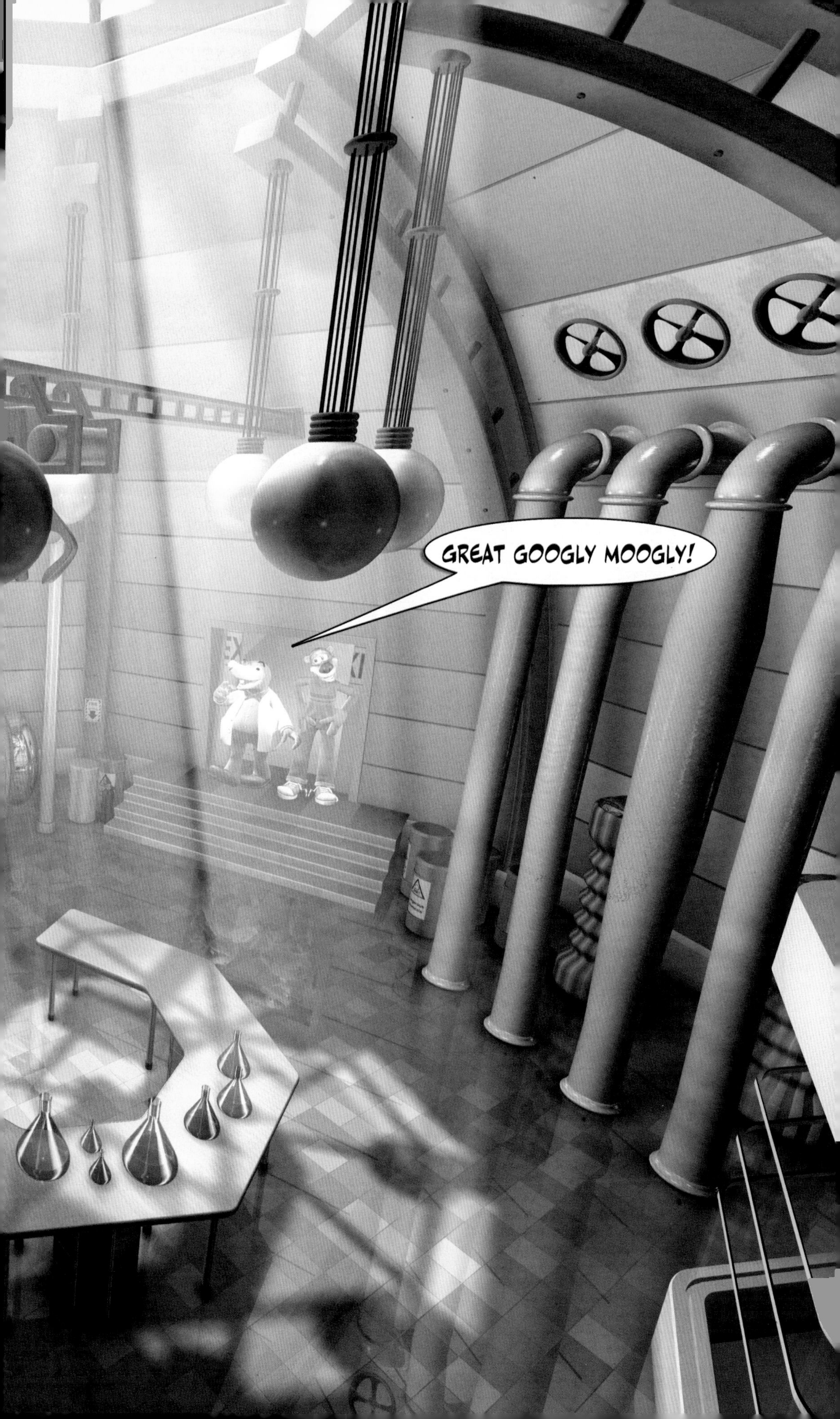
GREAT GOOGLY MOOGLY!

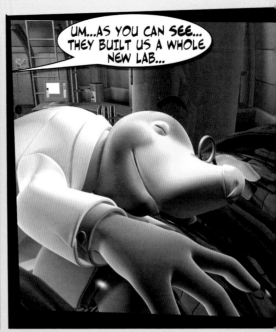

UM...AS YOU CAN SEE... THEY BUILT US A WHOLE NEW LAB...

LOT'S OF NEW GADGETS AND THINGS LIKE THAT...

LOOKS LIKE WE GOT HOOKED UP GOOD...EH?

OH YEAH! THIS IS SO COOL!!!

OOH! THERE'S A WHOLE SECOND LEVEL!

TEE HEE

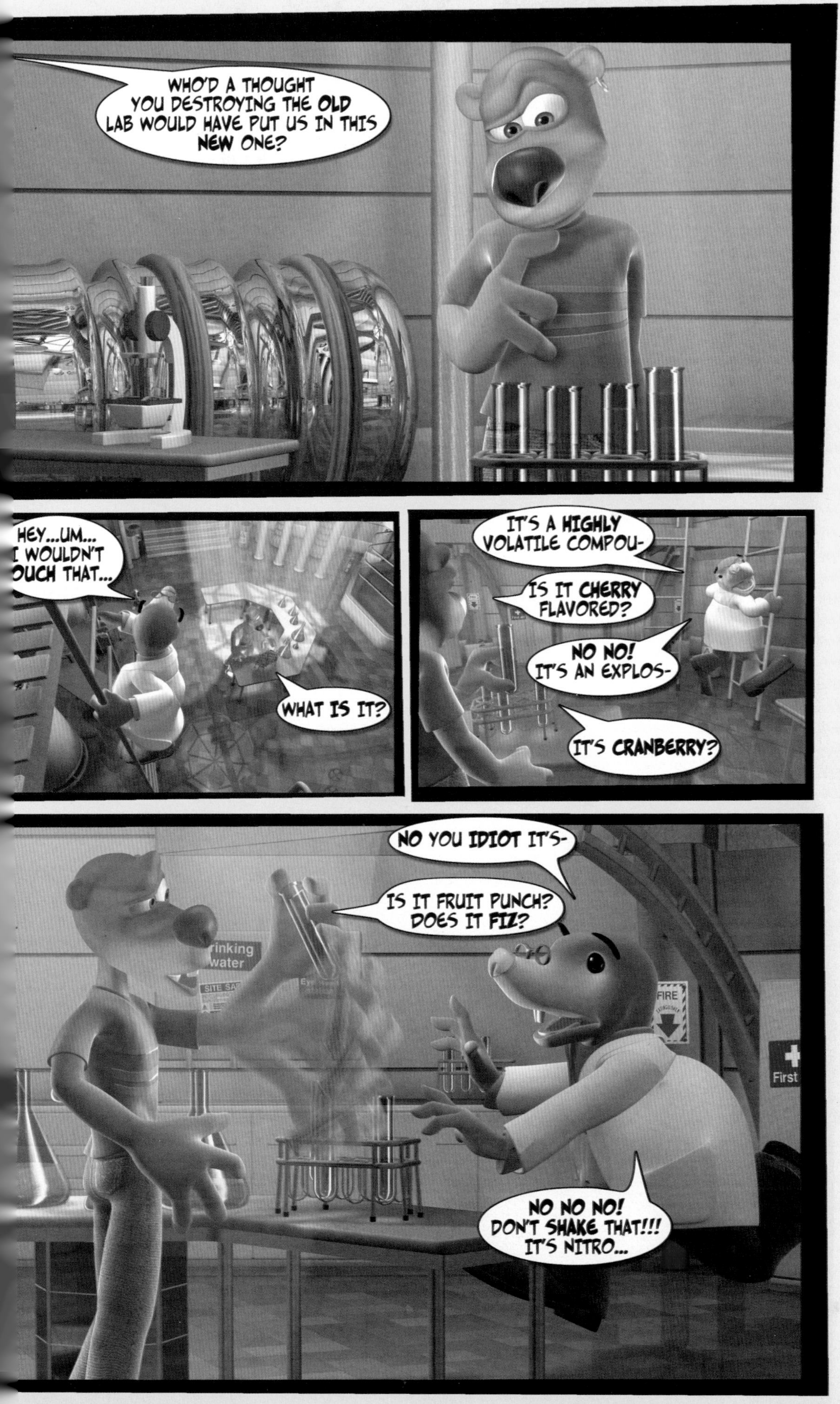
WHO'D A THOUGHT YOU DESTROYING THE OLD LAB WOULD HAVE PUT US IN THIS NEW ONE?
HEY...UM... I WOULDN'T OUCH THAT...
WHAT IS IT?
IT'S A HIGHLY VOLATILE COMPOU-
IS IT CHERRY FLAVORED?
NO NO! IT'S AN EXPLOS-
IT'S CRANBERRY?
NO YOU IDIOT IT'S-
IS IT FRUIT PUNCH? DOES IT FIZ?
NO NO NO! DON'T SHAKE THAT!!! IT'S NITRO...

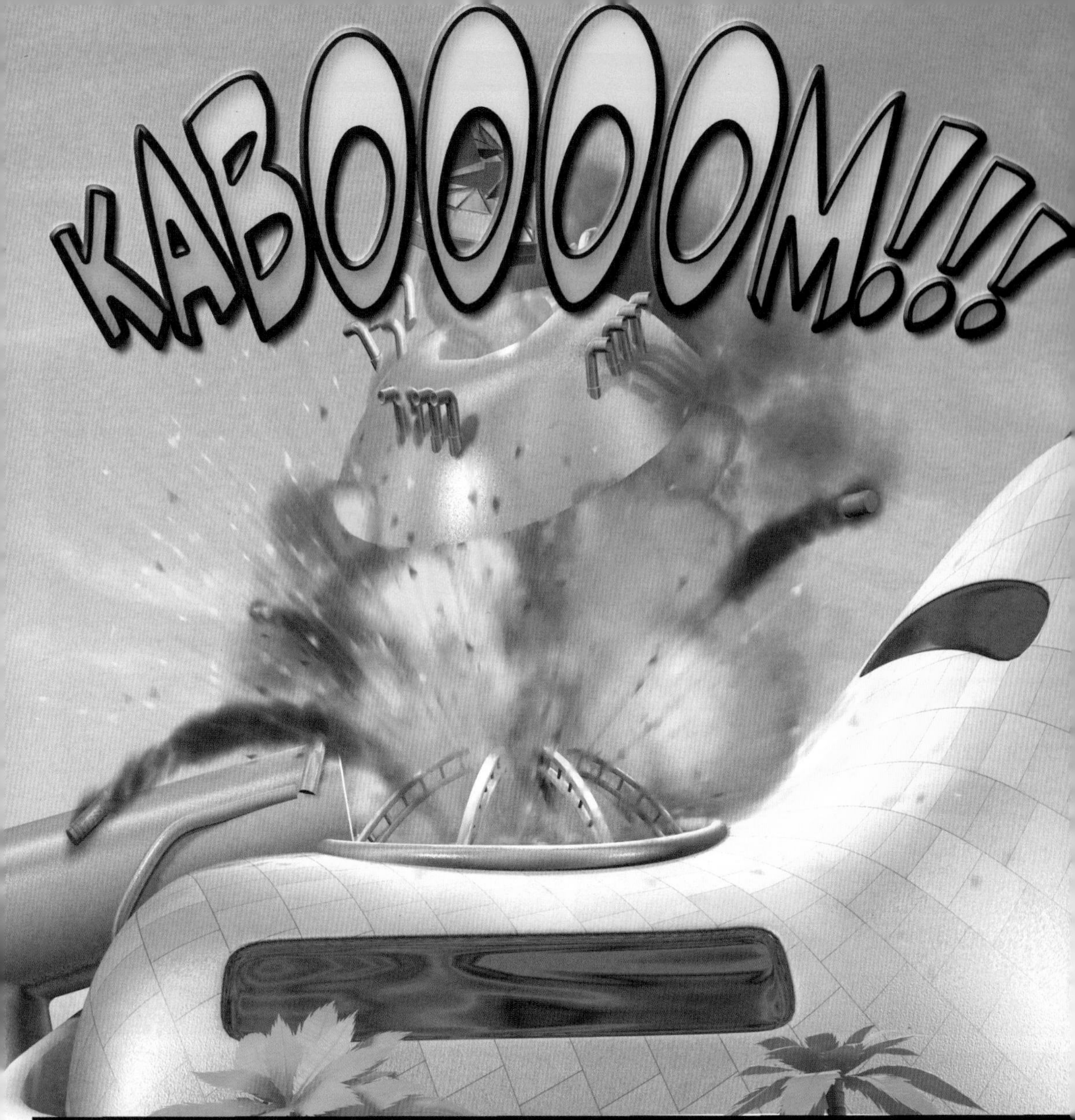
KABOOOOM!!!

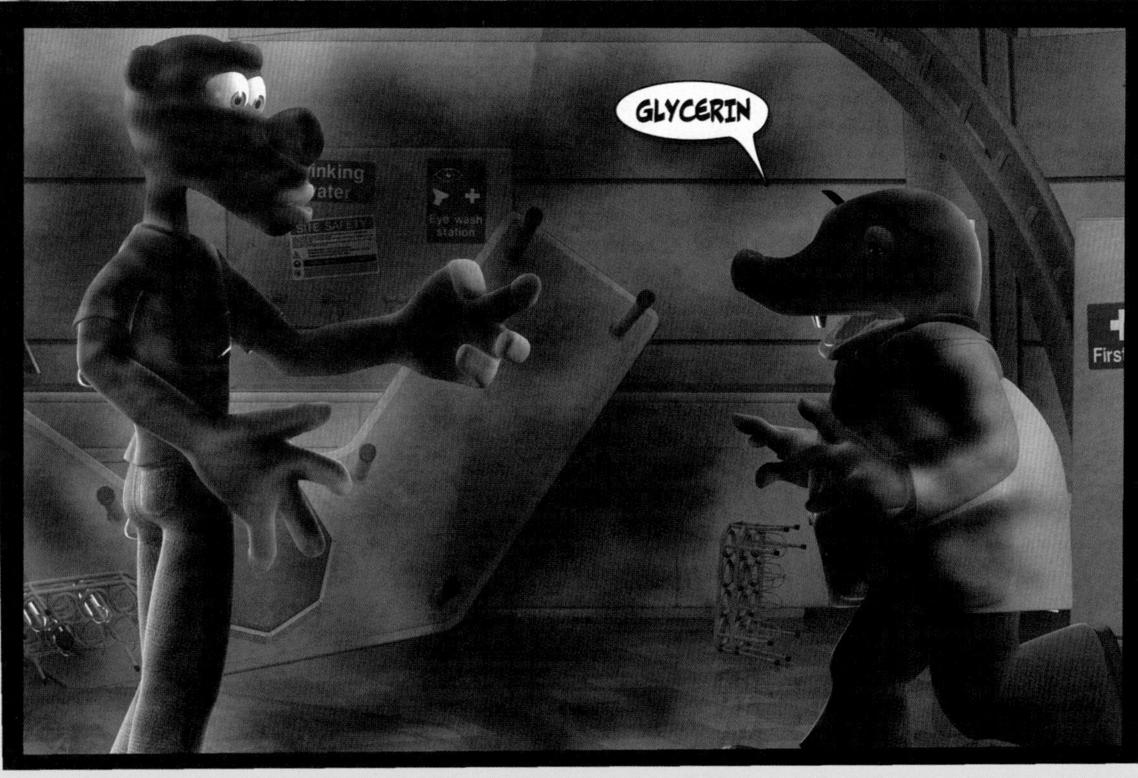
GLYCERIN
Drinking Water
SITE SAFETY
Eye wash station

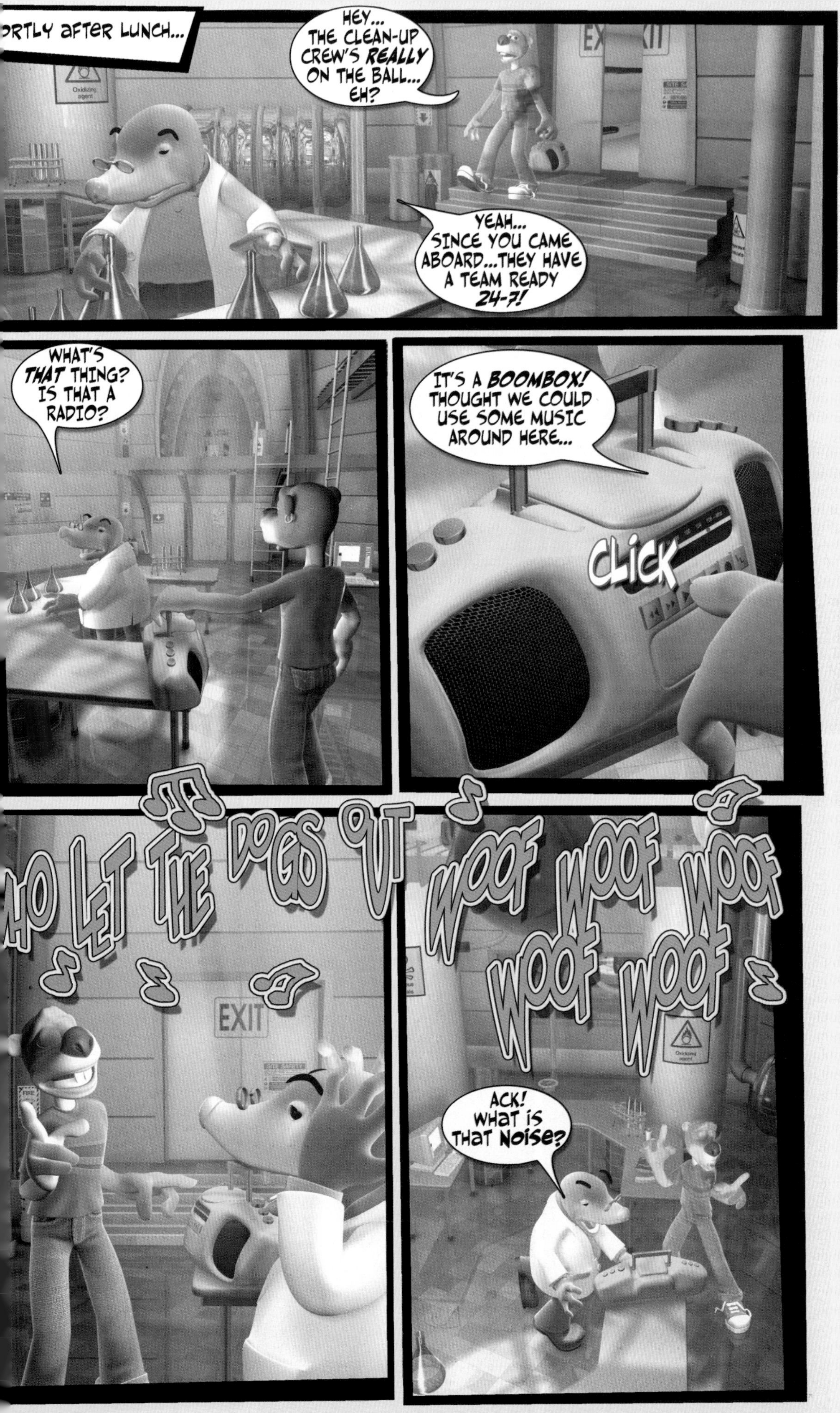
RTLY AFTER LUNCH...
Oxidizing agent
HEY... THE CLEAN-UP CREW'S REALLY ON THE BALL... EH?
YEAH... SINCE YOU CAME ABOARD...THEY HAVE A TEAM READY 24-7!
WHAT'S THAT THING? IS THAT A RADIO?
IT'S A BOOMBOX! THOUGHT WE COULD USE SOME MUSIC AROUND HERE...
CLICK
HO LET THE DOGS OUT
WOOF WOOF WOOF
WOOF WOOF
EXIT
Oxidizing agent
ACK! WHAT IS THAT NOISE?

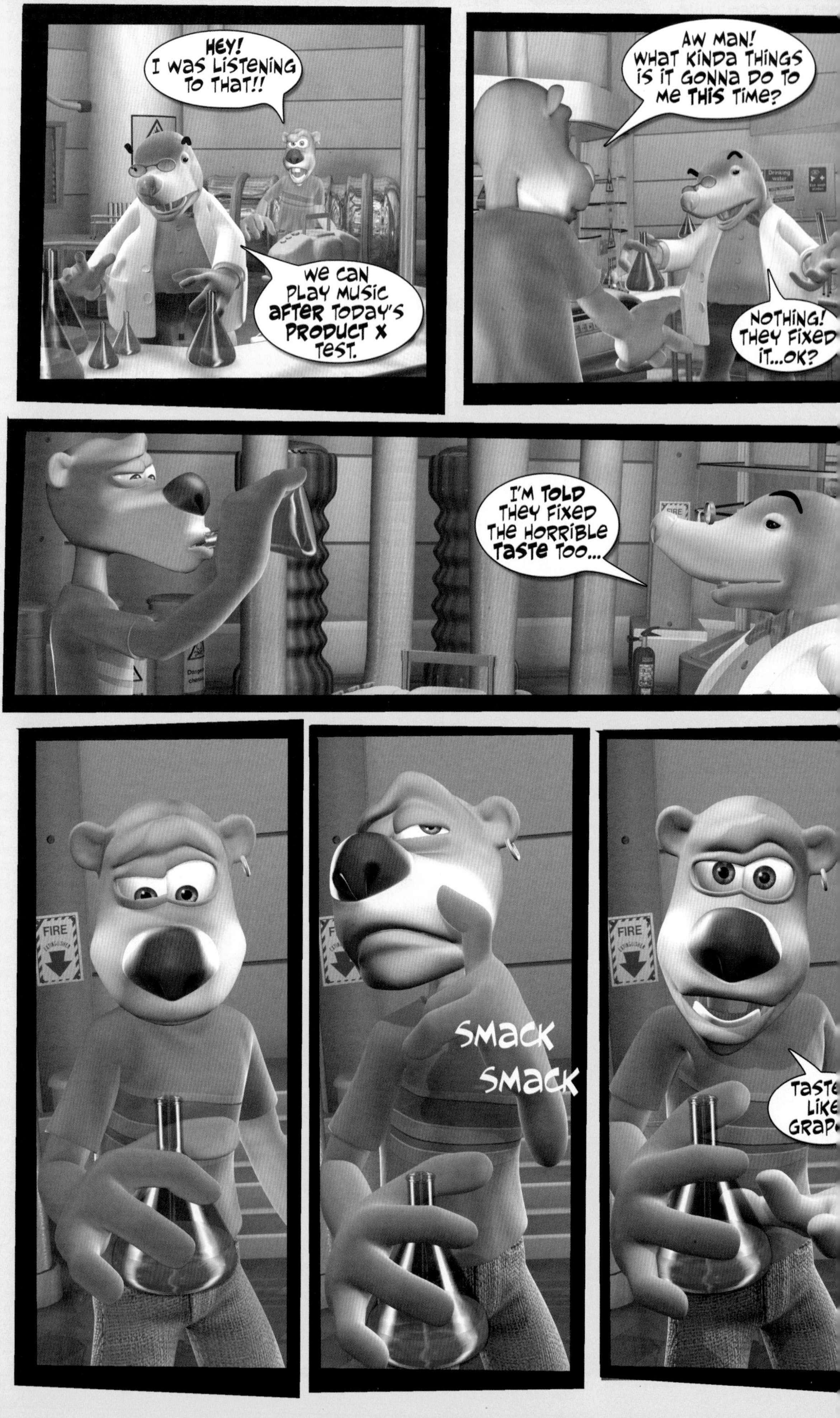
HEY! I WAS LISTENING TO THAT!!
WE CAN PLAY MUSIC AFTER TODAY'S PRODUCT X TEST.
AW MAN! WHAT KINDA THINGS IS IT GONNA DO TO ME THIS TIME?
NOTHING! THEY FIXED IT...OK?
I'M TOLD THEY FIXED THE HORRIBLE TASTE TOO...
FIRE
SMACK
SMACK
FIRE
TASTE LIKE GRAP

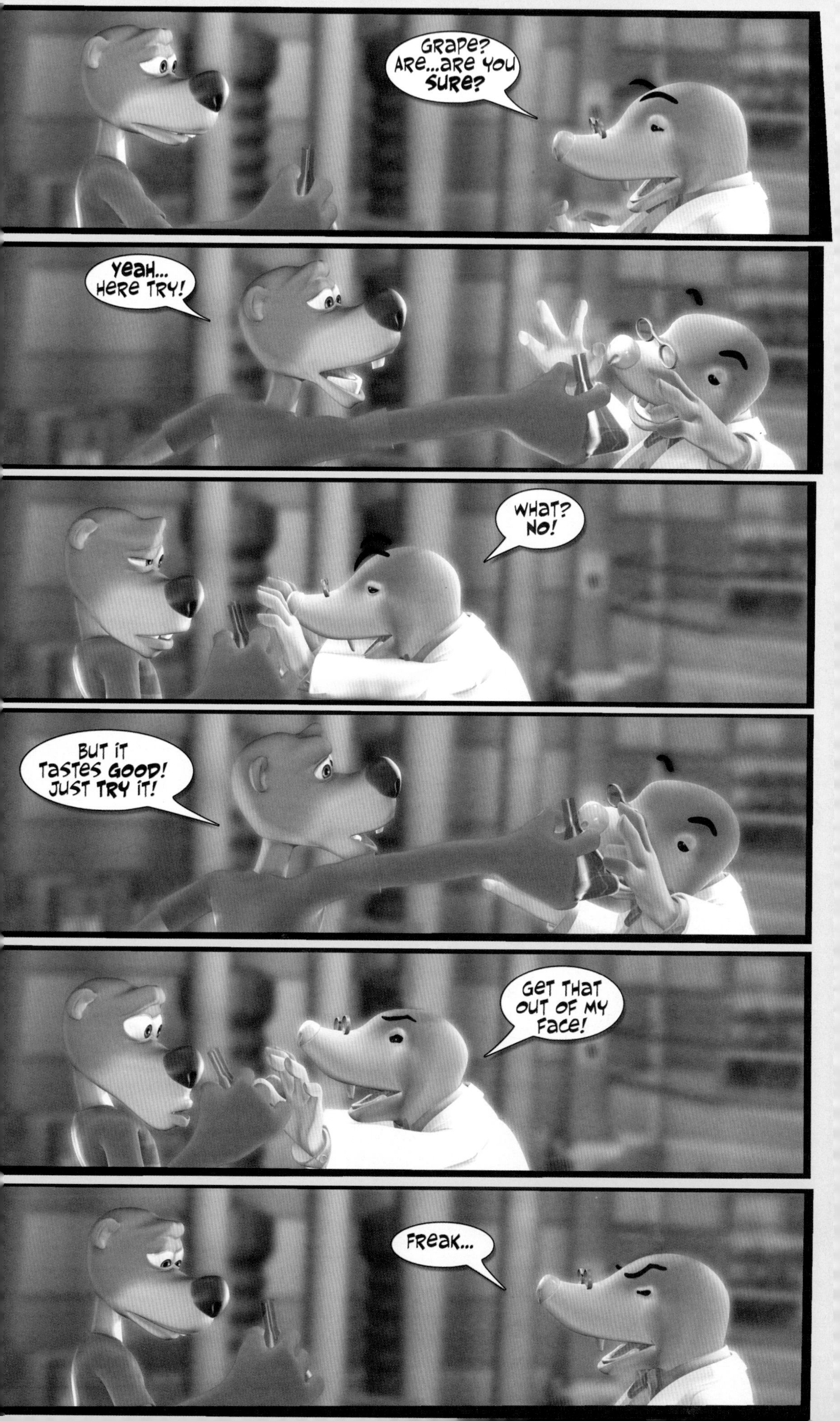
GRAPE? ARE...ARE YOU SURE?
YEAH... HERE TRY!
WHAT? NO!
BUT IT TASTES GOOD! JUST TRY IT!
GET THAT OUT OF MY FACE!
FREAK...

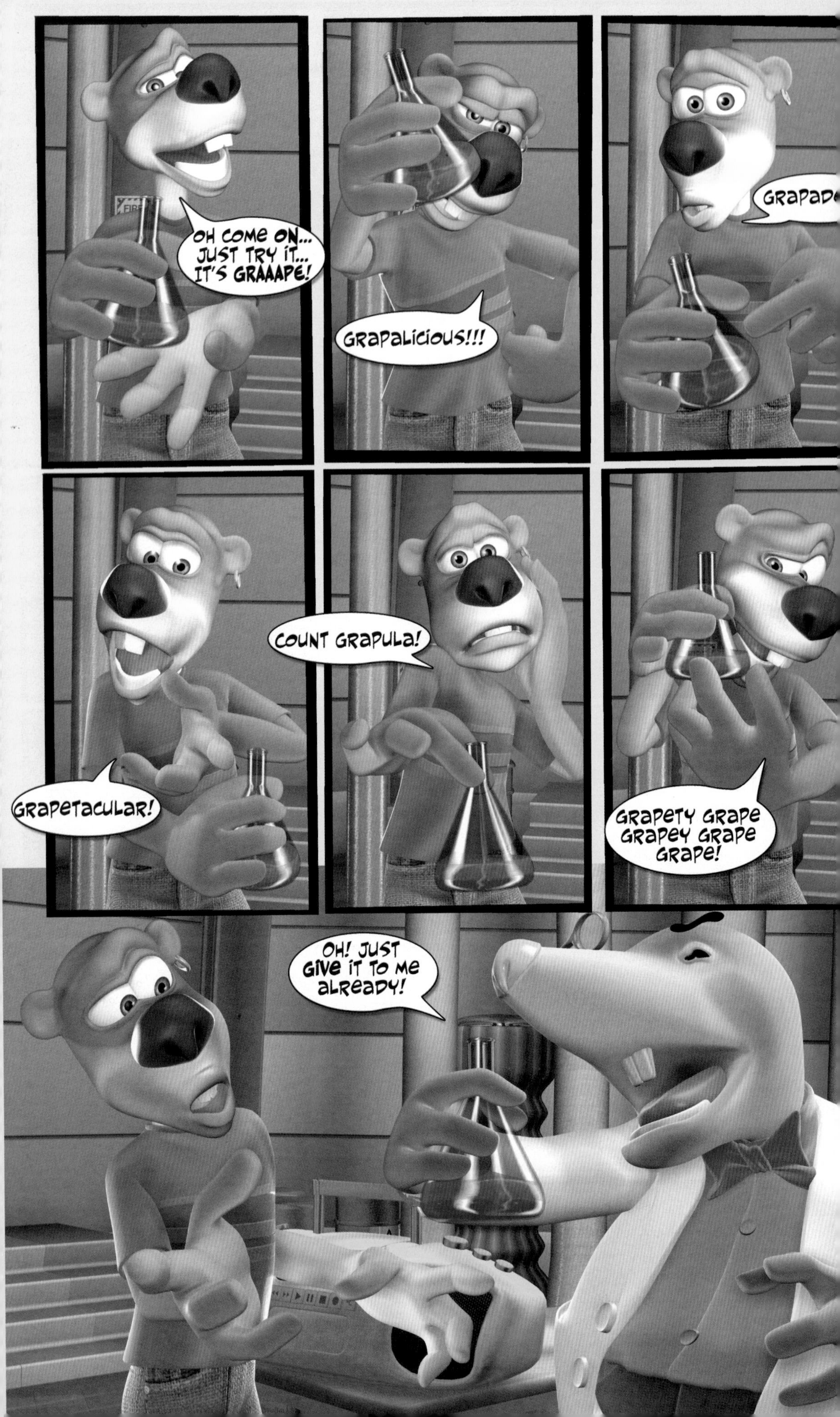
OH COME ON... JUST TRY IT... IT'S GRAAAPE!
GRAPALICIOUS!!!
GRAPAD
GRAPETACULAR!
COUNT GRAPULA!
GRAPETY GRAPE GRAPEY GRAPE GRAPE!
OH! JUST GIVE IT TO ME ALREADY!

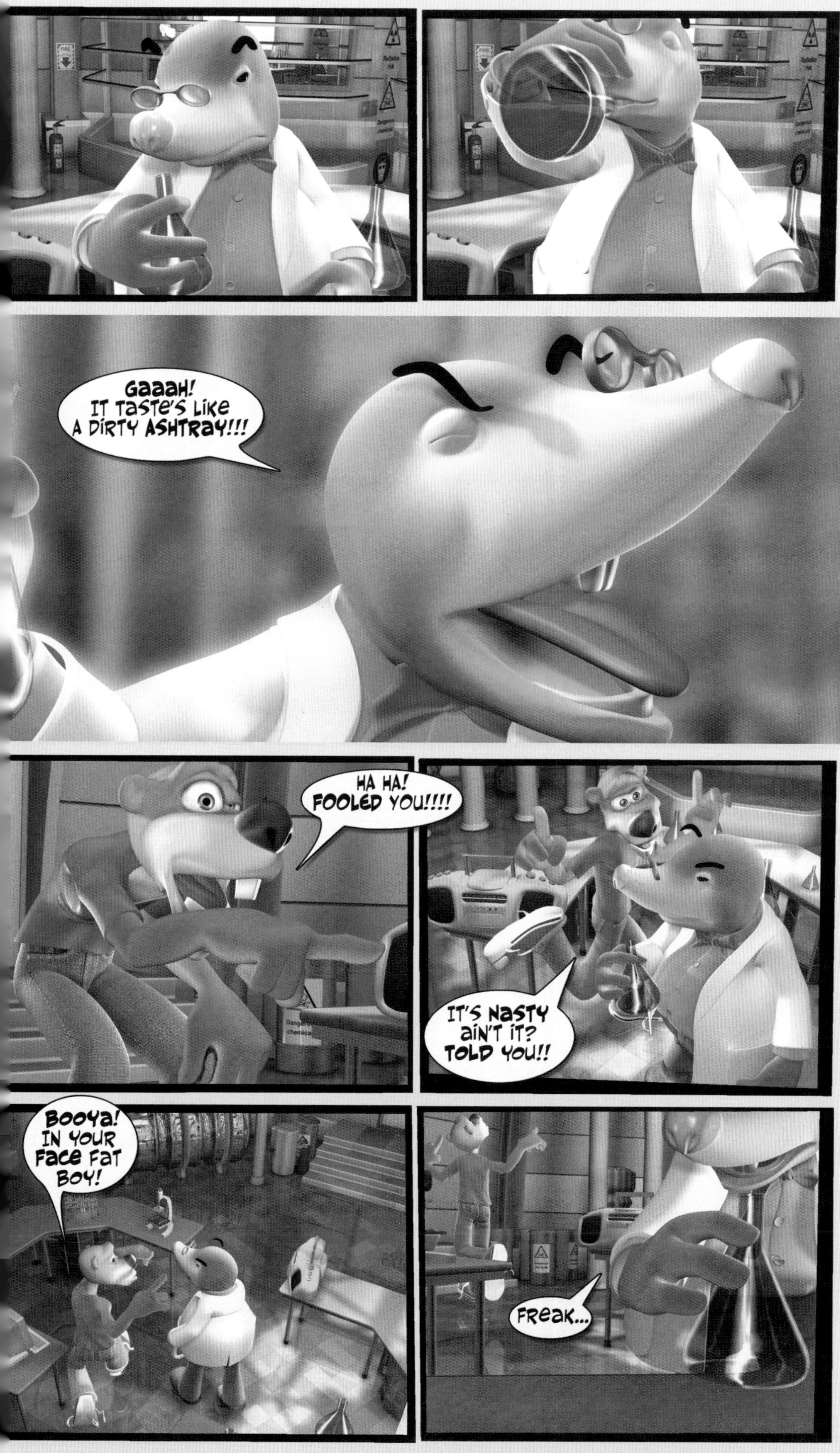
GaaaH! IT TaSTE'S LiKE A DIRTY ASHTRay!!!
HA HA! FOOLED YOU!!!!
IT'S NaSTY aiN'T iT? TOLD YOU!!
BooYa! IN YOUR Face FaT BOY!
FReaK...

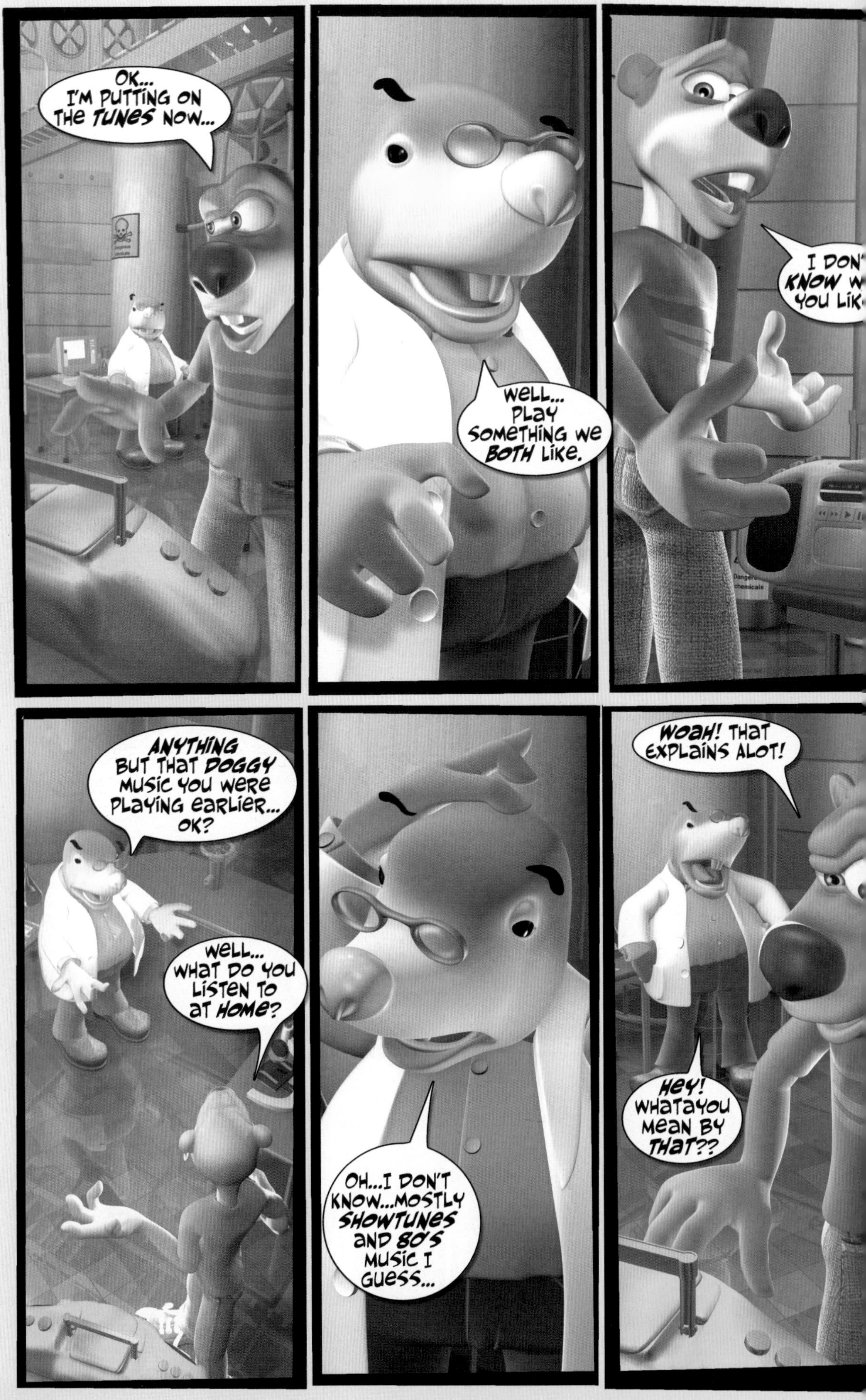
OK... I'M PUTTING ON THE TUNES NOW...
WELL... PLAY SOMETHING WE BOTH LIKE.
I DON' KNOW W YOU LIK
ANYTHING BUT THAT DOGGY MUSIC YOU WERE PLAYING EARLIER... OK?
WELL... WHAT DO YOU LISTEN TO AT HOME?
OH...I DON'T KNOW...MOSTLY SHOWTUNES AND 80'S MUSIC I GUESS...
WOAH! THAT EXPLAINS ALOT!
HEY! WHATAYOU MEAN BY THAT??

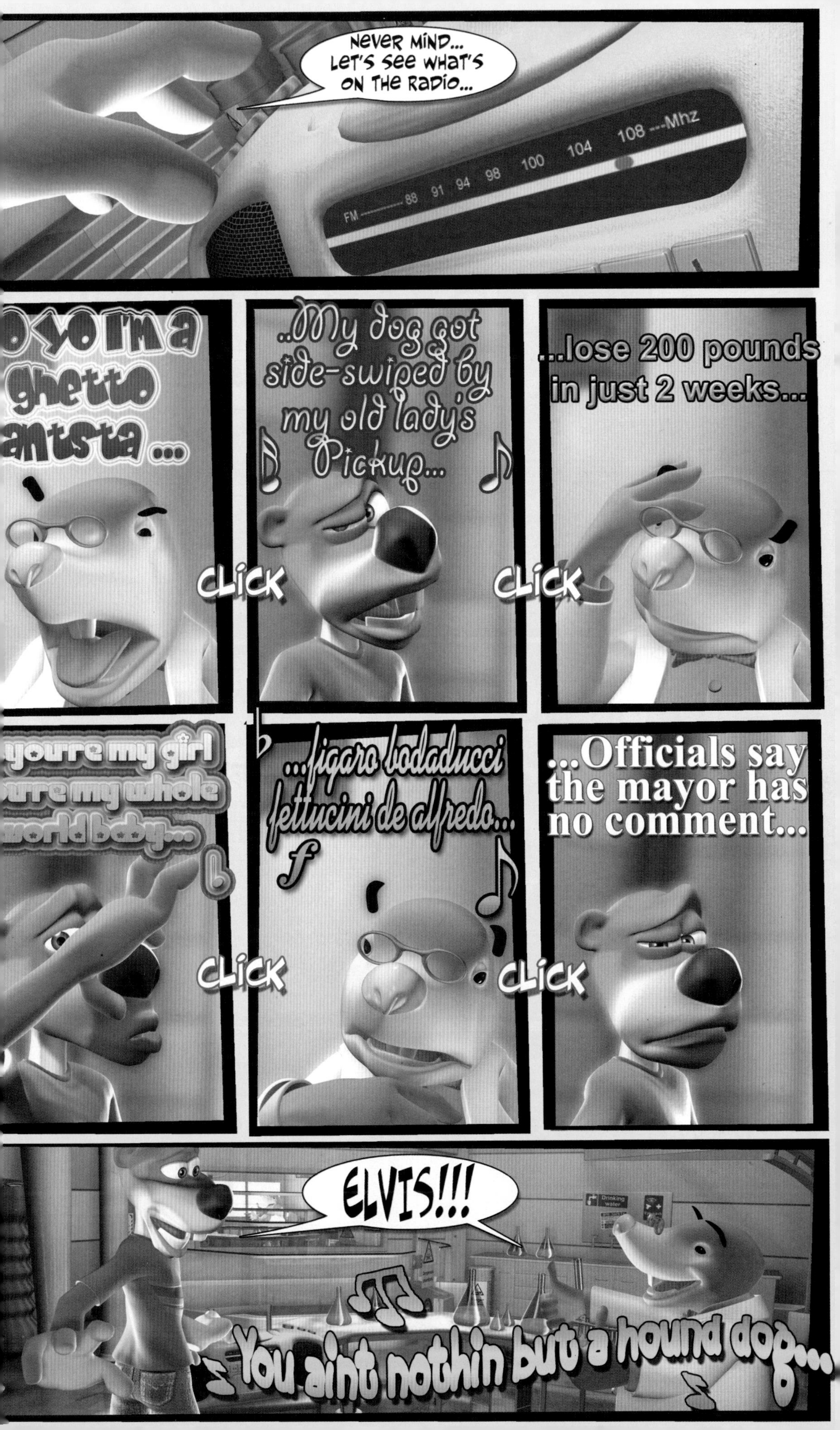
NEVER MIND...
LET'S SEE WHAT'S
ON THE RADIO...
FM 88 91 94 98 100 104 108 ---Mhz
o yo I'm a
ghetto
antsta ...
..My dog got
side-swiped by
my old lady's
Pickup...
CLICK
...lose 200 pounds
in just 2 weeks...
CLICK
youre my girl
urre my whole
world baby...
CLICK
...figaro bodaducci
fettucini de alfredo...
CLICK
...Officials say
the mayor has
no comment...
ELVIS!!!
Drinking water
You aint nothin but a hound dog...

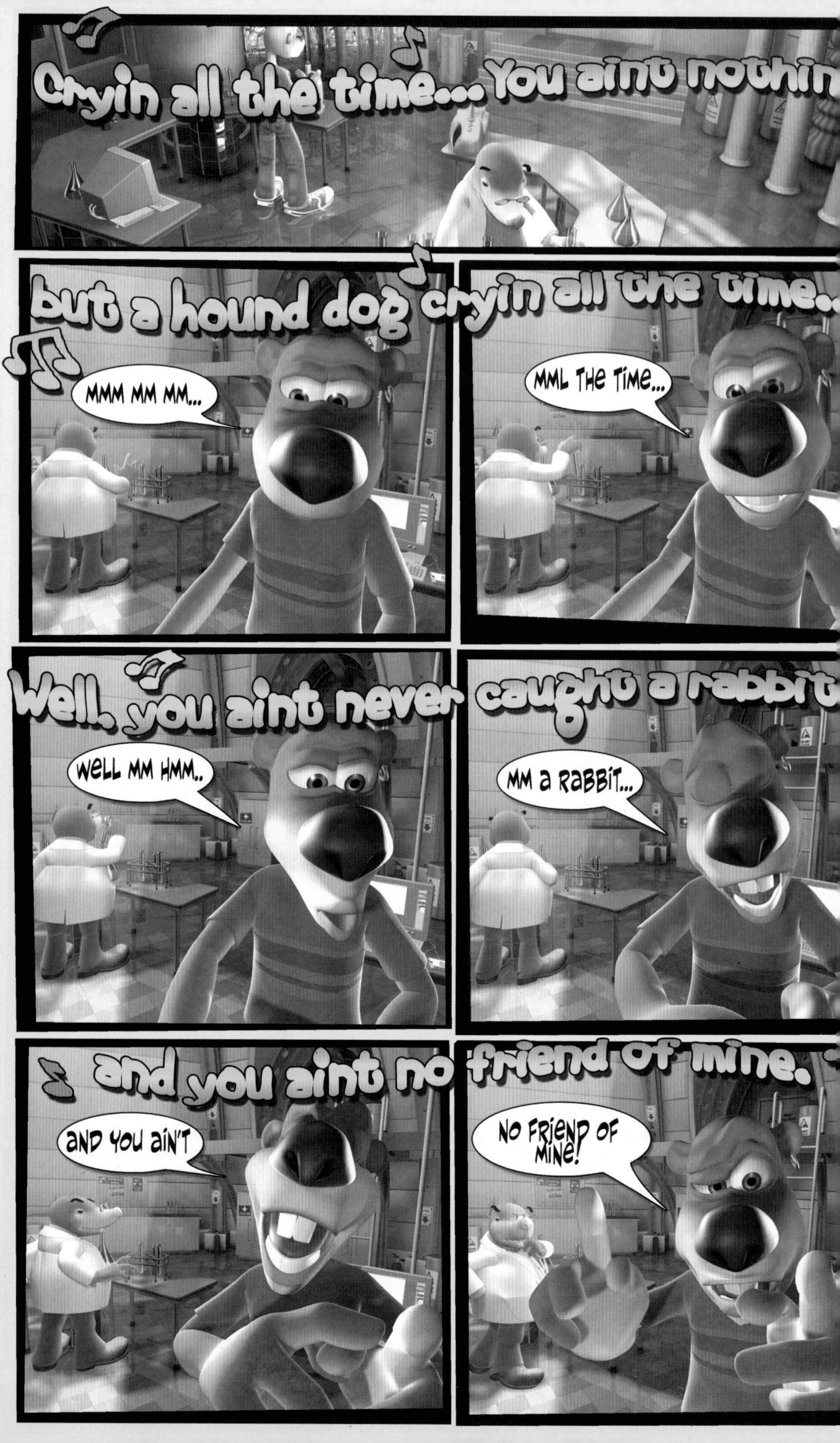
Cryin all the time... You aint nothin
but a hound dog cryin all the time..
MMM MM MM...
MML THE TIME...
Well, you aint never caught a rabbit
WELL MM HMM..
MM A RABBIT...
and you aint no friend of mine.
AND YOU AIN'T
NO FRIEND OF MINE!

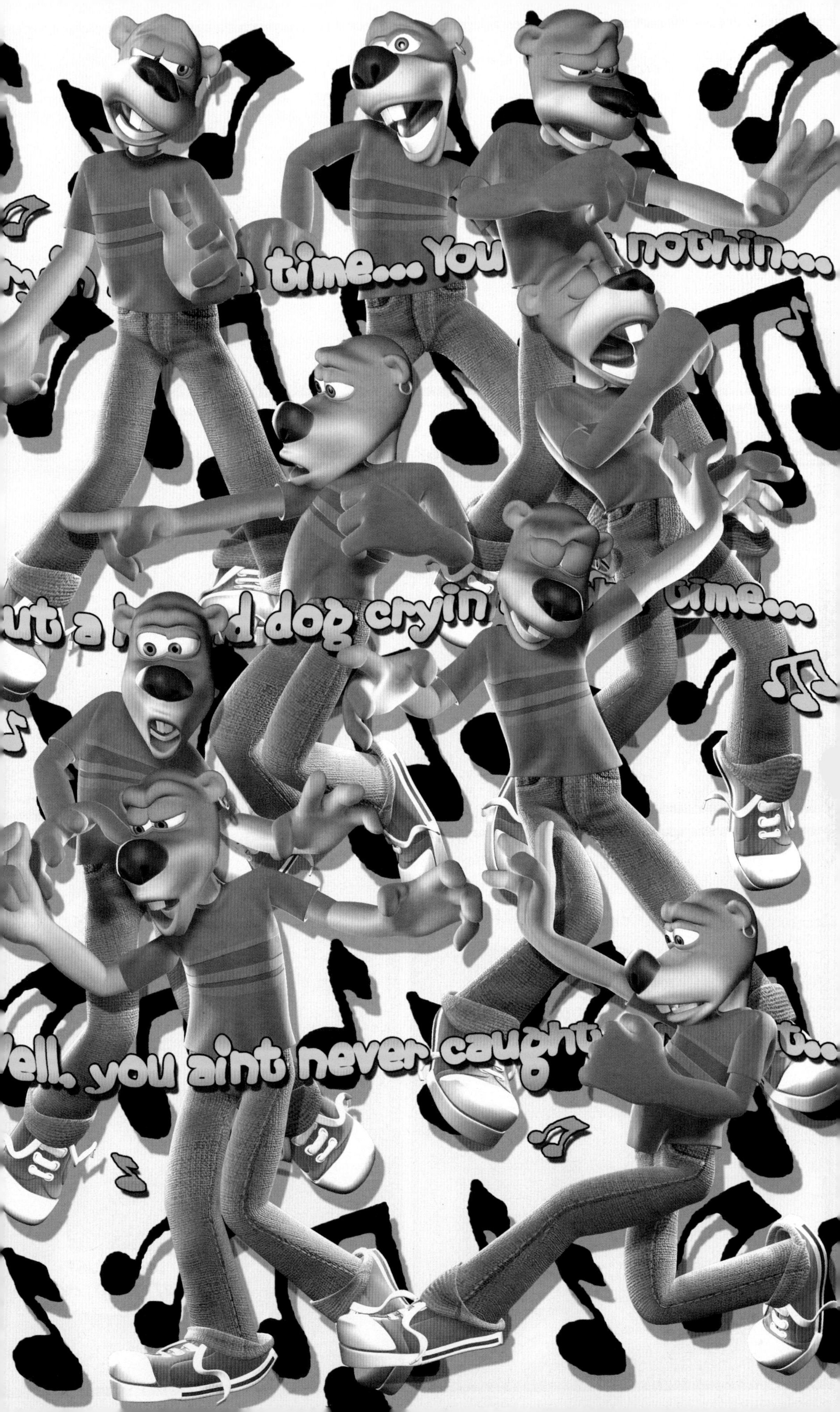
time... You
nothin...
ut a
d dog cryin
ime...
ell, you aint never caugh

CLICK

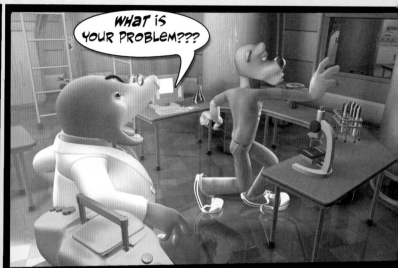

WHAT IS YOUR PROBLEM???

WHAT?

WHAT'RE YOU DOING?

WITH **WHAT**?

THE LAS VEGAS **LOUNGE** ACT YOU JUST PERFORMED!!

HUH? I WAS **SINGING**?

OF **COURSE**! AND IT WAS THE **WORST** ELVIS IMPERSONATION **TOO** I MIGHT ADD ! SHEESH.

SERIOUSLY?

LOOK...JUST **CUT** IT OUT...OK?

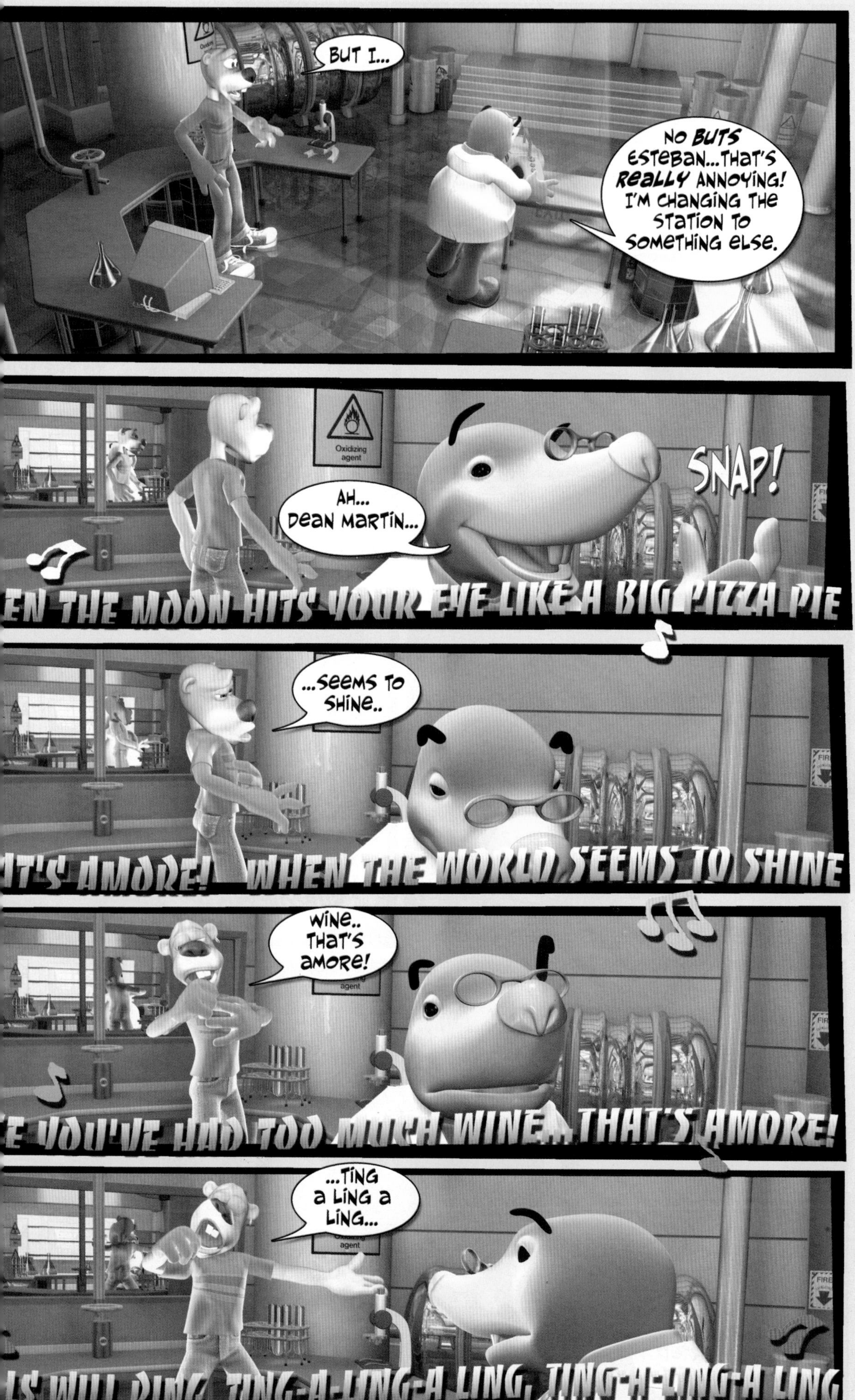
BUT I...
NO BUTS ESTEBAN...THAT'S REALLY ANNOYING! I'M CHANGING THE STATION TO SOMETHING ELSE.
Oxidizing agent
AH... DEAN MARTIN...
SNAP!
EN THE MOON HITS YOUR EYE LIKE A BIG PIZZA PIE
...SEEMS TO SHINE..
IT'S AMORE! WHEN THE WORLD SEEMS TO SHINE
WINE.. THAT'S AMORE!
E YOU'VE HAD TOO MUCH WINE..THAT'S AMORE!
...TING A LING A LING...
LS WILL RING, TING-A-LING-A LING, TING-A-LING-A LING

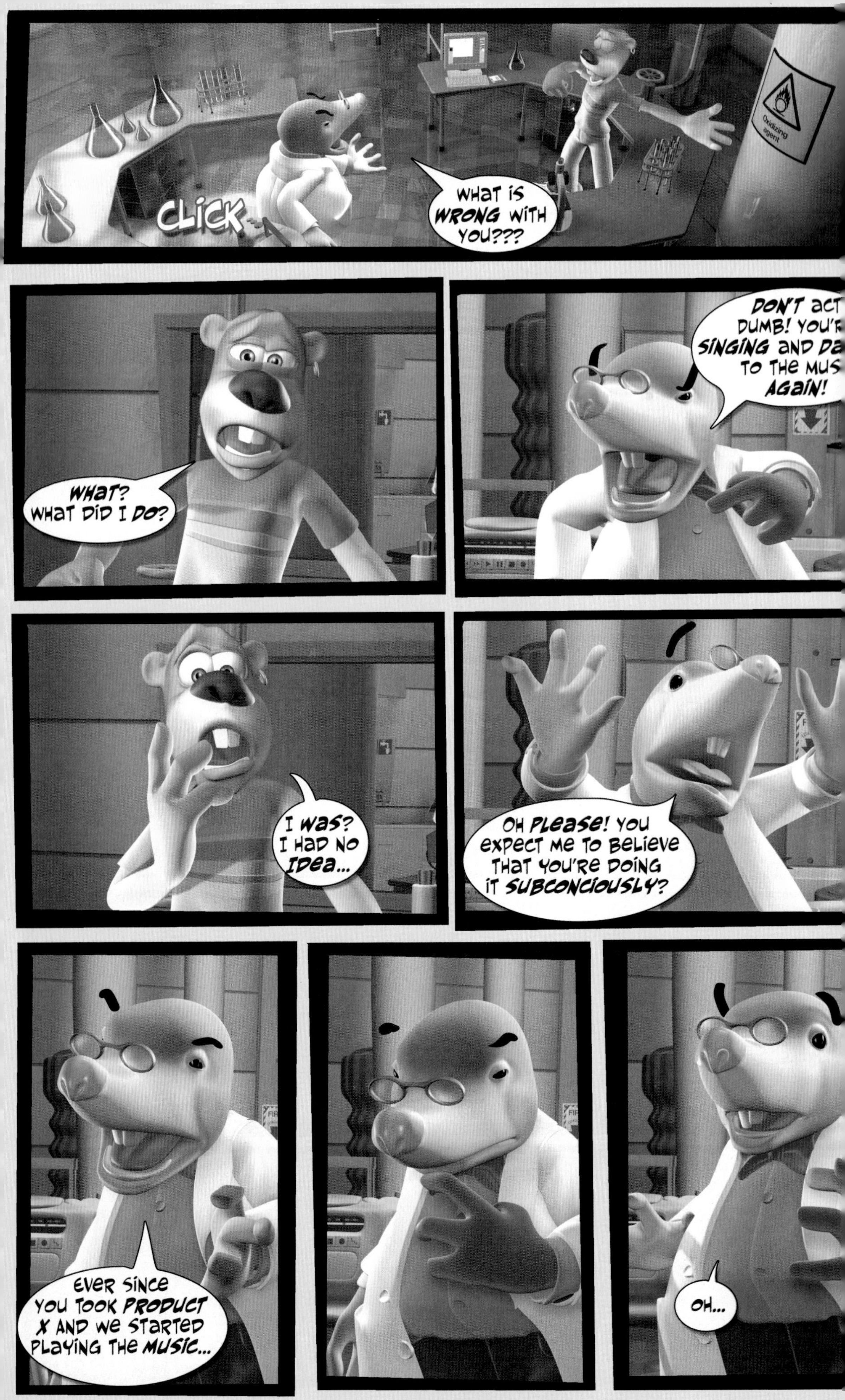

CLICK
WHAT IS WRONG WITH YOU???
WHAT? WHAT DID I DO?
DON'T ACT DUMB! YOU'R SINGING AND DA TO THE MUS AGAIN!
I WAS? I HAD NO IDEA...
OH PLEASE! YOU EXPECT ME TO BELIEVE THAT YOU'RE DOING IT SUBCONCIOUSLY?
EVER SINCE YOU TOOK PRODUCT X AND WE STARTED PLAYING THE MUSIC...
OH...

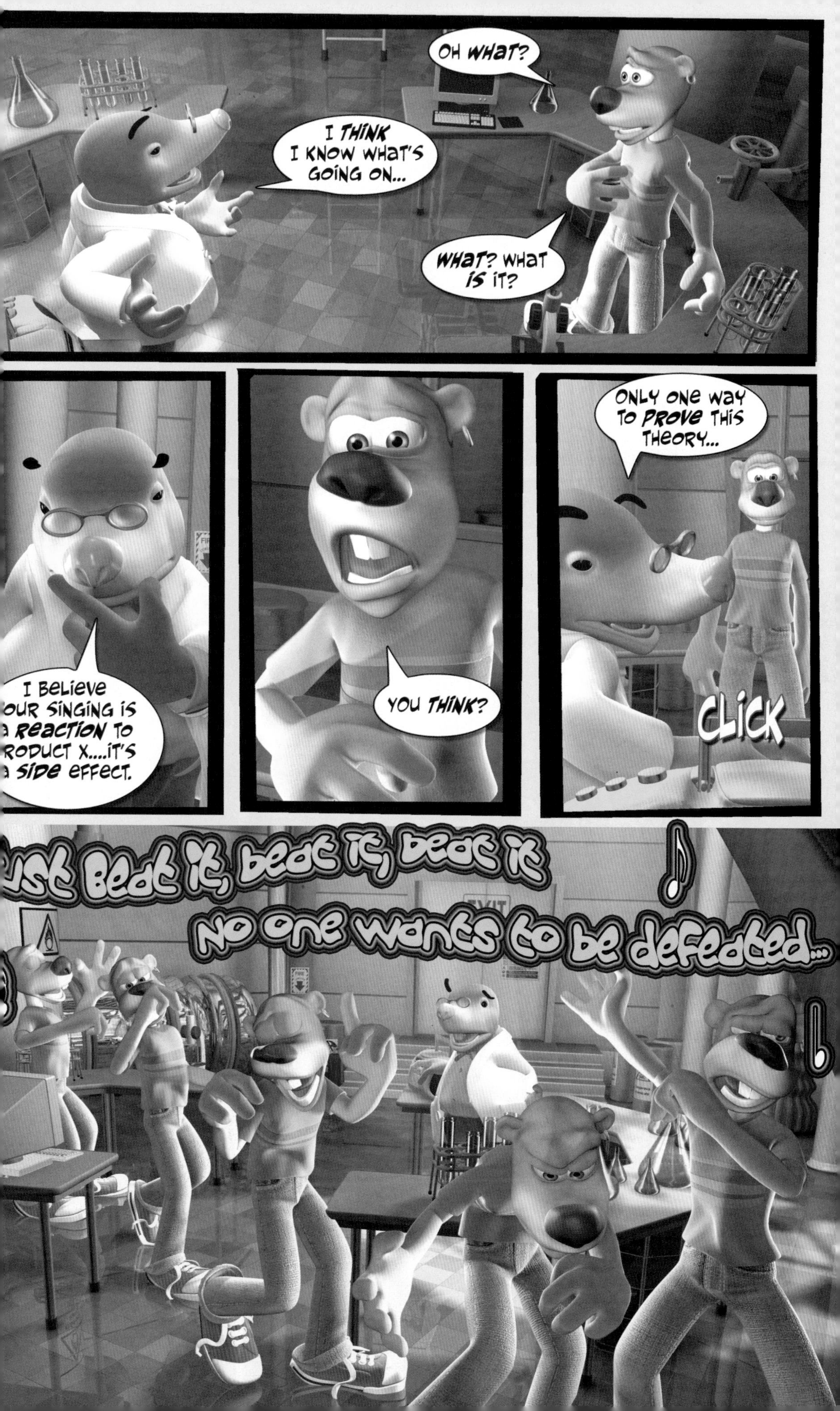
I THINK I KNOW WHAT'S GOING ON...
OH WHAT?
WHAT? WHAT IS IT?
I BELIEVE OUR SINGING IS A REACTION TO PRODUCT X....IT'S A SIDE EFFECT.
YOU THINK?
ONLY ONE WAY TO PROVE THIS THEORY...
CLICK
ust Beat it, beat it, beat it
No one wants to be defeated...

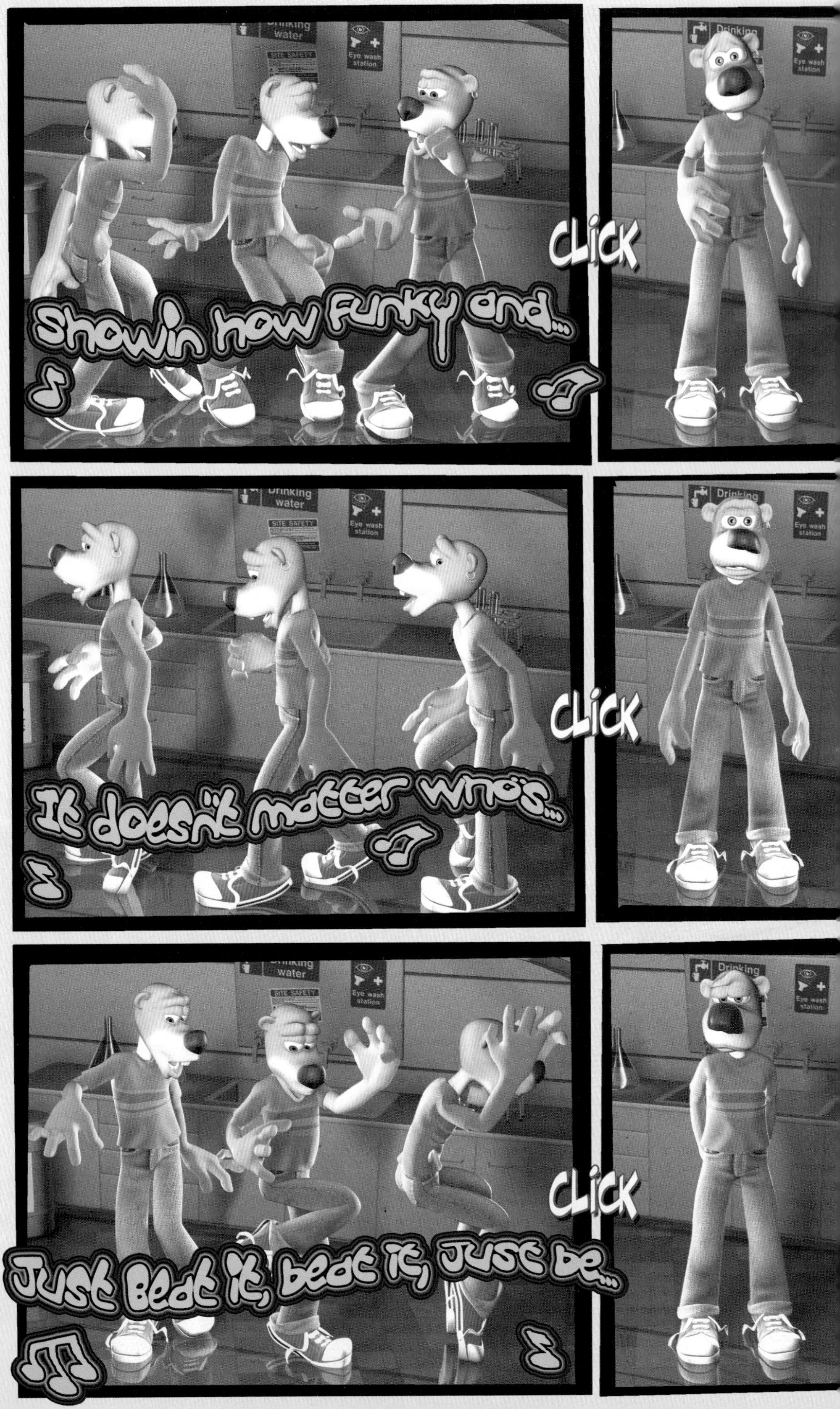
Drinking water
SITE SAFETY
Eye wash station
Showin how funky and...
CLICK
It doesn't matter who's...
CLICK
Just beat it, beat it, just be...
CLICK

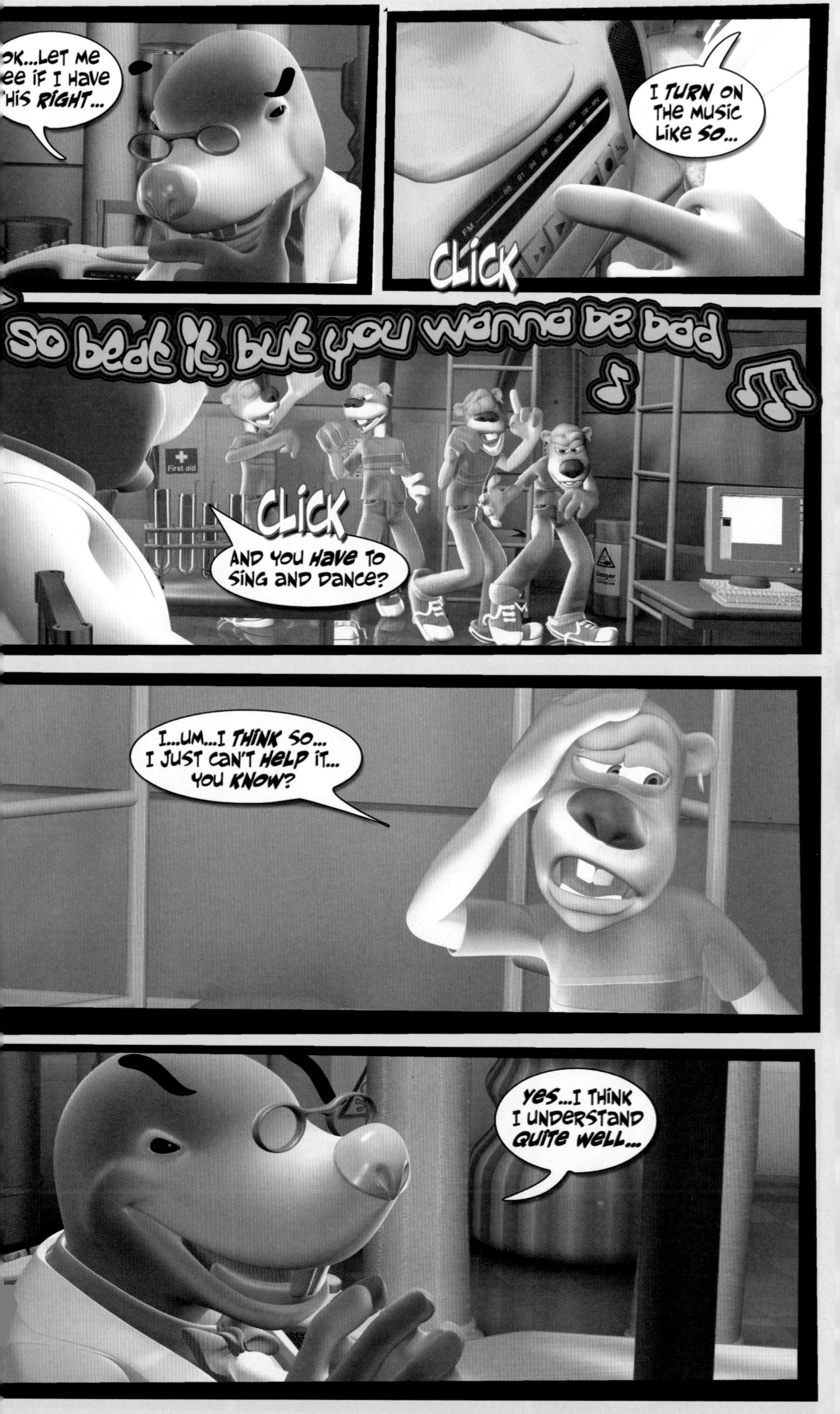
OK...LET ME
SEE IF I HAVE
THIS RIGHT...
I TURN ON
THE MUSIC
LIKE SO...
CLICK
SO BEAT IT, BUT YOU WANNA BE BAD
CLICK
AND YOU HAVE TO
SING AND DANCE?
I...UM...I THINK SO...
I JUST CAN'T HELP IT...
YOU KNOW?
YES...I THINK
I UNDERSTAND
QUITE WELL...

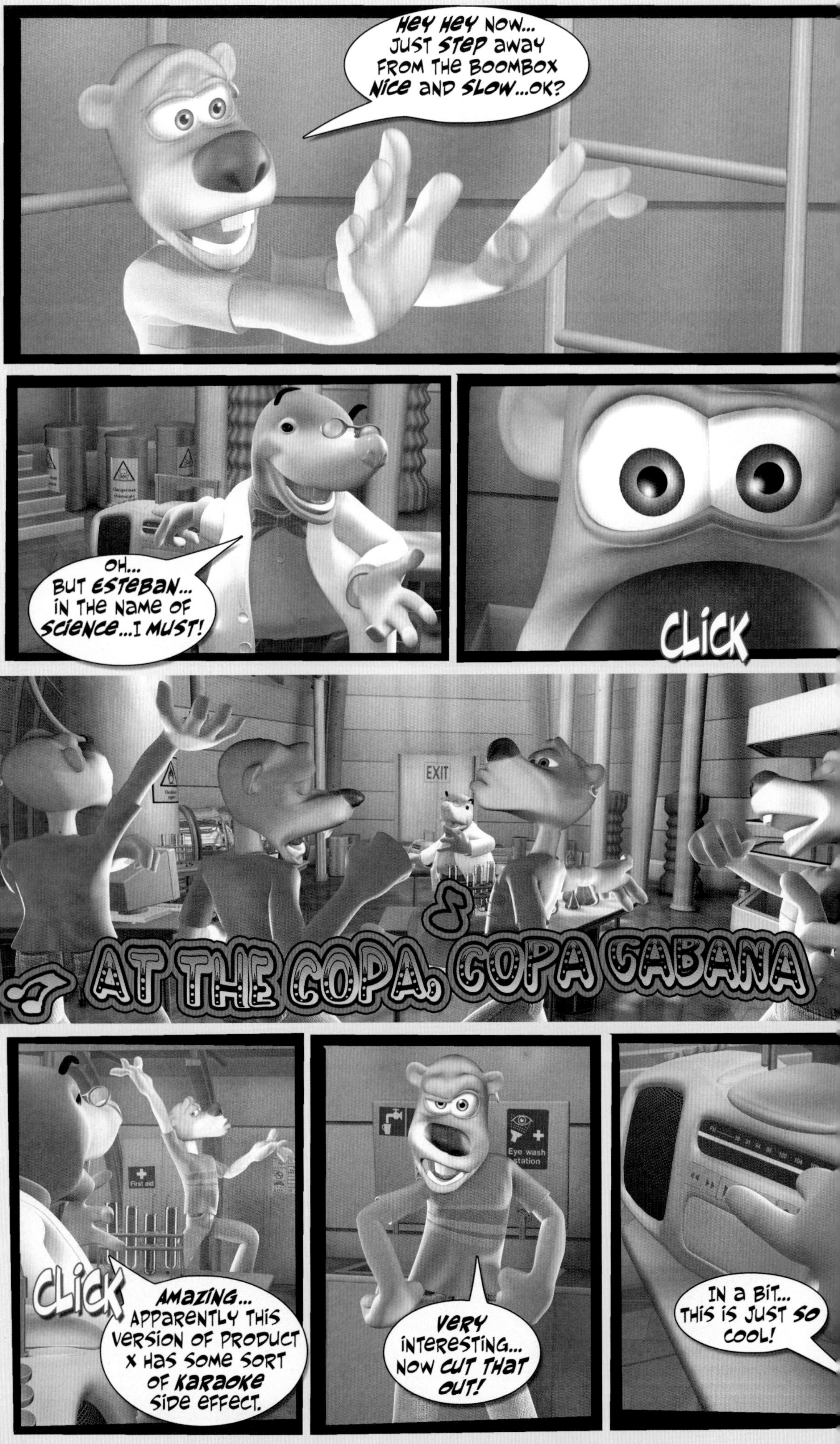
HEY HEY NOW... JUST STEP AWAY FROM THE BOOMBOX NICE AND SLOW...OK?
OH... BUT ESTEBAN... IN THE NAME OF SCIENCE...I MUST!
CLICK
EXIT
AT THE COPA, COPA CABANA
First aid
CLICK
AMAZING... APPARENTLY THIS VERSION OF PRODUCT X HAS SOME SORT OF KARAOKE SIDE EFFECT.
Eye wash station
VERY INTERESTING... NOW CUT THAT OUT!
IN A BIT... THIS IS JUST SO COOL!

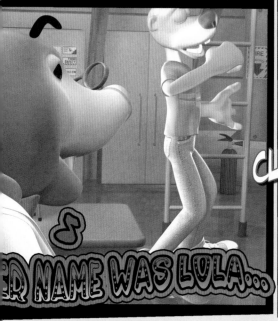

CLICK

...ER NAME WAS LULA...

OK... THAT'S ENOUGH!

CLICK

...E WAS A SHOWGIRL...

NOW CUT THAT OUT!!!

OOH OOH! WONDER IF E CAN GET Y FAVORITE TION...KSHW... ALL SHOW TUNES... L THE TIME!

YOU WOULDN'T DARE!!!

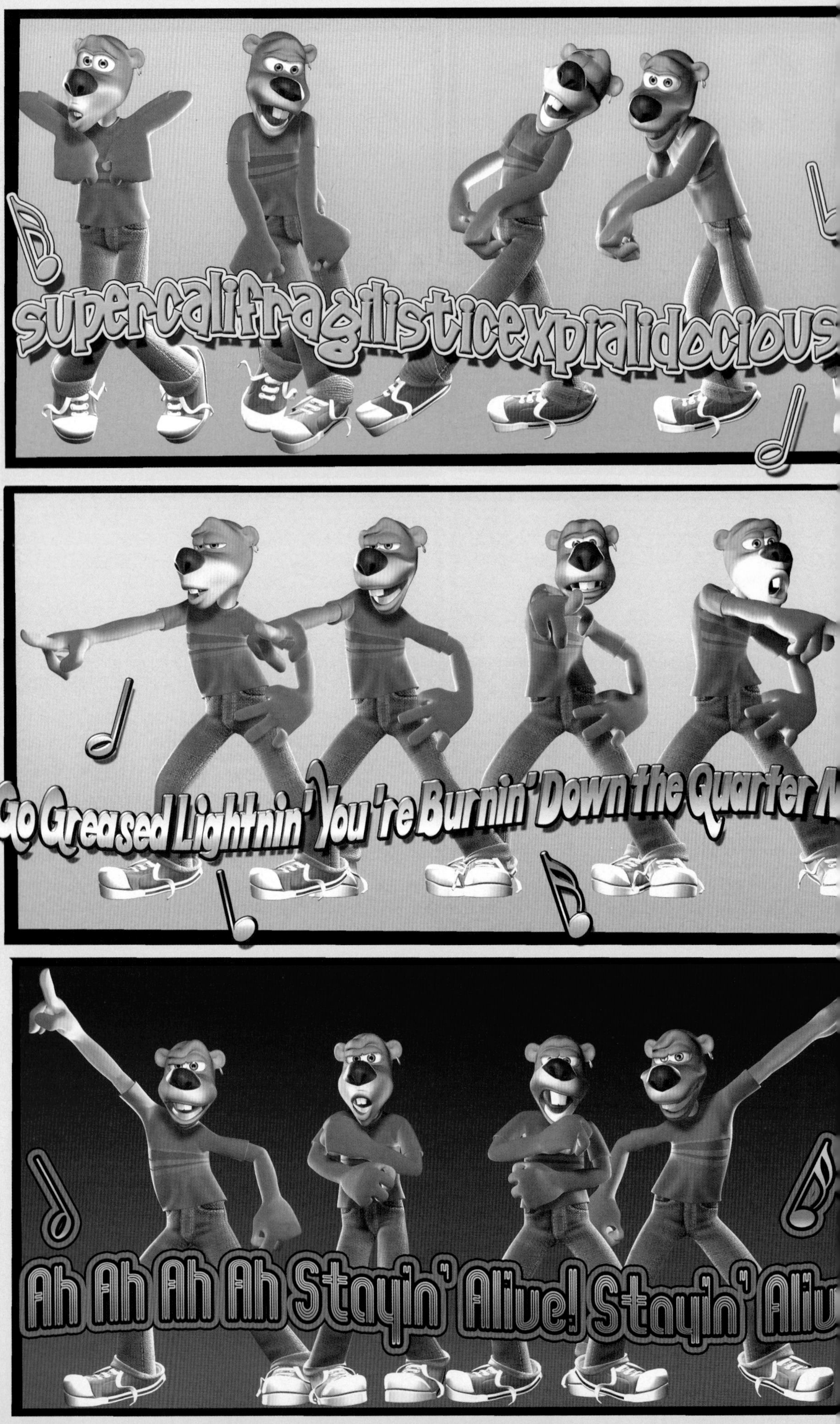
supercalifragilisticexpialidocious
Go Greased Lightnin' You're Burnin' Down the Quarter
Ah Ah Ah Ah Stayin' Alive! Stayin'

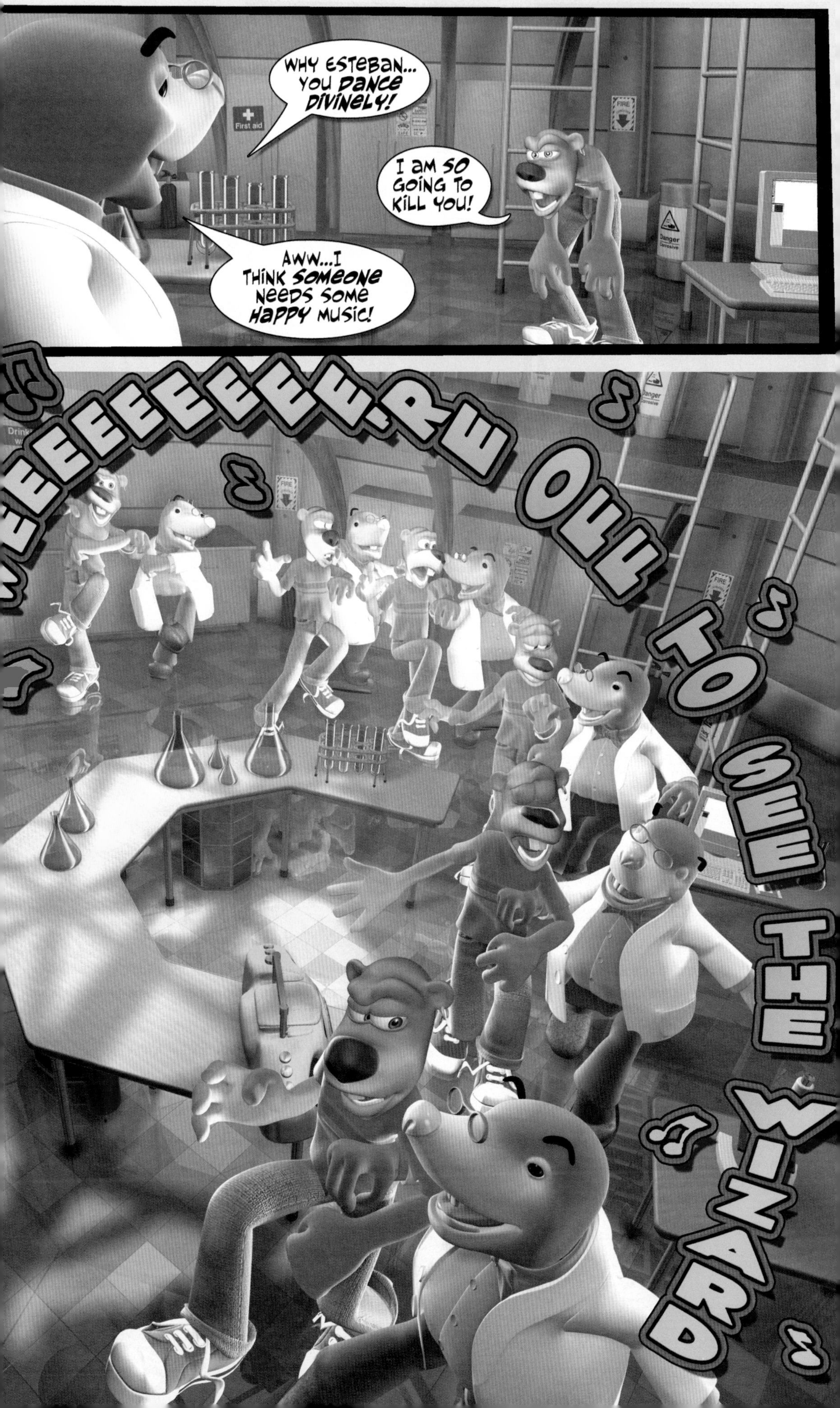
WHY ESTEBAN... YOU DANCE DIVINELY!
I AM SO GOING TO KILL YOU!
AWW...I THINK SOMEONE NEEDS SOME HAPPY MUSIC!
WEEEEEEEEE'RE OFF TO SEE THE WIZARD

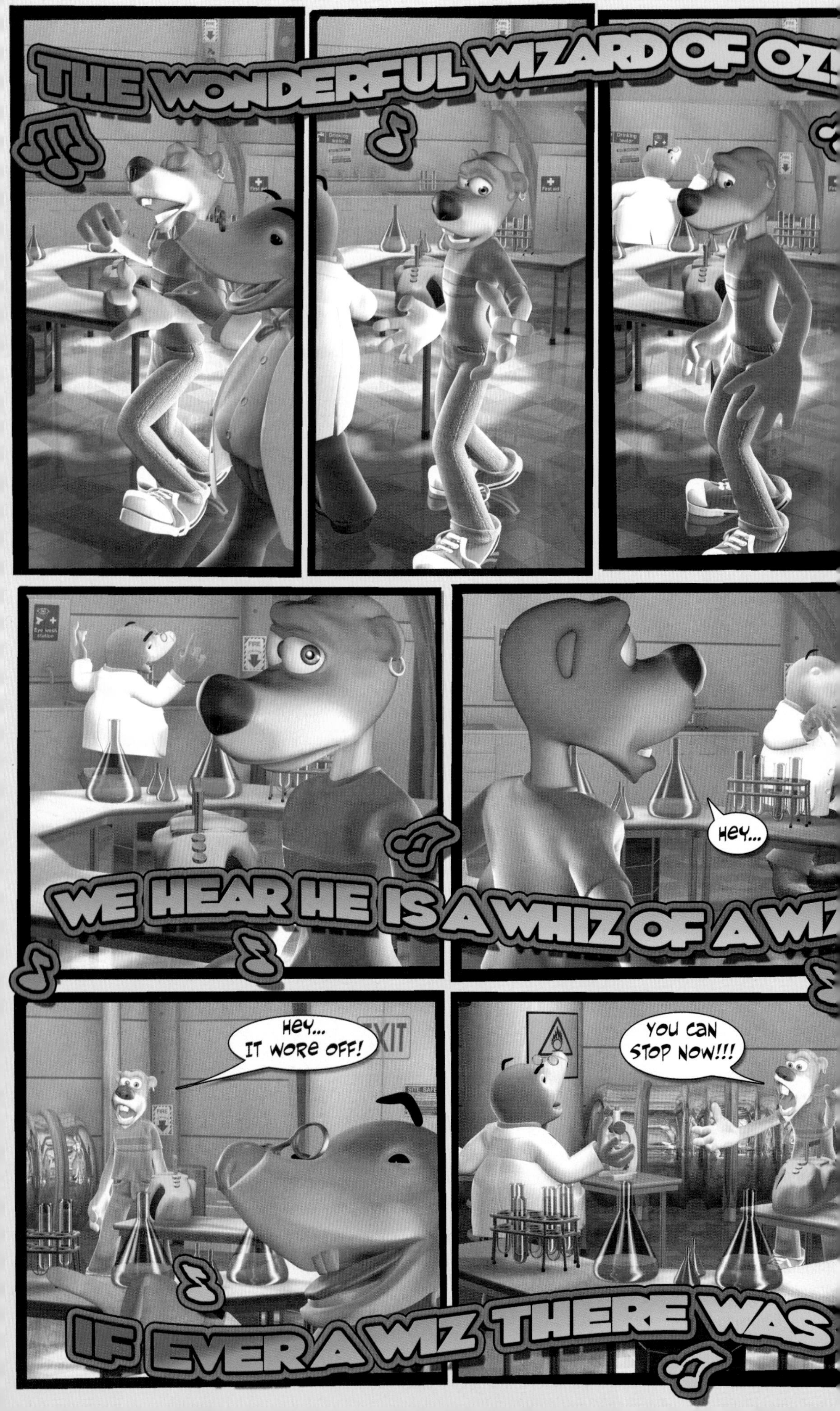
THE WONDERFUL WIZARD OF OZ
HEY...
WE HEAR HE IS A WHIZ OF A WIZ
HEY...
IT WORE OFF!
YOU CAN
STOP NOW!!!
IF EVER A WIZ THERE WAS

CLICK

WHAT'S **WRONG** WITH YOU? DIDN'T YOU **HEAR** ME?

WHAT? OH **YEAH**...BUT.. UM...

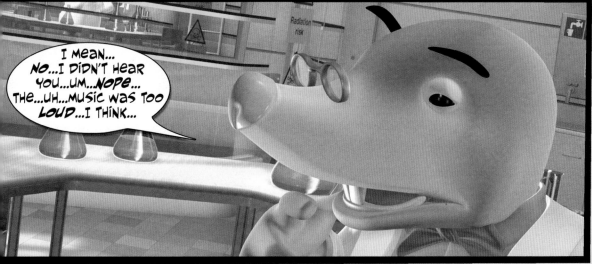

I MEAN... **NO**...I DIDN'T HEAR YOU...UM...**NOPE**... THE...UH...MUSIC WAS TOO **LOUD**...I THINK...

UM...HOW ABOUT THOSE **RED WINGS**... EH?

IS IT **WARM** IN HERE?

I WAS **TOTALLY** IN CONTROL... OK?

WHY DID I LET YOU TALK ME INTO DRINKING AN **EXPERIMENTAL** DRUG? UGH!

WHAT ARE YOU **LOOKING** AT? STOP **JUDGING** ME!

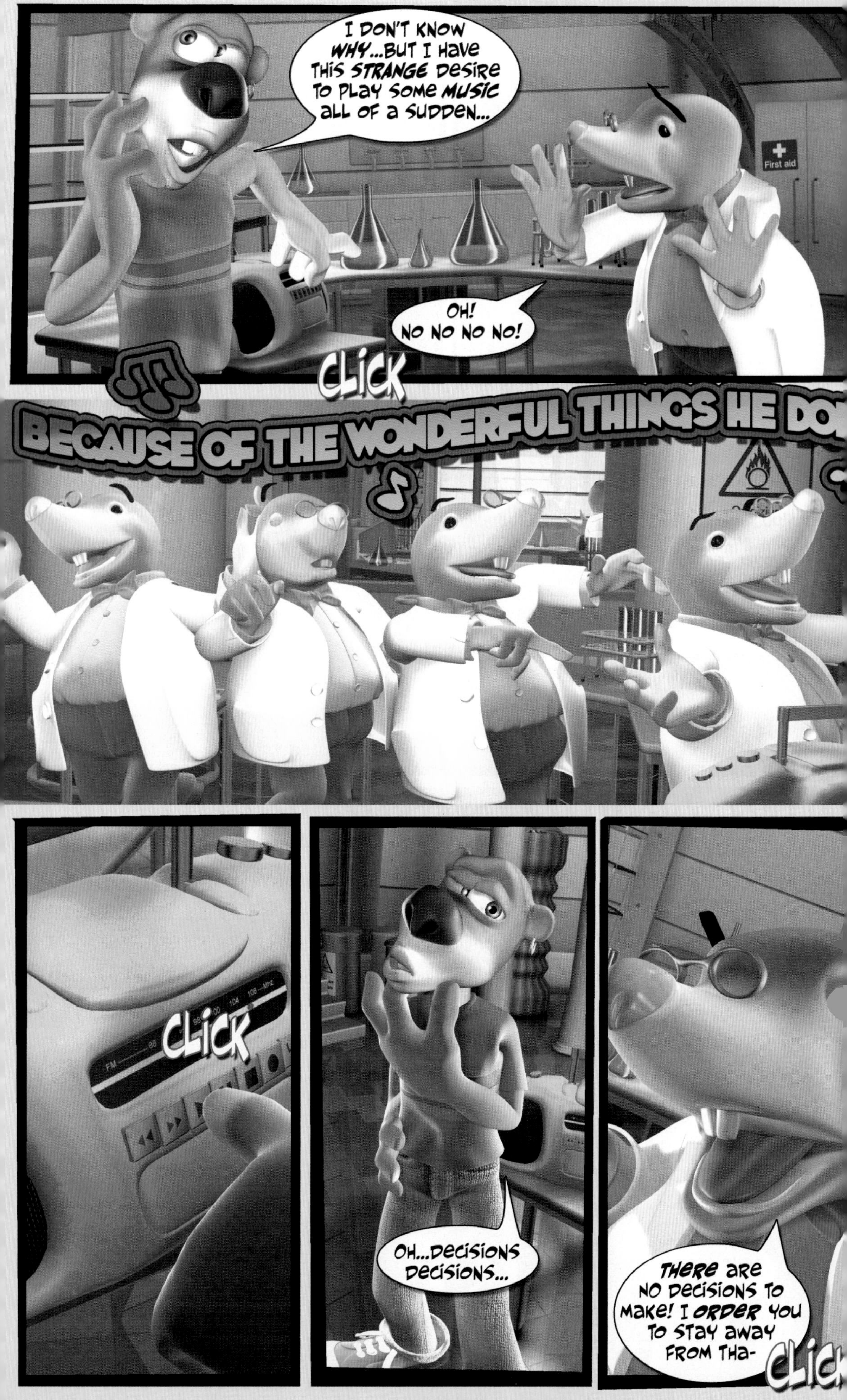
I DON'T KNOW WHY...BUT I HAVE THIS STRANGE DESIRE TO PLAY SOME MUSIC ALL OF A SUDDEN...
First aid
OH! NO NO NO NO!
CLICK
BECAUSE OF THE WONDERFUL THINGS HE DO
CLICK
OH...DECISIONS DECISIONS...
THERE ARE NO DECISIONS TO MAKE! I ORDER YOU TO STAY AWAY FROM THA-
CLICK

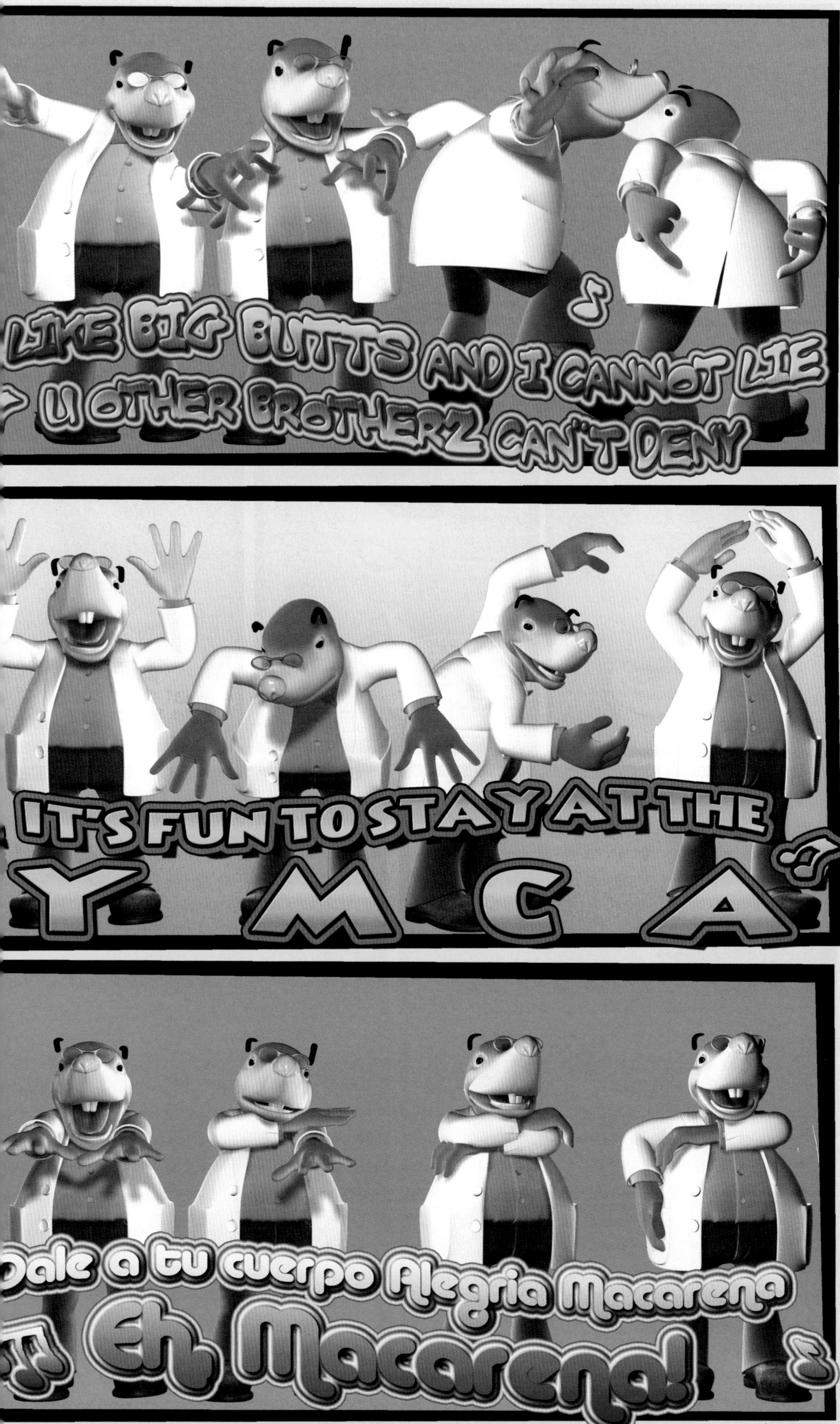
LIKE BIG BUTTS AND I CANNOT LIE
U OTHER BROTHERZ CAN'T DENY
IT'S FUN TO STAY AT THE
Y M C A
Dale a tu cuerpo Alegria Macarena
Eh Macarena!

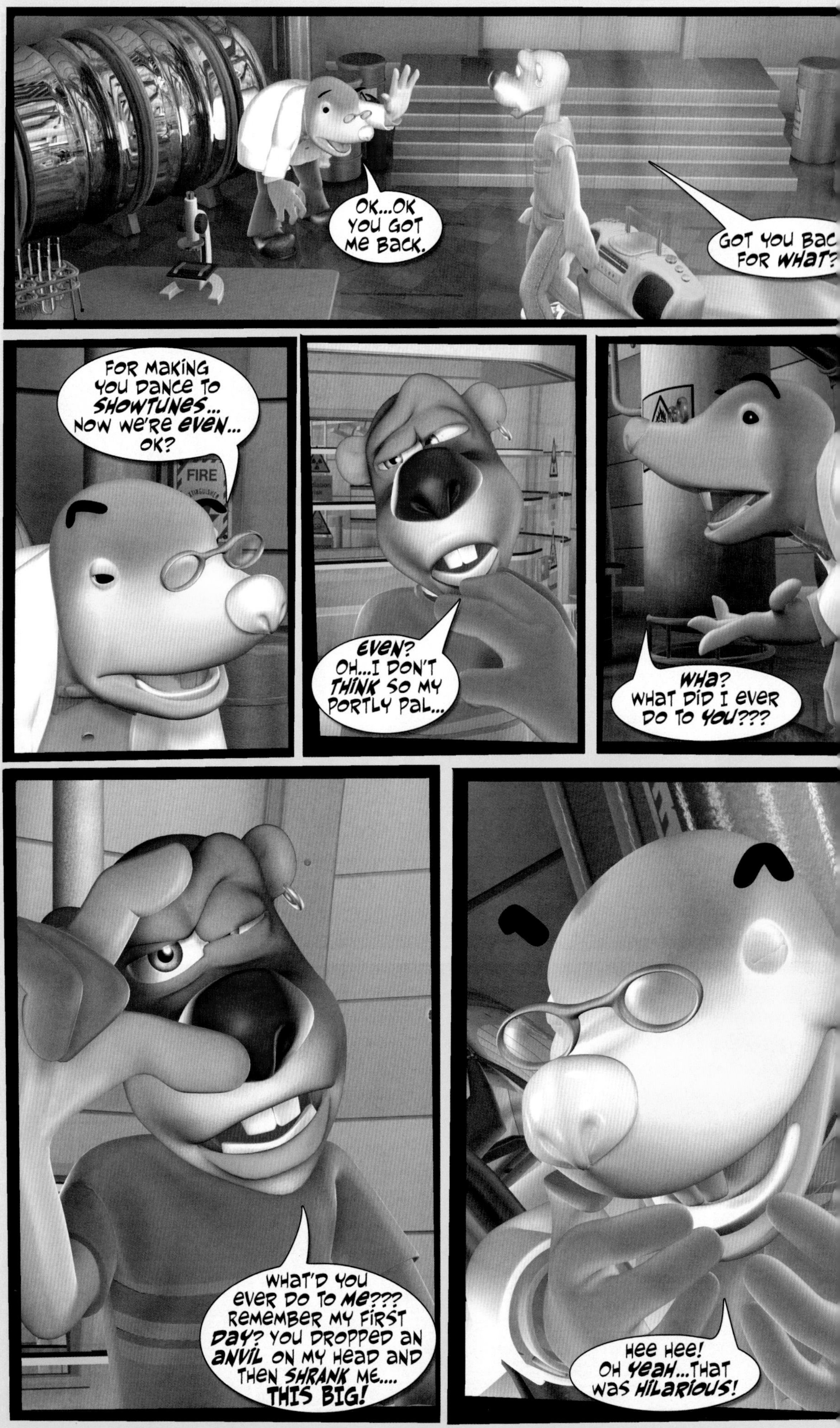
OK...OK
YOU GOT
ME BACK.
GOT YOU BAC
FOR WHAT?
FOR MAKING
YOU DANCE TO
SHOWTUNES...
NOW WE'RE EVEN...
OK?
FIRE
EVEN?
OH...I DON'T
THINK SO MY
PORTLY PAL...
WHA?
WHAT DID I EVER
DO TO YOU???
WHAT'D YOU
EVER DO TO ME???
REMEMBER MY FIRST
DAY? YOU DROPPED AN
ANVIL ON MY HEAD AND
THEN SHRANK ME....
THIS BIG!
HEE HEE!
OH YEAH...THAT
WAS HILARIOUS!

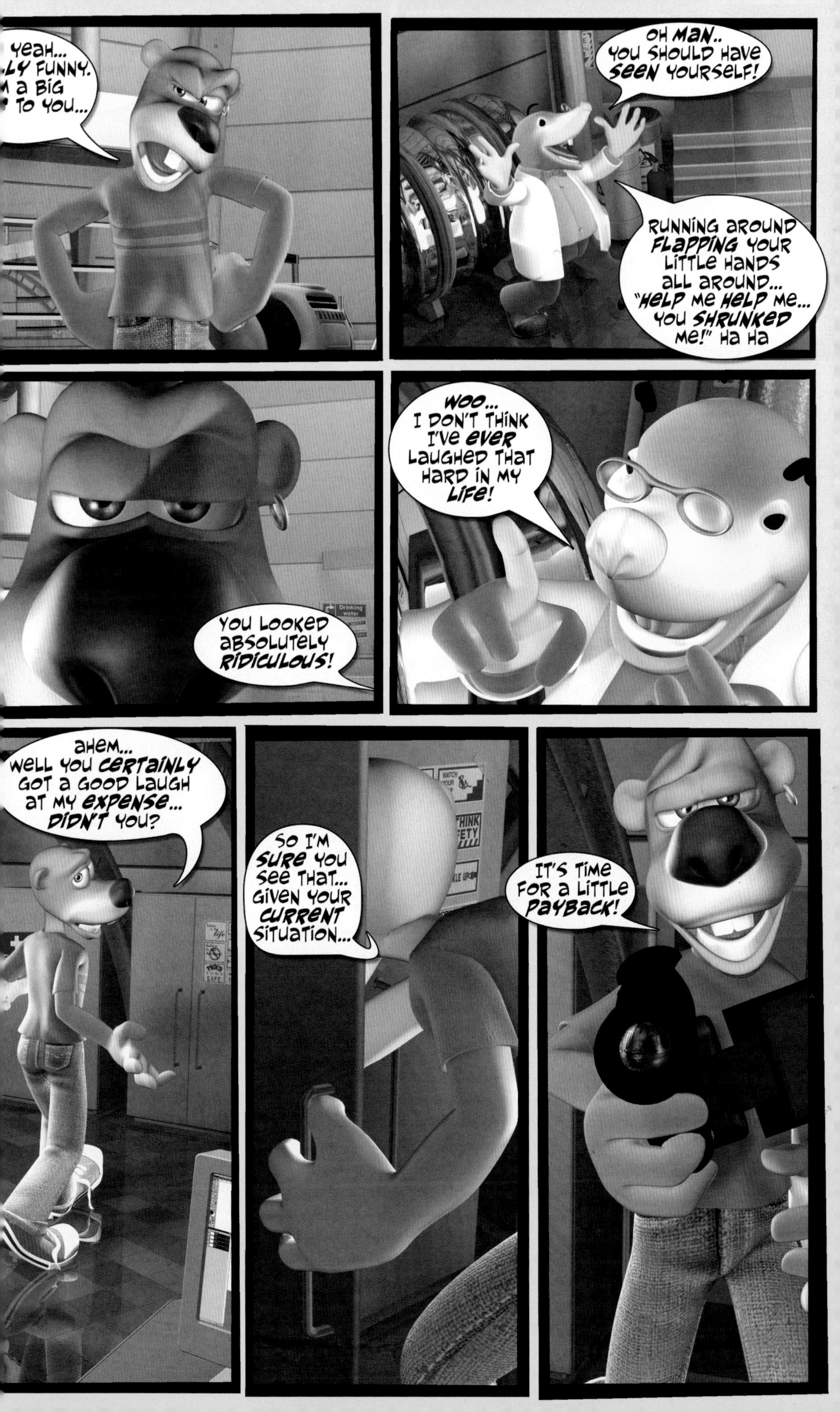
yeah... LY FUNNY. M a BIG TO YOU...
OH MAN.. YOU SHOULD HAVE SEEN YOURSELF!
RUNNING AROUND FLAPPING YOUR LITTLE HANDS ALL AROUND... "HELP ME HELP ME... YOU SHRUNKED ME!" HA HA
YOU LOOKED ABSOLUTELY RIDICULOUS!
WOO... I DON'T THINK I'VE EVER LAUGHED THAT HARD IN MY LIFE!
AHEM... WELL YOU CERTAINLY GOT A GOOD LAUGH AT MY EXPENSE... DIDN'T YOU?
SO I'M SURE YOU SEE THAT... GIVEN YOUR CURRENT SITUATION...
IT'S TIME FOR A LITTLE PAYBACK!

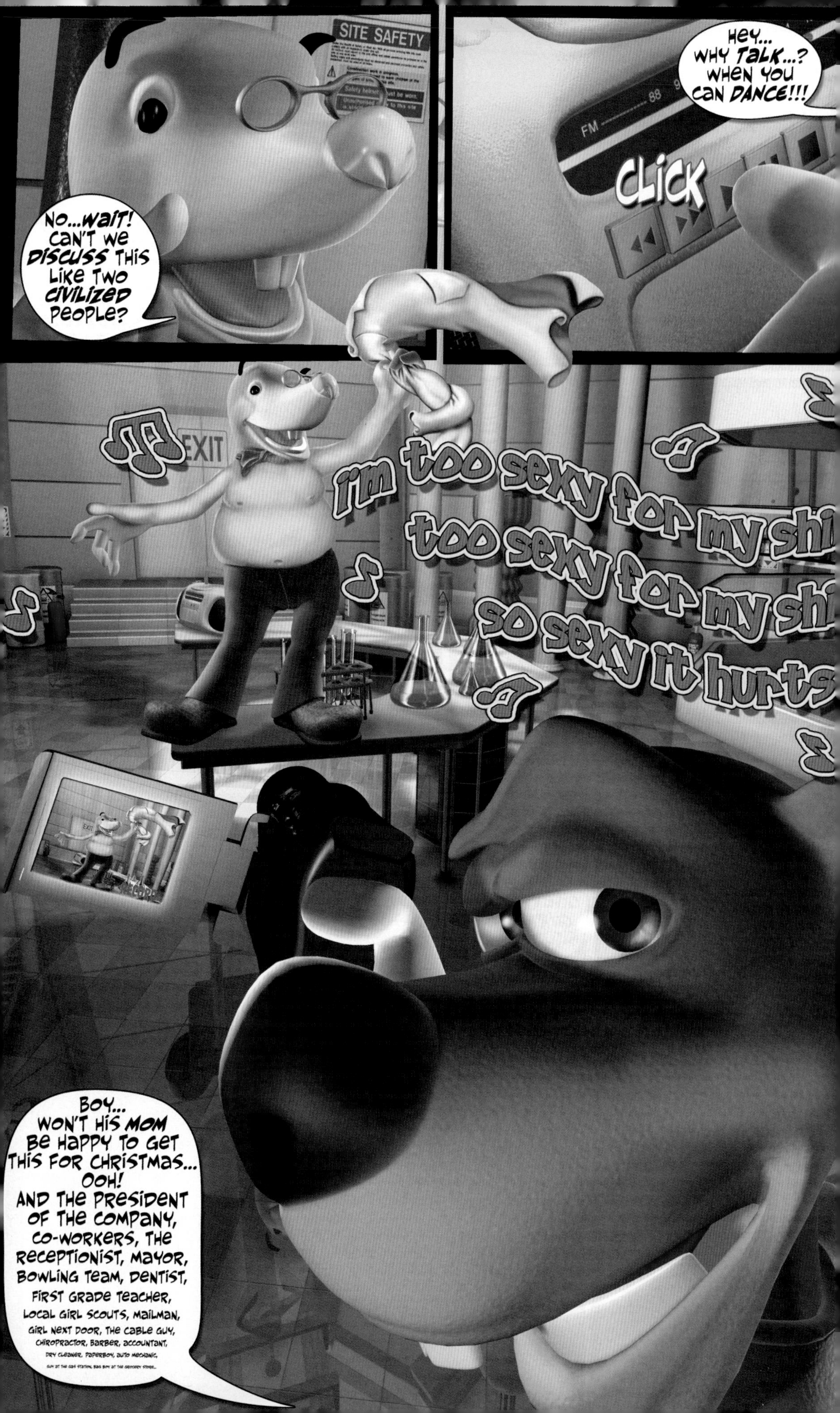
SITE SAFETY
NO...WAIT! CAN'T WE DISCUSS THIS LIKE TWO CIVILIZED PEOPLE?
HEY... WHY TALK...? WHEN YOU CAN DANCE!!!
FM 88
CLICK
EXIT
i'm too sexy for my shi
too sexy for my shi
so sexy it hurts
BOY... WON'T HIS MOM BE HAPPY TO GET THIS FOR CHRISTMAS... OOH! AND THE PRESIDENT OF THE COMPANY, CO-WORKERS, THE RECEPTIONIST, MAYOR, BOWLING TEAM, DENTIST, FIRST GRADE TEACHER, LOCAL GIRL SCOUTS, MAILMAN, GIRL NEXT DOOR, THE CABLE GUY, CHIROPRACTOR, BARBER, ACCOUNTANT, DRY CLEANER, PAPERBOY, AUTO MECHANIC, GUY AT THE GAS STATION, BAG BOY AT THE GROCERY STORE...

IT'S JOKE TIME!!!
WHAT DO YOU GET WHEN YOU CROSS A PARROT WITH A CENTIPEDE?
WHAT?
TURN THE PAGE FOR A HUMDINGER OF AN ANSWER!

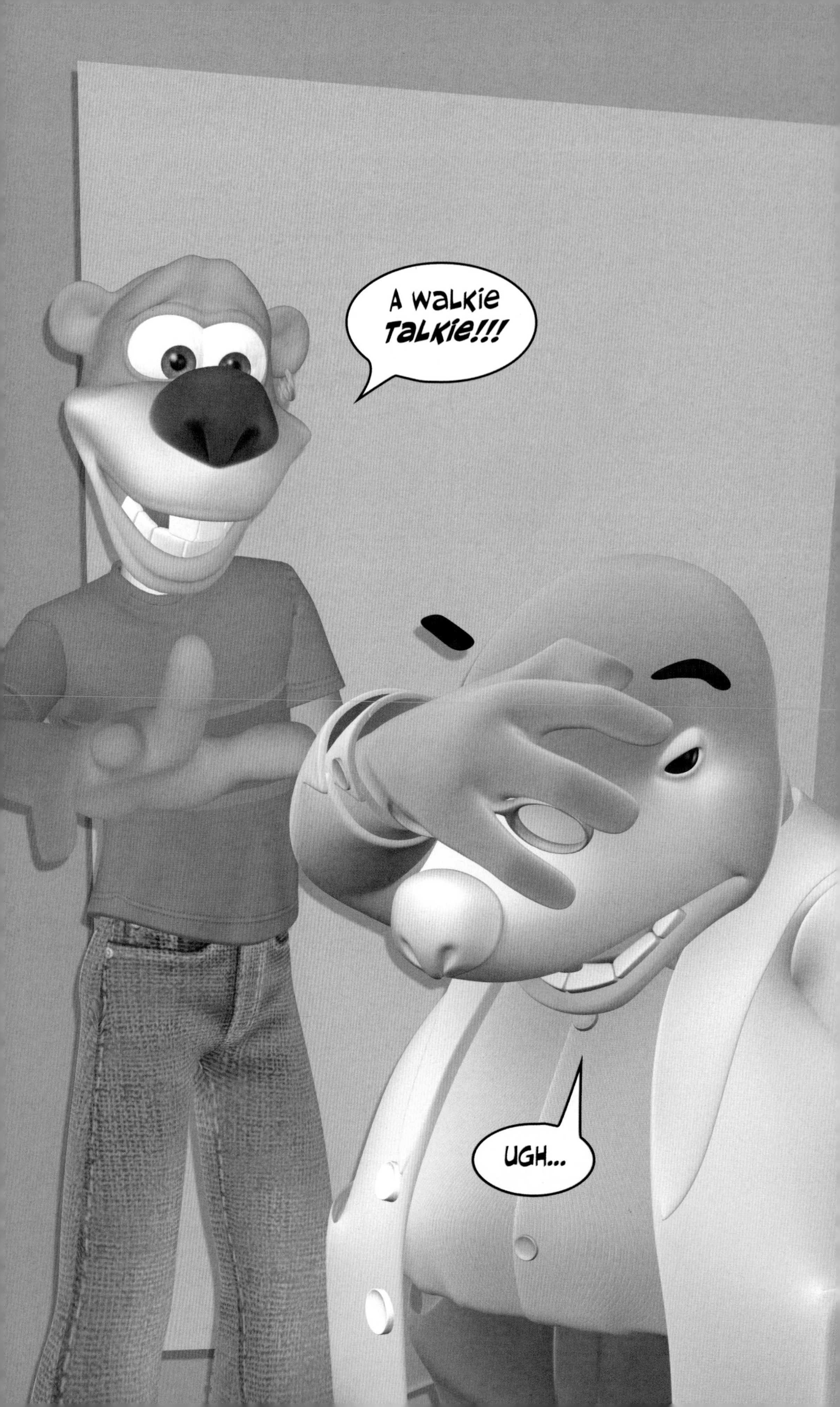
A WALKIE TALKIE!!!
UGH...

CRAZY SCIENCE EXPERIMENTS!

TRY THIS AT HOME WITH YOUR PARENTS...

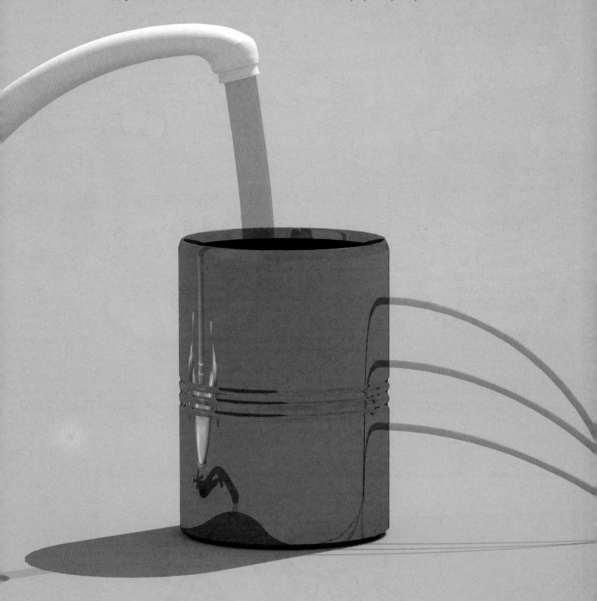

HAVE YOUR PARENTS USE A NAIL TO PUNCH THREE VERTICAL HOLES IN A CLEAN METAL CAN. FILL THE CAN TO THE TOP WITH WATER AND WATCH HOW THE LIQUID DRAINS OUT. SEE HOW THE WATER SHOOTS OUT FURTHER FROM THE BOTTOM HOLE THAN THE TOP?

THERE'S MORE PRESSURE AT THE BOTTOM BECAUSE THE WATER ON TOP IS PUSHING DOWN ON THE WATER ON THE BOTTOM.

FAN ART!

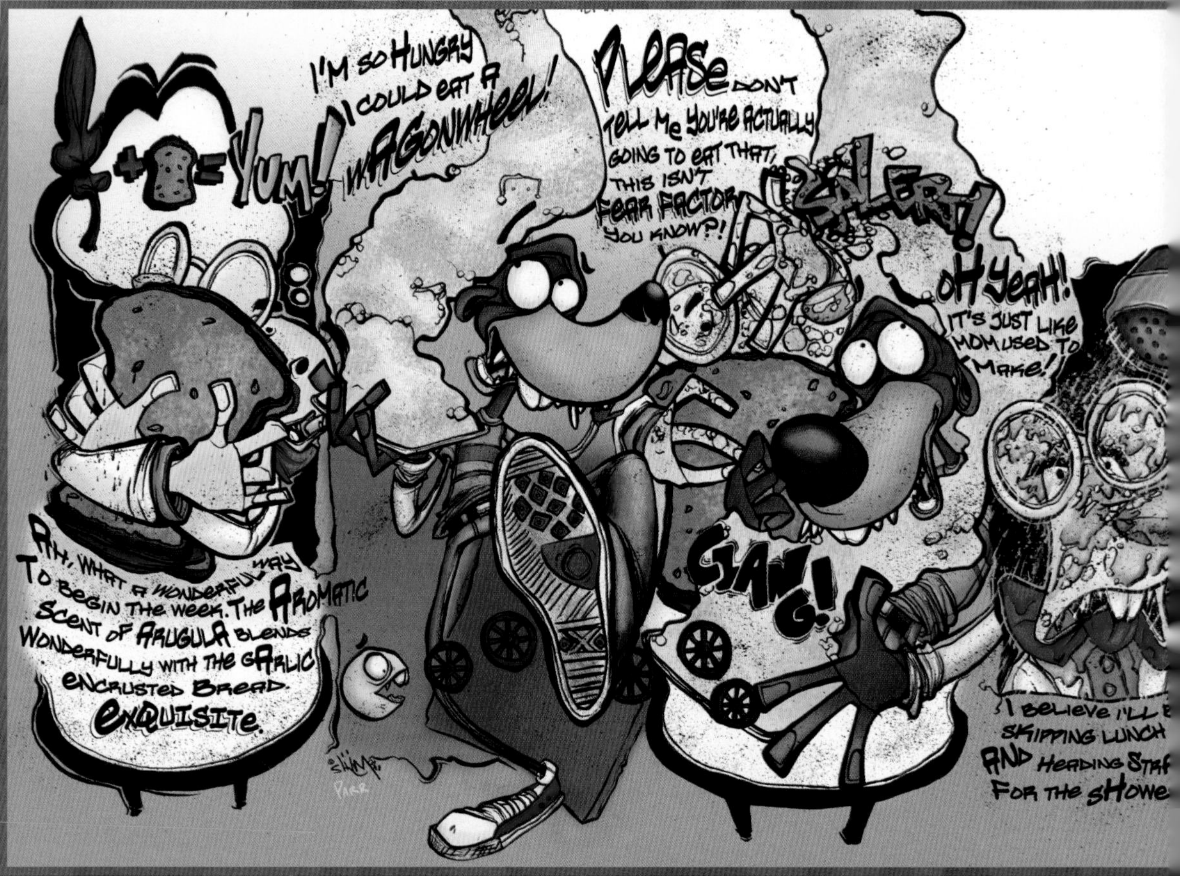

+ = YUM!
I'M SO HUNGRY I COULD EAT A WAGONWHEEL!
PLEASE DON'T TELL ME YOU'RE ACTUALLY GOING TO EAT THAT, THIS ISN'T FEAR FACTOR YOU KNOW?!
SPLERT!
OH YEAH! IT'S JUST LIKE MOM USED TO MAKE!
AH, WHAT A WONDERFUL WAY TO BEGIN THE WEEK. THE AROMATIC SCENT OF ARUGULA BLENDS WONDERFULLY WITH THE GARLIC ENCRUSTED BREAD. EXQUISITE.
CLANG!
I BELIEVE I'LL B SKIPPING LUNCH AND HEADING STR FOR THE SHOWE

CHRIS 'ESTLIN' SAWYER (RI) DERICK 'SLUM' BROOKS, AND SARAH 'SHIRO PARR (UK)

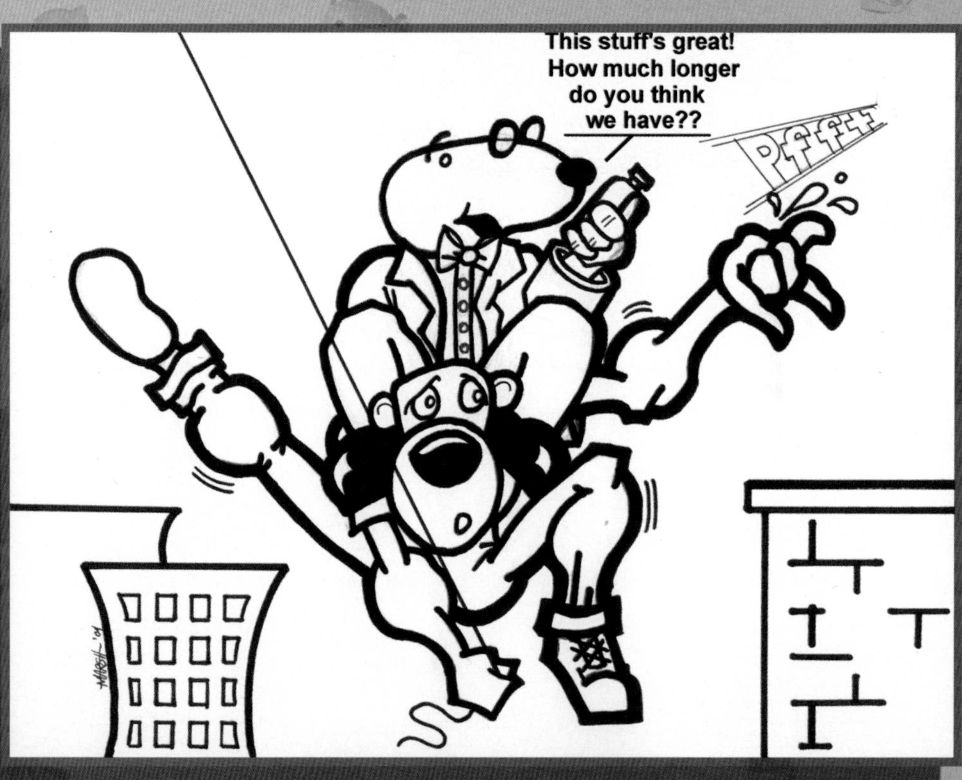

This stuff's great! How much longer do you think we have??
Pfffft

BY A GUY CALLED MAR (OZ)

FAN ART!

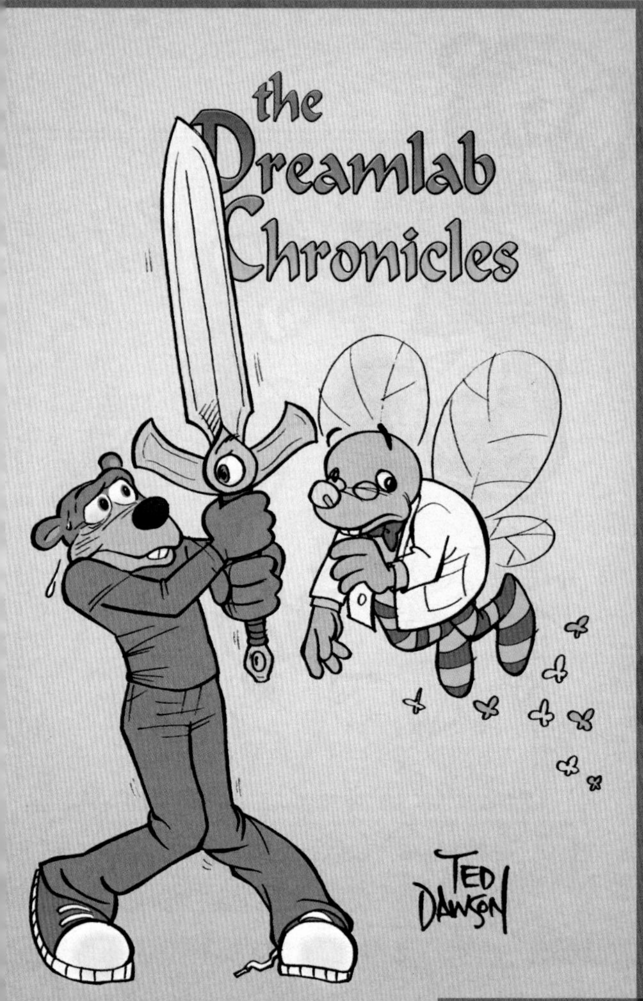
the Dreamlab Chronicles
TED DAWSON

TED DAWSON
BARTLESVILLE, OK
SPOONER CREATOR TED DAWSON FIGURES ONCE SCOTT GETS TOO BUSY TO DO BOTH OF HIS CREATIONS... THE DREAMLAND CHRONICLES AND THE LAB...HE'LL JUST GET LAZY AND MUSH EM ALL TOGETHER!
THIS IS THE RESULT.

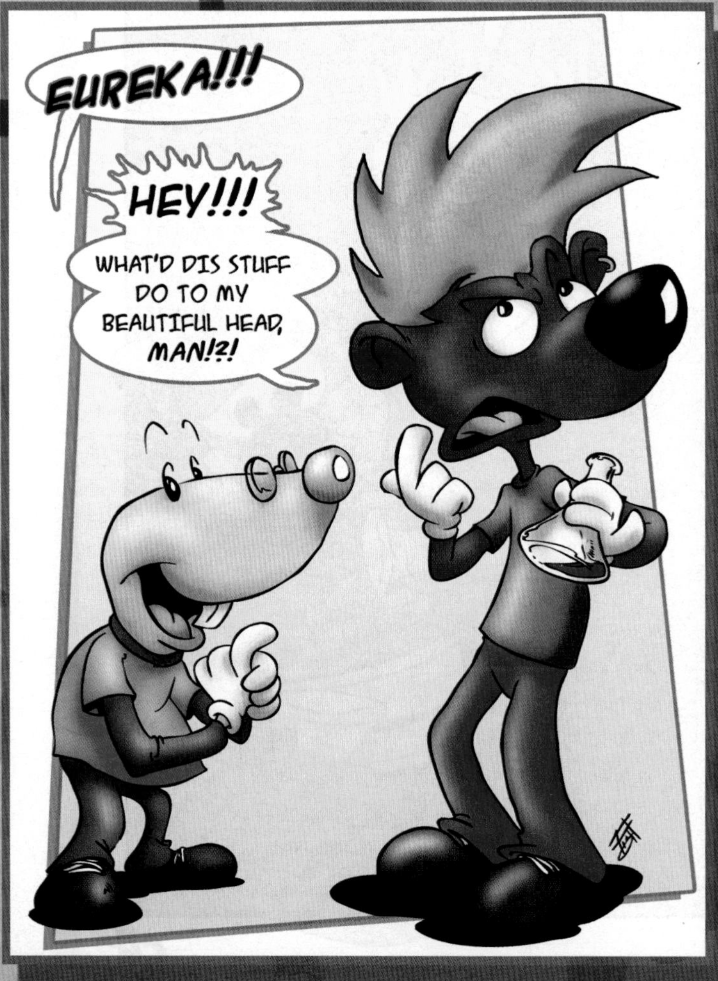
EUREKA!!!
HEY!!!
WHAT'D DIS STUFF DO TO MY BEAUTIFUL HEAD, MAN!?!

DERRICK FISH
A LAB HAIRY DAY! ESTEBAN'S SPORTING A VERY "DANDY" HAIRDO HERE, AND FRANKLY I DON'T THINK HE'S EVER LOOKED BETTER!

FAN ART!

MARK SPENCER REYNOLDS
(AKA. DOC GOT, BOO YAAH!)
HOLLAND, NEBRASKA
ESTEBAN IS ON ONE OF LIVINGSTON'S DIABOLICAL EXPERIMENTS DESIGNED TO ENTRAP INDIVIDUALS IN AN ETERNITY OF LITIGATION, THUS ALLOWING THE CREATOR MORE FREE TIME TO SURF, FROLIC WITH SEAGULLS AND KICK SAND ON WIMPY MEN.

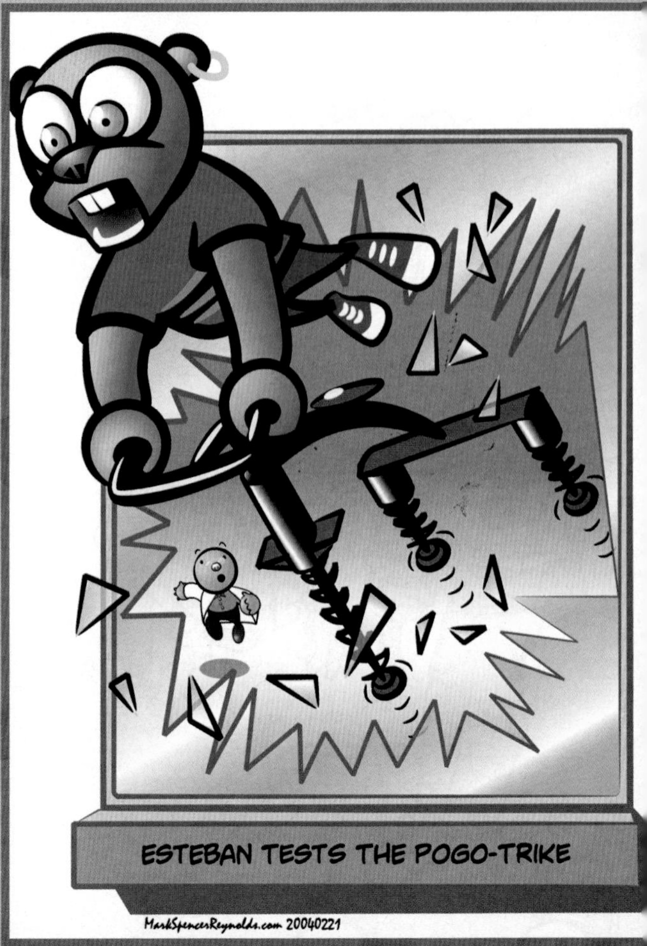

ESTEBAN TESTS THE POGO-TRIKE
MarkSpencerReynolds.com 20040221

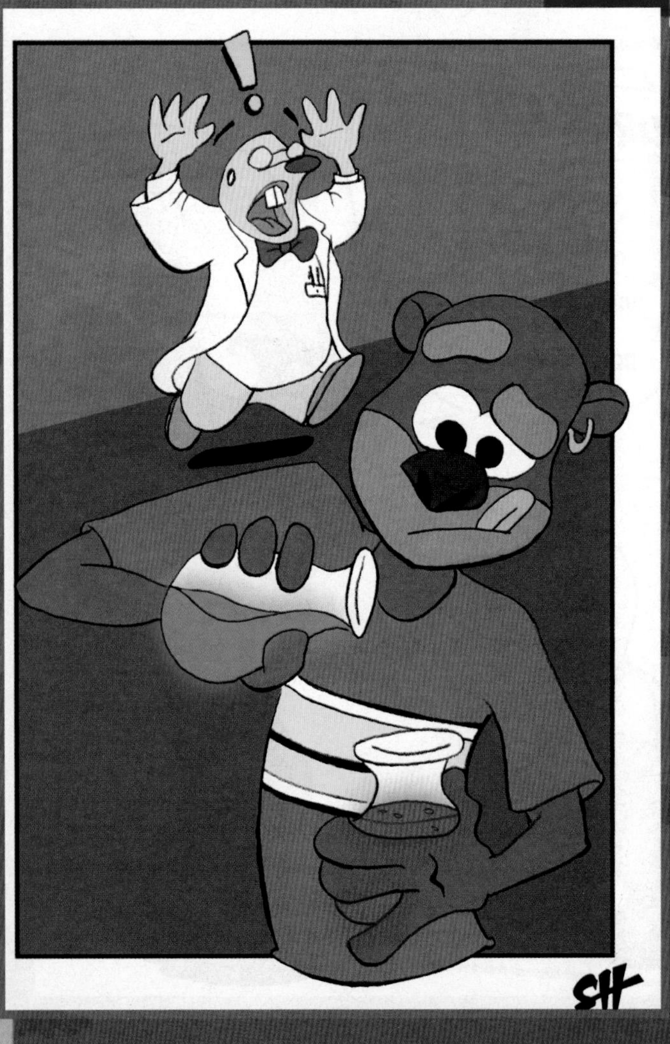

!
SH

SCOTT ZIRKEL
SAN ANTONIO, TX
IN THIS PIECE I REALLY WANTED TO STRESS THE DIFFERENCES WE HAVE AS PEOPLE, AND A WAY WE COULD ALL BRIDGE.. NO, NO WAIT.
I JUST LIKE BLOWING THINGS UP AND AS WE ALL KNOW...GREEN AND PINK ALWAYS GET YOU BLOWN UP.
IT'S A FACT, I LOOKED IT UP!

an ART!

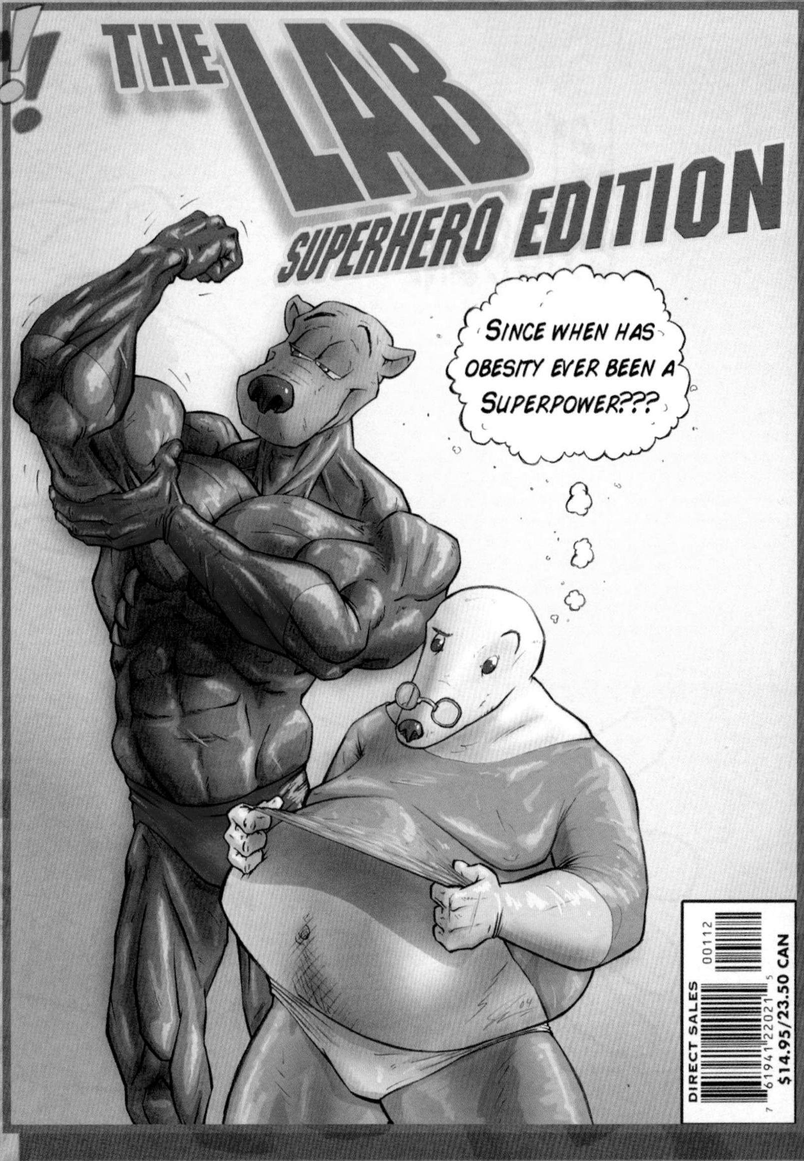
THE LAB
SUPERHERO EDITION
SINCE WHEN HAS OBESITY EVER BEEN A SUPERPOWER???
DIRECT SALES
$14.95/23.50 CAN

JOEL AARON CARLSON
VANCOUVER, CANADA
A DEPICTION OF WHAT "THE LAB" WOULD LOOK LIKE IF IT WERE A REAL COMIC BOOK, INSTEAD OF... WELL...YOU KNOW.

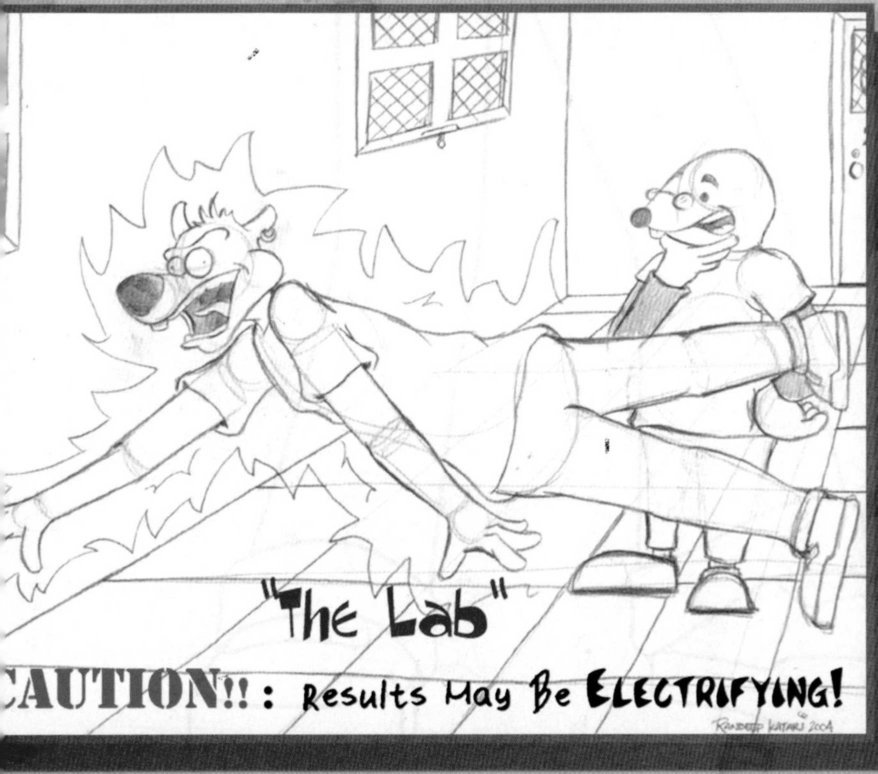
"The Lab"
CAUTION!! : Results May Be ELECTRIFYING!
Randeep Katari 2004

RANDEEP KATARI
RICHMOND HILL, ONTARIO
I'VE DECIDED TO DO A LITTLE RENDITION OF LIVINGSTON SHOWING HOW HE'S GOTTEN USED TO ESTEBAN'S LITTLE "ACCIDENTS".

LET'S COLOR ESTEBAN!

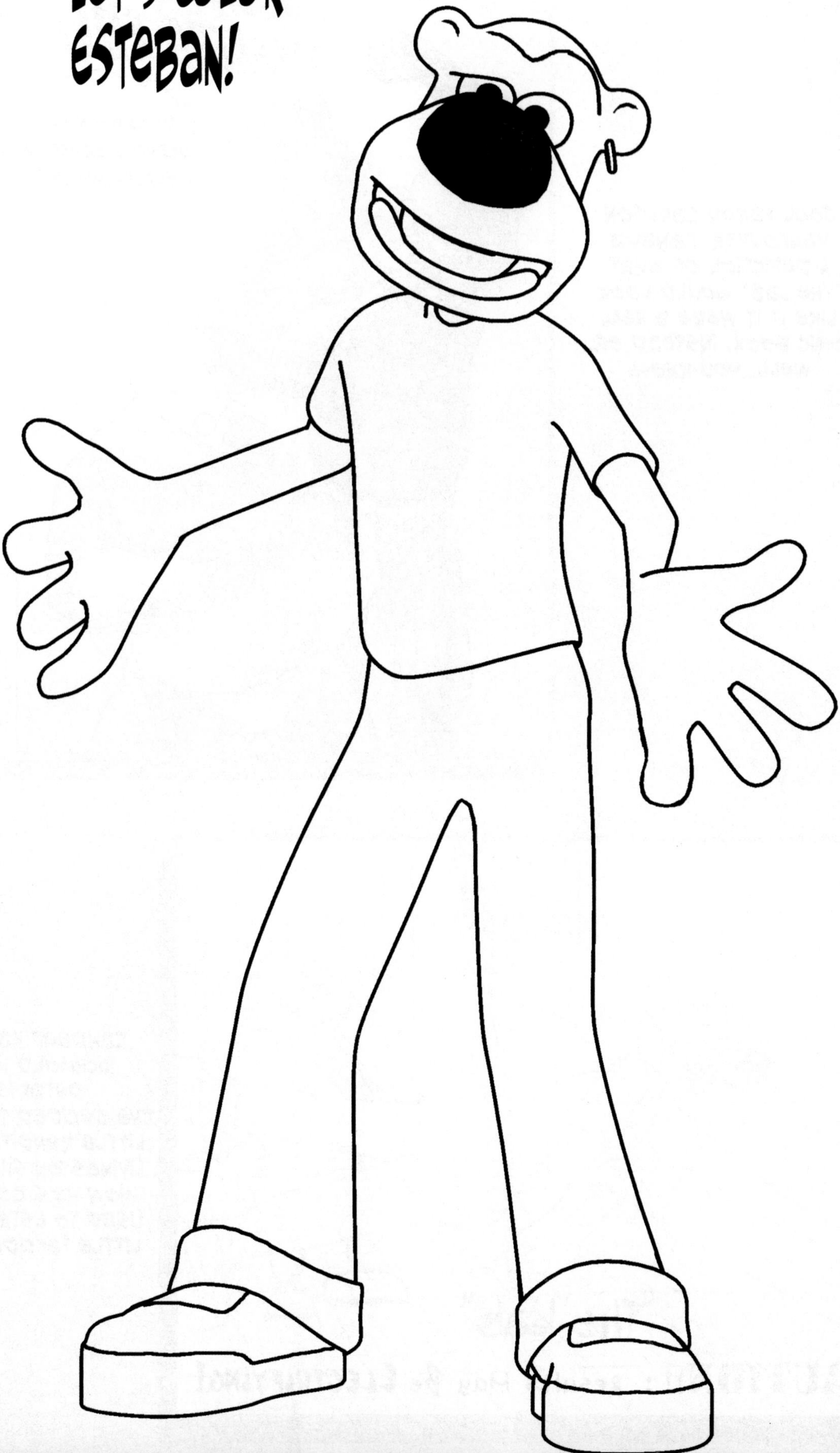

CRAZY SCIENCE EXPERIMENTS!

TRY THIS AT HOME WITH YOUR PARENTS...

TAKE A HARD BOILED EGG AND PEEL IT. ASK YOUR PARENT TO DROP TWO LIT MATCHES INTO THE BOTTLE. NOW SET THE EGG ON THE NECK OF A GLASS BOTTLE. AS THE MATCHES GO OUT...THE EGG WILL BE SUCKED INTO THE BOTTLE!

WOW...HOW DID THAT HAPPEN? WELL...THE AIR INSIDE THE BOTTLE GOT THINNER WHEN THE FLAME FROM THE MATCHES USED UP THE OXYGEN. THIS CAUSED A VACUUM! THE AIR ON THE OUTSIDE ACTUALLY PUSHED THE EGG THROUGH!

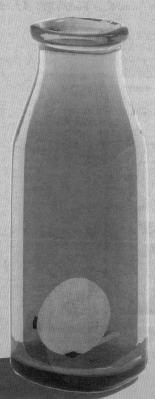

IT ALL STARTED WITH AN ARMPIT...

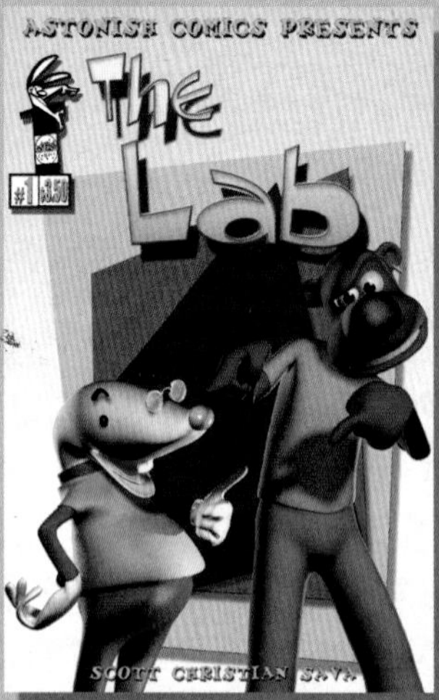
ASTONISH COMICS PRESENTS
The Lab
SCOTT CHRISTIAN SAVA

The cover for the Lab issue 1
2001

IT ALL STARTED WITH AN ***ARMPIT?*** WELL...MORE OR LESS I GUESS
THERE WAS AN OLD MAGAZINE...***TIME*** I THINK THAT HAD AN ARTICL
WITH WAR-TIME JOBS I BELIEVE. THEY HAD A PICTURE OF THESE
POOR WOMEN WHO'S SOLE JOB WAS TO ***SNIFF*** THESE MEN'S
ARMPITS AND SEE IF THEIR ***DEODORANT*** WAS WORKING...
FOR SOME STRANGE REASON THIS STAYED WITH ME....

NOW...IN 1999 I WAS TRYING TO COME UP WITH A FUN NEW IDEA FOR A TV SHOW...AND HAD WORKED OUT A ***MOLE*** AND A ***WEASEL***. I CALLED MY CHILDHOOD FRIEND ***ROBERT DIAZ*** AND WE PLAYED AROUND WITH SOME FUN QUIRKS FOR THEM LIKE ***OPERA SINGING*** AND ***ACCENTS***...BUT IT STILL NEEDED A CATCH....THEN I REMEMBERED THE ***ARMPITS!***

ONCE I HAD THAT...THE LAB WAS BORN...AND THE REST FELL INTO PLACE. WE ADDED THE FUNNY ACCENTS WITH ROBERT DOING HIS BEST ***THICK HISPANIC ACCENT*** FOR ESTEBAN AND MY GOOD FRIEND ***ROBERT TOONE*** DOING THE ***BRITISH*** VOICE FOR LIVINGSTON. AN ANIMATED SHORT WAS IN THE WORKS WHEN I MET ***MIKE KUNKEL.***

MIKE HAD STARTED HIS OWN COMIC COMPANY CALLED ***ASTONISH COMICS***...AND HE ASKED ME IF I'D LIKE TO DO THE LAB AS A COMIC BOOK. I HADN'T THOUGHT ABOUT IT UP UNTIL HE ASKED...BUT....IT MADE SENSE.

IN THE WINTER OF 2001 THE LAB HIT SHELVES WORLDWIDE AND WAS VERY WELL RECEIVED.

AFTER A BRIEF STINT ON ***SPIDER-MAN*** IN 2002 I WENT BACK TO THE LAB FOR THE ***LAB 2 ELECTRIC BOOGALOO!***

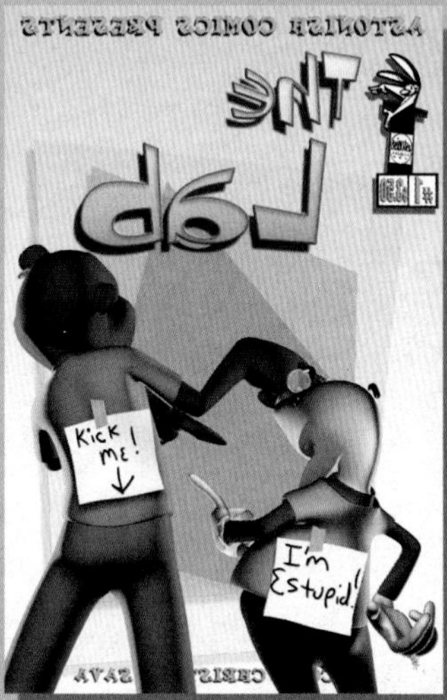
Kick me!
I'm Estupid!

The back cover for the Lab issue
2001

WITH EVERYTHING I HAD LEARNED ON THE FIRST BOOK... COUPLED WITH WHAT HAD BEEN LEARNED ON SPIDER-MAN, THE LAB 2 WAS A ***GREAT LEAP*** IN STORYTELLING AND TECHNOLOGY. IT HIT STORES IN EARLY 2003 TO ***GREAT*** REVIEWS AND A WARM FAN WELCOME!
ONE THING WAS MISSING THOUGH...***THE ACCENTS!*** FOR SOME...IT WAS PART OF THE ***CHARM*** OF THE BOOK... FOR OTHERS...IT WAS A ***DISTRACTION***....SOME THINGS WORK BETTER IN ANIMATION...AND I REALIZED THIS WAS ONE OF THEM.
CURRENTLY WE'RE IN TALKS WITH A FEW STUDIOS ABOUT MAKING THE LAB AN ANIMATED SERIES (COINCIDENT WHAT IT WAS ORIGINALLY INTENDED TO BE) AND OF COURS THE 2 ISSUES ALONG WITH ***60*** MORE PAGES OF NEW STOR AND FUN IS COLLECTED RIGHT HERE IN YOUR HOT LITTLE HANDS!

SO...***THANKS*** FOR READING! ESTEBAN, LIVINGSTON, AND MYS HOPE YOU LAUGH OUT LOUD AND HAVE A ***GREAT*** TIME!

SCOTT CHRISTIAN SAVA
APRIL, 2004

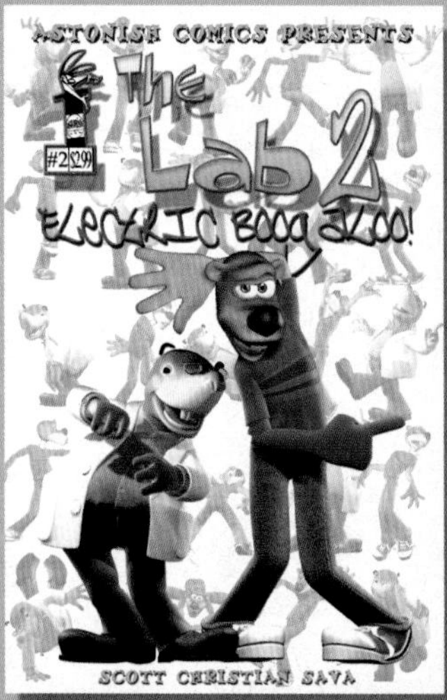
ASTONISH COMICS PRESENTS
The Lab 2
Electric Boogaloo!
SCOTT CHRISTIAN SAVA

The cover for the Lab 2 Electric Boogaloo
2003

IT'S ALIVE...it's ALIVE!!!!

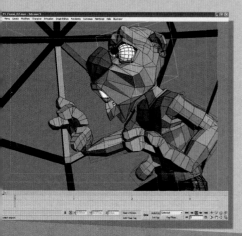

IN THE YEAR OF 2000 I HAD THE GREAT
FORTUNE TO MEET **MIKE KUNKEL**. HE WAS DOING THIS
COMIC BOOK CALLED **HEROBEAR AND THE KID**
(MAYBE YOU'VE HEARD OF IT)
AND HE WAS PRODUCING
IT ALL ON HIS **OWN**. THIS **ONE** GUY...SITTING IN
HIS HOME WITH HIS
PENCIL AND **PAPER**...DOING IT ALL BY
HIMSELF....INCREDIBLE.

WELL...I FIGURED...IF **THIS** POOR SLOB COULD
DO IT...**I** SURELY COULD!
HA HA....BOY...I DIDN'T KNOW WHAT I WAS **IN** FOR!
SEE...MIKE WAS AN EX-DISNEY ANIMATOR...DOING HIS WORK
IN **PENCIL** AND **PAPER**...WHERE I CAME FROM
3D ANIMATION...
DOING THE WORK ON THE **COMPUTER**.

I CAN SEE HERE THE POLYGONS...THOSE
SQUARES THAT ESTEBAN IS MADE OF.

WHERE ART SEEMS TO **FLOW** FROM MIKE'S PENCIL
AS HE DRAWS EACH FRAME...I HAD TO FIRST
MODEL EACH CHARACTER AND ENVIRONMENT ON THE
COMPUTER. YOU SEE...ALL OF THE THINGS YOU FIND
THE LAB HAVE TO BE **BUILT FIRST**...BEFORE THEY GET
POSED. ESTEBAN AND LIVINGSTON ARE MADE OF
GONS. THAT'S A SERIES OF SQUARES PUT TOGETHER
A VIRTUAL LEGO SET. IT'S A WIERD WAY TO WORK...
I ENJOY THE RESULTS...SO...WHAT AM I GONNA DO?

...HOW EXACTLY **DOES** IT ALL COME TOGETHER?
WELL...FIRST I **DESIGN** THE CHARACTERS...THAT
OOK ACTUAL PAPER AND PENCIL. THEN I **MODEL**
HARACTERS...FIRST ESTEBAN...THEN I DID LIVINGSTON.
THEIR SHAPE IS GOOD...I HAVE TO **TEXTURE** THEM...
THIS IS ESSENTIALLY PAINTING THE MODELS.

ER THIS IS **MORPH TARGETS**...THAT'S MAKING THE
DIFFERENT **FACIAL EXPRESSIONS** I USE.
ND LASTLY...I ADD **BONES**. THE BONES ALLOW
ME TO POSE THE CHARACTERS.

SEE THOSE BOXES AROUND HIS HEAD,
ARMS, AND SUCH? THOSE ARE HIS BONES!
I MOVE THOSE TO POSE HIM.

AS I MOVE THE BONES...THE BODY FOLLOWS.
ONCE I HAVE THE LAB BUILT...I THEN **POSE**
THE CHARACTERS IN IT...ADD **LIGHTS** TO THE
SCENE...THEN RENDER.
WHAT'S RENDERING? WELL...SINCE THIS IS
STILL DONE IN THE EARLY YEARS OF
COMPUTERS...THE PROCESSING
SPEED ISN'T **FAST** ENOUGH TO
CALCULATE ALL OF THE
THINGS NECESSARY LIKE **SHADOWS**,
REFLECTIONS, AND
TRANSPARENCY. SO I HAVE TO HIT
RENDER...AND LET
THE COMPUTER FIGURE IT ALL OUT...
USUALLY TAKES ABOUT
20 MINUTES PER FRAME.
OK...NOT AS EASY AS PENCIL AND PAPER...
BUT HEY...
IT'S FUN.

AFTER THE COMPUTER HAS CALCULATED
EVERYTHING...HERE'S WHAT I GET.

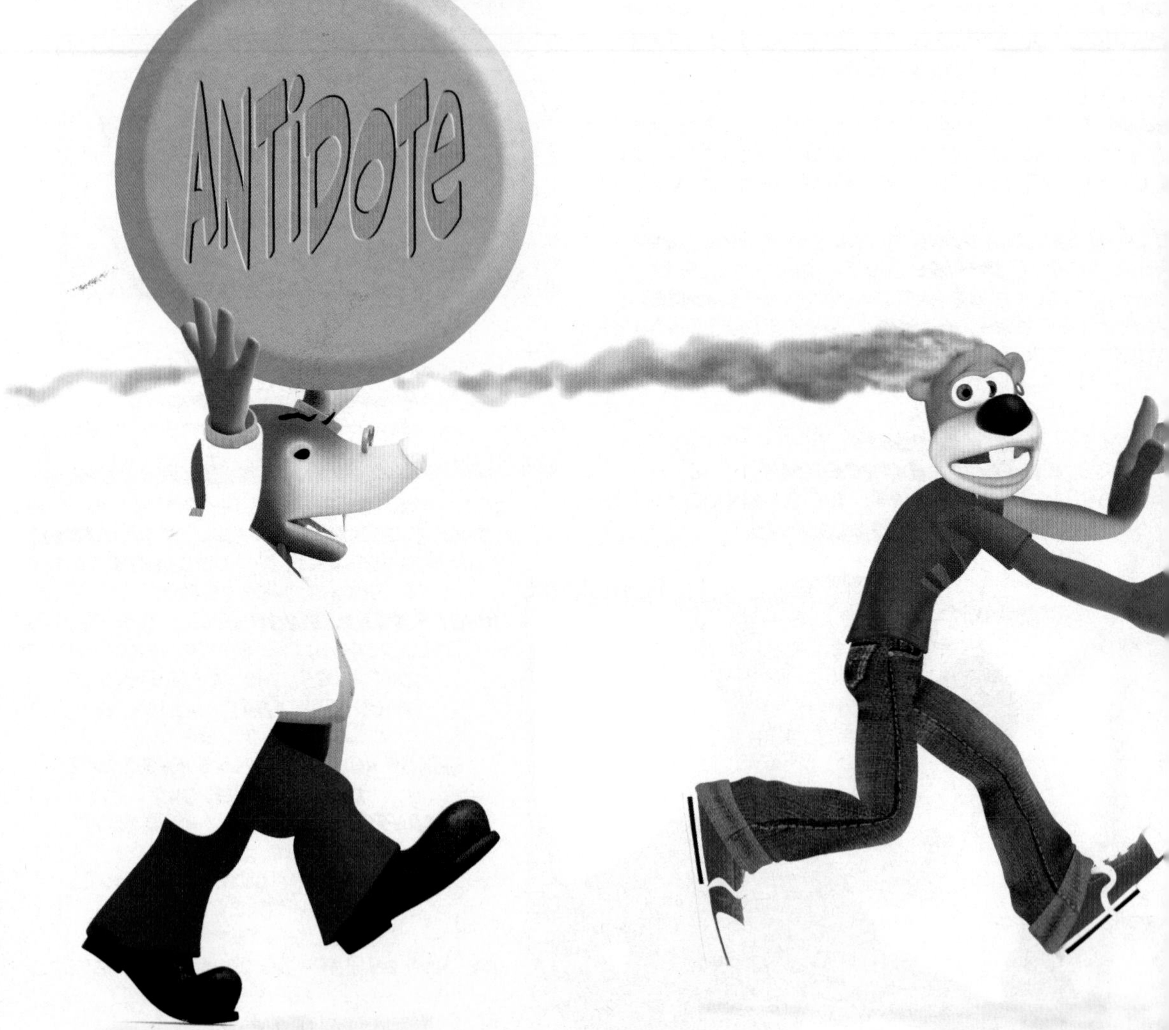
ANTIDOTE